Steppenwolf and Everyman

☙ Steppenwolf and Everyman

by Hans Mayer

Translated and with an Introduction by
Jack D. Zipes

Thomas Y. Crowell Company

New York · Established 1834

Contents

Translator's Introduction

Hans Mayer is one of those extraordinary critics who manage to have a firm grasp on the key issues of their times and also to be ahead of their times. This accounts for his provocative ideas and unusual style, which are rooted in Marxist dialectical materialism. As one of the leading Marxist critics of the twentieth century, he has broken new ground in the field of literary criticism, engaged in stimulating debates with Marxists and anti-Marxists alike, and postulated new theories about the bourgeois tradition that reverse the traditional views. A master of dialectics, Mayer has the uncanny gift of answering questions by raising even more valid and challenging questions which lead to a higher state of consciousness. This art of raising questions and consciousness has also proved dangerous: Mayer was chased from Nazi Germany, and he abandoned East Germany because of political differences. He has made it clear that he will suffer no repression, and his critical views on modern literature stem from a razor's edge type of living which in turn emanates from a firm belief in Marxism that refuses to make concessions to either party or state.

Born in Cologne in 1907, Mayer was raised in a good bourgeois home which, despite its disadvantages considered from a socialist point of view, provided him with the opportunity to school himself thoroughly in the arts and experience the proper German rituals of order, property, and culture. After studying modern history, philosophy, and law at the universities of Cologne, Bonn, and Berlin, Mayer received a law degree and wrote a doctoral dissertation, *The Crisis of the German Doctrine of the State and*

Rudolf Smend's Concept of the State. This was in 1931, and it was followed soon after by his own personal crisis with the Hitler regime in 1933, incurred as a result of his political activities as a lawyer. Mayer avoided arrest by storm troopers, left Berlin, and made his way first to Strasbourg, then to Paris, and finally to Switzerland, where he remained until 1945.

It was in Switzerland that Mayer began to devote more time to his literary studies and to establish contacts with most of the important European writers of that time. His literary essays appeared in such magazines as Thomas Mann's *Mass und Wert* and *Die Neue Schweizer Rundschau.* Along with Stephan Hermlin and Michael Tschesno, he edited the journal *Über die Grenzen,* which published works by Bertolt Brecht, Else Lasker-Schüler, Georg Kaiser, and other leading German writers in exile. Aside from participating in various seminars on politics and literature in Geneva and Zurich, Mayer also completed two books during his stay in Switzerland: *From the Third to the Fourth Republic: Intellectual Currents in France 1939–1945,* and *Georg Büchner and His Times,* a pioneer work which ushered in the Büchner renaissance.

In 1945 Mayer returned to Germany, where he first accepted a position with the German Associated Press and soon afterward was appointed a director of the state radio station in Frankfurt am Main. Then, in 1948, he moved to East Germany to become professor of German literature at the University of Leipzig. Mayer soon established a reputation as one of the finest educators in the German Democratic Republic, and some of the most talented writers (Uwe Johnson and Christa Wolf) and critics came under his tutelage at the university. In addition, he continued his remarkable rate of production, which was aimed at giving a new historical focus to modern German literature. A partial list of the translated titles includes: *Thomas Mann* (1950), *Studies in German Literary History* (1953), *Schiller and the Nation* (1953), *German Literature and World Literature* (1957), *From Lessing to Thomas Mann* (1959), *Bertolt Brecht and the Tradition* (1961), *Heinrich von Kleist: The Historical Moment* (1962), *Views About the Literature of the Times* (1962), and *On German Classicism and Romanticism* (1963). By 1963, Mayer had become dissatisfied with the restrictions placed upon him as critic and educator in East Germany, and he decided to remain in the West during one of his visits. Soon after this he was offered the chair as professor of German literature at the Technical University of Hannover, a position which he presently holds.

Commenting on Mayer's critical works up to 1963, George Steiner has remarked: "There is a gray, flat reasonableness about a good deal of Mayer's work. As if the constant effort toward mediation and equilibrium between dialectical pressures had blunted the edge of feeling . . . . This blurring at the edges, the sense of argument muted, is obviously part of Mayer's survival. That he should have accomplished so much under the conditions so abrasive is itself a very high achievement. His style, moreover, has precisely those virtues of scruple and modesty which sometimes diminish the bite of his criticism. It has remained delightfully intact from the somber jargon which mars so much present German prose, Marxist or academic . . . . It will be exciting to see what a mind so orderly and wide-ranging will produce now that certain pressures are off."

Though complimentary, Steiner's essay misses the mark, for it assumes that Mayer did not write as freely and critically as he could while in the German Democratic Republic (GDR) and that he might even change the tone and sharpen his criticism once in the "free" West. However, it must be noted that Mayer, who was in the West when the Berlin Wall was erected in 1961, chose to return to East Germany and that he was always allowed to publish his works in the West. There is no doubt that Mayer was under pressure while living in the GDR, but one might ask, When hasn't he been under pressure? Or better yet, Can a Marxist who refuses to compromise and whose writings reflect a critical attitude toward party, state, and culture ever rid himself of harassment in either East or West? Mayer is not compromising. His dialectical manner of presenting arguments is subtle and always to the point, and the works he has produced since leaving East Germany have continued a much-needed tradition of reassessing European bourgeois literature along Marxist lines.

This tradition of reassessment was begun by Franz Mehring and G. V. Plechanov toward the end of the nineteenth century and in the early twentieth century and was carried forth by the Hungarian scholar Georg Lukács. Lukács is primarily responsible for establishing a theoretical basis for the "para-Marxists," who respect the integrity of a work of art while endeavoring to interpret its socioeconomic relevance. This approach is opposed by the orthodox Marxists, who have followed the lead of Andrei Zhdanov and declared (in the name of Lenin) that a work of art must be tendentious and comply with socialist doctrine. Mayer has essentially followed the broad principles laid down by Lukács, but at the same time he has questioned the grand master of Marxist criticism and in many instances gone beyond him.

It would take a study in itself to bring out the differences between Lukács and Mayer, and such a study might be worth the undertaking, for Mayer's criticism reflects the remarkable and diverse direction that the best "para-Marxist" literary critics, such as Walter Benjamin, Theodor Adorno, Ernst Fischer, Lucien Goldman, Roger Garaudy, Edmund Wilson, and others have taken. Here it is sufficient to remark that Lukács tends to be more doctrinaire and didactic when it comes to studying forms of literature in relation to reality and the economic modes of production. He is more strict in his economic and class analysis, and his writing is philosophically oriented and pontifical. Mayer's starting point is his material and the peculiar constellation of the writer and his times. He is more the historical empiricist. His dialectical method shuns simple economic determinism for a more sophisticated materialistic interpretation of history which encompasses the economic foundation of society, its peculiar social structure, and its value systems. Like Sartre, whom he has translated, he is also a superb essayist with an eye for unusual "situations."

Perhaps the key difference between Lukács and Mayer is in their attitude toward the purpose of criticism. The Hungarian scholar seeks to provide a theoretical framework for literature in an Aristotelian manner and to dictate the concern and forms of literature from the standpoint of the class struggle. The German essayist suggests relative guidelines for interpreting literature in a Hegelian manner and endeavors to throw light on the contemporary development of the arts in view of changing socioeconomic factors. Both claim to be heirs of Marx. Both are bourgeois European intellectuals with enormous learning and insights, and both have turned away from their bourgeois tradition—Lukács with disdain, Mayer with sympathy.

Ironically, it is because Mayer had by chance the "privilege" of undergoing initiation into the bourgeois value system and because he had learned the meaning of all the rituals and fetishes that he was drawn to Marxist dialectical materialism. In the course of his development as a Marxist critic, he has both perceived and experienced the disturbing contradictions in the late stage of bourgeois capitalism, and he has geared his writing to preserve the humanitarian aspects of bourgeois culture while moving in the direction of socialism. Most of Mayer's essays deal with German bourgeois writers who took a critical stance from their society. In one collection of essays, *Von Lessing bis Thomas Mann*, Mayer runs the German gamut, including Johann Gottfried Schnabel, Lessing, Schiller, Goethe, Hoffmann, Hegel, Heine, Karl Immermann, Conrad Ferdinand Meyer, Hauptmann, and Thomas Mann. In each one of these eminently bourgeois writers he seeks the antibourgeois seed which will bear fruit in the proletarian age. "The characteristics of the bourgeois literary development in Germany, which has constantly sought to avoid the inadequacies of the outer life by prescribing for itself a 'safeguarded inwardness,' reveal why the theme 'the chronic complaint about Germany' plays a role which has no parallel and can scarcely be found in any other great literature. The theme of German self-criticism is one of the leitmotifs of the German literary development."

Like the development of German literature, Mayer's own literary criticism stems from a "chronic complaint about Germany," and consequently, it mirrors what Heine (and Marx after him) termed *die deutsche Misere*. This term refers to the oppressive conditions in Germany during the nineteenth century, which resulted largely from the failure of the German bourgeoisie to liberate itself from the aristocracy in the eighteenth century and to overthrow the feudal system that cultivated patriarchism, militarism, and bureaucracy. Where most writers and critics of the German bourgeois tradition have turned inward in search of ideal metaphysical realms for relief from the *deutsche Misere*, Mayer has followed Hegel, Marx, Engels, and other radical thinkers who have turned outward and sought a subject-object relationship to resolve the contradictions in the German society. This approach has enabled Mayer to shed new light on some of the more paradoxical figures in German literature, place them in their correct historical context, and reutilize their writings in respect to the socialist tradition and Marx's scientific theories.

Mayer's studies of Kleist, the romantics, Büchner, Kafka, and Brecht are particularly important because they view these authors from a materialistic standpoint that is at odds with the accepted interpretation in bourgeois literary history. Mayer has demonstrated that Kleist's works and suicide were not determined by his reactionary and decadent attitude as aristocrat but by his extreme idealism (stamped by Rousseau) and his disillusionment with the French Revolution. Kleist was, according to Mayer, a man out of step with his own times, beyond help in his own times. The romantics, Kleist's contemporaries, are similar: they are not reactionary escapists longing for refuge in the bosom of the Catholic Church. There are radical components to their paradoxical position related to the Sturm und Drang movement, and this has yet to be explored (*Fragen der Romantikforschung*). The radical components were brought to fruition by Heinrich Heine and Georg Büchner. This is not to imply that they were followers of the romantics. In fact, Heine and Büchner disassociated themselves from the romantics, that is, from the conservative side of the romantics. Essentially, they developed the radical innovations in style and thought which the romantics had conceived but never concretized because of the Napoleonic Wars and Restoration. Mayer portrays Heine as a writer without a tradition who was therefore free to depict the world as an outsider and to react in an exceptionally realistic manner to the "miserable" conditions in his day. Büchner is more the German poet in and of his times who never shied away from taking a stand against the oppressors. Though his work is fragmentary, it is not to be considered incomplete, for he gave complete answers to the questions raised by the conflicts in his epoch. This is also true of Kafka. In fact, the Kafka legend, which enshrouds the writer has been created by literary critics who are hampered by their nonhistorical approach. Mayer is in accord with the more recent criticism that places Kafka as a German-Jew in a Slavic milieu at a time when the Hapsburg Empire was in a state of collapse. Kafka used art as a lever against his own consciousness of this collapse, and in the process, art itself became "relativized." To a certain extent, Mayer also sees Brecht's literary works and practice as experiments in relativity. That is, they seek to reutilize the bourgeois tradition for socialist ends. Brecht cannot be understood, in Mayer's view, without understanding his relation to tradition.

There is also something traditional in Mayer's own relation to writers he favors such as Lessing, J. M. R. Lenz, Kleist, Heine, Büchner, Kafka, Heinrich Mann, Wedekind, and Brecht, not to mention Marx and Engels: they are all outsiders, all influenced greatly by a French democratic tradition. This does not mean that Mayer rejects the mainstream of bourgeois writers from the Goethe-Schiller nexus down through Thomas Mann. It points more to Mayer's own origins—Cologne, his native city, was greatly influenced by the French Revolution—and his admiration for French culture and objectivity. In his criticism, he constantly compares the German outsiders with the insiders, the outsiders with French writers, the French culture with the German culture. The movement is toward a synthesis, toward developing a critical vantage point relying on the objectivity of the French and the subjectivity of the Germans, which might provide the basis for understanding and changing the social realities.

Though not a theoretician in a strict sense, Mayer is greatly concerned with the function of criticism. In his essay *On Realism and Decadence*, he studies how the meanings of literary terms and the role of writers, poets, and critics have been determined by the economic division of labor and specialization. The numerous changes in society have resulted in a loss of universality in literature and historical perspective in criticism. Mayer cites the need for a clarification of literary terms which have become divorced from their subject matter and no longer serve a literary historical function. In stressing the significance of history, Mayer never neglects aesthetic questions. One of his most recent books, *Zur deutschen Literatur der Zeit (On German Literature of the Times,* 1969), studies in part the importance that Marxist critics such as Franz Mehring, Siegfried Jacobsohn, Paul Rilla, Ernst Bloch, and Lukács had for his own development. He then analyzes the extent to which changing socioeconomic conditions determined the function and meaning of language and generated crises in the lives of such different writers as Thomas and Heinrich Mann, Gottfried Benn, Hesse, Musil, Kurt Tucholsky, Kafka, Ludwig Renn, Max Frisch, and Dürrenmatt. As he proceeds, he derives his own theory: the art of criticism consists in appreciating the integrity of a literary work and posing the correct questions in a historical context, which in themselves reflect literature's capacity to offer ontological alternatives. The ideal critic must possess experience, artistic sensitivity, the ability to enjoy, in addition to a keen mind. He must also have a thorough grasp of the classics and history understood in terms of Marxist dialectical materialism. Without these qualities, it is impossible to interpret contemporary literature.

The fact that Mayer deems it necessary that a "scholar" address himself to contemporary literature reveals how sharply he himself breaks from the bourgeois tradition of academic scholarship, which looks down on the criticism of contemporary literature as unprofessional and mere journalism. More than any other European Marxist literary critic, he has concerned himself with contemporary trends in the arts, and not only in Germany. This universality is most unusual for a German critic, and he has distinguished himself by uncovering certain European and American writers for provincial German audiences and encouraging younger critics to take a second, more comparative look at western literature. Mayer was one of the first critics outside of France to study Sartre and one of the first to contend with Gombrowicz. Add to this a list of essays which deal with Aragon, Durrell, Giraudoux, Ionesco, Pasternak, Arbuzov, and Wilder, then his translations of Aragon and Sartre, finally his writings on philosophy, music, and painting, and the vast scope of his critical achievement in the Marxist tradition of reassessment becomes clear.

In his more recent criticism of contemporary literature, *Zur deutschen Literatur der Zeit* and *Das Geschehen und das Schweigen (The Happening and the Silence)*, Mayer reveals just how quickly he reacts to changes in historical trends with great perspicacity.

His analysis of the postwar situation in Germany and the works of such writers as Wolfgang Koeppen, Heinrich Böll, Martin Walser, Uwe Johnson, Günter Grass, Peter Weiss, Wolf Biermann, Christa Wolf, and Günter Kunert leads him to two interesting prognostications: (1) there are two German literatures which have been determined by the political-economic situation and the social rules of the game in the German Federal Republic and the German Democratic Republic; (2) these two literatures mirror the final decadent period—decadence understood as ideological decay —of bourgeois capitalism and the prevailing ideas of the two different states. In West Germany the writers do it with mannerism; in East Germany, with a "slave language." The alternatives vary in each society. They depend on the socioeconomic constellation.

The alternatives in the socioeconomic constellation for the Marxist critic Mayer have never caused him confusion or limited his perspective. With his dialectics and his art of raising questions, he has endeavored to trace the connection of the present condition of society and literature to the past and future. In doing so, he has focused on the tasks of art and criticism within the entire historical process. Mayer's position is taken as an outsider, from the razor's edge. This is a position that he has taken with hope. A position he relentlessly holds wherever he goes and whatever he writes.

The essays in this book have been selected by Professor Mayer and represent part of his more recent endeavors to reassess bourgeois literature along Marxist lines. The focus here is on twentieth-century literature. Professor Mayer wrote the chapter "Steppenwolf and Everyman: Literary Types of the Outsider" exclusively for this volume. "Hermann Hesse's Steppenwolf" and "Robert Musil: A Remembrance of Things Past" appeared in *Zur deutschen Literatur der Zeit* (Reinbek: Rowohlt Verlag, 1967); "Bertolt Brecht and the Tradition" was taken from the unabridged edition *Bertolt Brecht und die Tradition* (Munich: Deutscher Taschenbuch Verlag, 1965); "Friedrich Dürrenmatt: The Worst Possible Turn of Events" was printed in the *Zeitschrift für deutsche Philologie*, 87 (1968), pp. 482–498; "Günter Grass and Thomas Mann: Aspects of the Novel" was published in *Das Geschehen und das Schweigen* (Frankfurt/M: Suhrkamp Verlag, 1969); and "Ionesco and Ideologies," "Observations on the Situation of Sartre," "The Views of Witold Gombrowicz," "Doctor Zhivago," and "Literature and Daily Life: Everyman in the Soviet Union and the United States" were collected in *Ansichten zur Literatur der Zeit* (Reinbek: Rowohlt Verlag, 1962).

In many instances, the original texts and titles were revised and changed with Professor Mayer's approval. One section of the essay on Sartre was taken from Professor Mayer's afterword to his translation of *The Words,* published by Rowohlt Verlag. All translations of the material in this book are mine. The only exception is the Pasternak poem taken from *Doctor Zhivago* (New York: Pantheon, 1958). I have generally used the English titles of European works when they are well known. Otherwise I refer to the original title. In the case of poetry in translation, I have often sacrificed meter and rhyme for the literal meaning since the substance has more significance for the points that Professor Mayer wants to make.

I should like to thank Miriam Koerner and Barry Batorsky for helping me with parts of the translation. I also want to express my gratitude to Abbey Dodge for intangibles that made my work possible.

JACK D. ZIPES

৯৯ Steppenwolf and Everyman

Hermann Hesse's

Steppenwolf

A book about a personal crisis, the crisis of the artist, a social crisis. Only after the indissoluble link between the poetic self-revelation and the cultural criticism is recognized can the book be fully comprehended and properly interpreted. Not everything in it has weathered the times, and Hesse himself would have been the first one to admit this. In fact, he would have called upon Mozart to sentence him in the Magic Theater just like Johannes Brahms and Richard Wagner, who had to redeem themselves in the life hereafter by leading "a massive parade of thousands of men dressed in black," and these thousands were "the musicians who were to play all those notes and parts in their scores which were deemed superfluous by divine judgment." This is exactly what would have happened to the creator of *Steppenwolf*, for even Harry Haller, the Steppenwolf himself, must learn to take such criticism from Mozart, who talks exactly like the real Mozart in his letters to his cousin in Augsburg: "God be with you! The devil's coming to get you. He'll slice you and splice you to pieces for your writings and lousy plagiarizings."

It is difficult to determine whether Mozart's verdict on Harry Haller's writings is correct. Nor are we obliged to read this as a judgment of Hesse. However, there is some truth here, particularly in regard to this one novel, *Steppenwolf*. The pathos in many parts is no longer convincing. The erotic scenes may have had their importance for the fifty-year-old writer Hermann Hesse seeking to emancipate himself in the year A.D. 1927. Yet, today they have a somewhat puerile effect—and this is not merely due to the fact that the modern reader is accustomed to a more spicy diet of novels. The sex scenes are portrayed in a remarkably unsensual manner. It is actually stylized eroticism. Even the cultural criticism—when taken by itself—gives the strange impression in numerous spots of being meek. Hesse treated these themes much more extensively in his portrayal of the "feuilletonistic age" in *The Glass-Bead Game,* written approximately fifteen years after *Steppenwolf.*

Each of these three themes—the personal crisis, the problem of the artist, the cultural criticism—suffers from obvious weaknesses in formal conception and realization in *Steppenwolf.* Despite this, the unusual combination of the themes did give rise to a most remarkable book, and it has retained its appeal.

It is a known fact that the figure of Harry Haller, who has the initials of the author, bears many of Hesse's own traits, and this would be easy to recognize in the course of reading the book even if one did not know the details of his life. The publication of poems, letters, and autobiographical accounts have sufficiently proven that Hesse was undergoing a personal and creative crisis in his fiftieth year, that is, about the time that *Steppenwolf* was being written. The effectiveness of the volume of poems entitled *Krisis* (*Crisis*), which takes its place right next to the Steppenwolf novel as a poetical document of self-revelation, is due not alone to the fact that Hesse's unusually bold fantasies balance his attacks against slick and didactic lyricisms and save them from dilettantism. *Krisis* is also a journal about sickness, and it records great physical and mental sufferings. To a certain extent, this is also true of *Steppenwolf.* Some situations in the novel can be considered a recapitulation of real events in Hesse's life. Many of the erotic parts in the book are clearly reproductions of his experiences, as well as reflections of psychoanalytical studies. However, these very same passages, which were viewed as bold in his time, are the ones which often prove to be somewhat comical, like the fashions of a bygone era. Everything is there: the connection between the libido and the death wish, the ambivalence of sexual desires, infantile eroticism, and the transformation of Haller's boyhood friend Hermann into the long desired, ideal partner Hermine. Moreover, the names Hermine and Hermann recall Hesse's own first name, so Sigmund Freud's remarks concerning the figure of the Greek youth Narcissus form an integral part of the novel. A well-versed psychoanalyst could, in the end, diagnose the relationship between Harry Haller and Hermine-Hermann as the exclusive process of autoeroticism. This would then explain why the ostensibly "bold" sex scenes have such a strange, unsensual, and ethereal effect. Those parts in the book which were fashionable, if not avant-garde, in Hesse's times are funny and quaint in our times.

Yet, Hesse knew even then that this would happen. He wrote a book of spiritual catharsis as another "part of a great confession," to use Goethe's words, and the psychoanalytical apparatus of *Steppenwolf* is integral to the novel, just as the somewhat similar psychoanalytical and philosophical-gnostic structure fits his earlier work *Demian*. He alone sensed from the beginning that the present events and fashions which were important for him would eventually pass for artistic weaknesses. This is clearly expressed in the scene where Mozart uses Brahms and Wagner to instruct Steppenwolf: "The law must take its course. Until they have paid the debt of their time, it cannot be known whether things of a private nature will retain their value." Insofar as this concerns Hesse and his novel written during the critical year 1927, the autobiographical features which Haller received from his author and the erotic behavior and misbehavior correspond to the parts in the scores of Brahms and Wagner that Mozart criticized as bombastic instrumentalization and an unnecessary waste of material.

Hesse had to take into account these cumbersome leftovers of a Magic Theater (which he knew would lose its magic) in order to create a novel that would have enough things of a private nature "to retain its value" even after the fashionable parts had been taken away.

The Steppenwolf novel has retained the value placed upon it in the late 1920's. Goethe, Mozart, the Magic Theater. Haller's love life and relation to his environment can be explained by examining the change in his attitude from obsequiousness and insolence to humorous detachment, and this must be understood as the depiction and solution of the real *problem of the artist*. Hesse does not mean to focus on the split between the Steppenwolf and his bourgeois surroundings so much as on the collapse of Haller's cultural ideals and the breakdown of the cultural rituals, such as the general political beliefs, which he must encounter. This split between Steppenwolf's artistic sense of values determined by Handel, Mozart, and the real (not the misunderstood) Goethe, and the affairs of his contemporaries brought about a painful, almost unbearable alienation. Hermine makes this clear to Haller, her friend and disciple of love: "You had a picture of life within you, a faith, a challenge, and you were ready for deeds and sufferings and sacrifices, and then you became aware by degrees that the world did not demand any deeds and sacrifices from you whatsoever and that life is not a poem of heroism with heroic parts to play and so on, but a tidy bourgeois home where people are quite content with eating and drinking, coffee and knitting, cards and radio. And whoever wants the other life and has got it in him—the heroic and the beautiful and the reverence for great poets or saints—he's a fool and a Don Quixote."

Actually it was in 1919 at the end of World War I that Hesse became concerned with painting this contrast between the great tradition behind his artistry and the "culinary" era of the contented consumer. Two years before *Steppenwolf*, in 1925, he wrote something quite similar in the introduction to the book *Kurgast* (*The Convalescent*): "It is not important to me if the majority is against me. I always blame the majority for being wrong before I blame myself. This is also my position when judging the great German writers whom I continue to admire, love, and need, even though most Germans now do exactly the opposite, preferring rockets to stars. Rockets are pretty. They're delightful. Let them live forever! But stars! Just one glimpse or thought filled with their silent lights, filled with their encompassing world music—you must admit, oh friends, that this is something different!" In that same year Hesse had also published *Kurzgefaßter Lebenslauf* (*A Brief Biography*), and this was an attempt to use Jean Paul's example and compose a bold "conjectural biography" that was to anticipate the future. This engrossing prose narrative began with the words: "I was born toward the end of modern times, right before the middle ages were about to return." The conjectural biography reached its climax with this statement: "This world was unbearable without magic."

What world? *Steppenwolf* appeared in the world of 1927, which Hesse was compelled to feel as a dire contradiction to all his emotions and values. In this particular case, it is necessary to distinguish quite carefully between the conservative prejudices that the Steppenwolf Harry Haller holds against his times and the social criticism that is justifiable. Haller has to learn that the antithesis cannot be terminated in the following manner: for Mozart, against jazz; for traditional chamber music, against the saxophone. Genuine cultural criticism cannot be slanted to take the form of praise for the good old days. This is what Steppenwolf learns from the musician Pablo. The real antithesis continues to operate between Haller's ideal of an artist (which is also Hesse's) and the society in which the artist lives and is supposed to create art. The meaning here is conveyed by the grandiose vision of the "Great Hunt in Automobiles," which forms a part of the Magic Theater: "Cars, some of them armored, were raced through the streets chasing pedestrians. They ran them over and either mashed them into the pavement or squashed them into the walls of the houses. I understood at once that it was the long-prepared, long-awaited, and long-feared war between men and machines which had finally erupted. Dead bodies and bodies torn to pieces lay everywhere, and cars, too, lay smashed, disjointed, and half-burned all over the place. Planes circled above the wasteland turned upside down while rifles and machine guns fired at them from numerous roofs and windows." There are definitely features of anarchy and the machine-breakers in this vision, but it is the hard language and the powerful images, gradually developing the climactic picture of modern man as a lone wolf, that lend these scenes such frightening credibility. All this is integral to the novel and cannot be considered as superfluous musical notes to be repented. Furthermore, these visions recall Picasso's treatment of the war and the Minotaur themes, and so we can see from the form used by Hesse that he was anything but a mere imitator of the great poets, a latter-day romantic. On the contrary, he was a passionate artist of his times. Embittered and desperate.

In addition to all of this, *Steppenwolf* is a particularly German book. Or one could say that it is mainly a novel filled with *criticism of conditions in Germany*. At one point the reactionary professor who invites Haller to dinner tells Harry, who appears to be a friendly, cultivated dinner guest, that he evidently has a quite evil-minded relative, a rotten patriot: "He made fun of the Kaiser and expressed the view that his own country was no less responsible for the outbreak of the war than the enemy nations. What kind of a man says things like this? Well, he's getting what he deserves—the editor has cut him down a peg or two and put him on the rack." However, the honored guest is himself this disreputable individual—unfortunately so for all concerned.

This theme is continually repeated. One time Hesse also quotes the recitative of the *Ninth Symphony's* closing sentence: "O friends, not this way!" This was the title of his famous essay which appeared in the newspaper *Neue Zürcher Zeitung* on November 3, 1914, and lamented the current ecstatic rage of the nationalists and chauvinists. Hesse's exasperation with the epidemic of hate coming from Germany and the Germans rises to the surface time and again in *Steppenwolf*. Whenever this occurs, Haller speaks entirely in behalf of his author. As both cultural critic and artist, Hesse recognized a definite danger in this fermentation of German nationalism and bourgeois superciliousness. Because of it, the development of literature is also threatened: "There was another attack, poorly written, partly by the editor himself, partly plagiarized from the numerous essays in newspapers which all held and repeated the same views. As is well known, no one writes as poorly as the defender of a dying ideology, and no one practices his trade with greater sloppiness and irresponsibility." Once more we can see that *Steppenwolf* belongs to still another important German tradition—one of self-criticism. Here, too, Hesse is anything but a mild, smiling neoromantic. One may debate about the artistic conception, but the intellectual contents of the book and the critical concern about the disgraceful conditions in Germany places *Steppenwolf* in the tradition of Hölderlin's *Hyperion,* Heine's *Wintermärchen* (*Winter Tale*), and Heinrich Mann's *Der Untertan* (*The Loyal Subject*). The writing of this strange novel in 1927 was not intended merely to bring about a spiritual catharsis but to serve as a warning. Mention is made frequently of a new war in preparation. Twenty years later, in 1947, Hesse had to confirm this when he sadly recalled that *Steppenwolf* was actually "among other things an anxious cry of warning about the coming war," and this was the reason why it was "appropriately treated as pedantic and ridiculous" by the bourgeois public and press in Germany at that time.

It is rather remarkable, by the way, that Hesse expressed the very same ideas in *Steppenwolf* concerning the Germans' warped relationship to reality because of music as Thomas Mann did exactly twenty years later in *Doctor Faustus.* When the Steppenwolf Haller reaches the lowest point in his depression and appears to play with the idea of suicide more seriously than usual, he confirms this point: "I had reflected upon the significance of music at length during this night's walk, and once again, I saw the destiny of the entire German spirit connected to this appealing as well as fatal relationship to music. In the German spirit the matriarchal link with nature rules in the form of the hegemony of music to an extent unknown in any other people. We intellectuals, instead of fighting against this tendency like men, and rendering obedience to the spirit, the Logos, the word, and gaining a hearing for it, are all dreaming of a speech without words that utters the inexpressible and gives form to the formless. Instead of playing his part as truly and honestly as he could, the German intellectual has constantly rebelled against the word and against reason and courted music. Therefore, the German spirit, carousing in music, in wonderful creations of sound, and wonderful beauties of feeling and mood that were never pressed home to reality, has neglected the majority of its real tasks." This observation began with a generalization which was too vague, and consequently, it was immediately modified and qualified. "We intellectuals," writes Haller, and by using this phrase, he demonstrates that the problem concerns a species in Germany which has a warped relationship to reality and has not been able to change reality with its ideas because of this. Such action on the part of intellectuals would not be possible anyway because their ideas were secretly musical ideas even where the score had never been written. If, like Heinrich Mann, one were to try in spite of this to bring about the unity of spirit and action in works of fiction after a difficult war, then it could only amount to lamentation.

Haller does not name Heinrich Mann but refers to those efforts to remedy the conditions in Germany after World War I, and he also refers to the efforts of the writer Hermann Hesse about 1920. The result? "It always ended in resignation, in a surrender to destiny. The generals and the captains of industry were quite right: there was nothing to worry about from us 'intellectuals.' We were nothing but a bunch of superfluous, irresponsible, ingenious talkers who knew nothing about reality." Many of these meditations from the year 1927 became part of Thomas Mann's novel *Doctor Faustus* in 1947, and here, too, it was necessary to link the complex features of autobiographical material, the problem of creativity, and the social crisis in a highly unusual epic form. In his journal *Die Entstehung des Doktor Faustus* (*The Origination of Doctor Faustus*), Mann noted at the very beginning that it had been a mistake on the part of Goethe to portray Faust as a professor and a man of science and not a musician. He himself tried to correct this alleged error. In the subtitle he began to speak about the "German musician," which was somewhat tautological for Mann since a reference to music was already contained in the word German. It is not much different in *Steppenwolf*. There the musicality of German intellectuals also takes the shape of a disturbed relationship to reality.

This makes it even more astounding that the apparent solution to Harry Haller's mental crisis and life dilemma should be seen in a logical separation of intellect and reality. When the immortals Goethe and Mozart attempt to help Steppenwolf in his existential conflict, they teach him that he must begin to separate the Magic Theater of art from the depressing daily routine of life. The most serious accusation that can be brought against

Haller by the state's attorney reads as follows: "Gentlemen, before you stands Harry Haller, accused and convicted of the willful misuse of our Magic Theater. Haller has not only insulted the sublimity of art by confusing our beautiful picture gallery with so-called reality and stabbing the reflection of a girl with the reflection of a knife, but he has moreover demonstrated the intention of using our theater as a mechanism for suicide without a sense of humor." Whoever acts in this manner is to be subjected to the frightful laughter of the immortals.

Of course, these immortals, with no less of an artist than Mozart at their head, appear to be dedicated Schopenhauerians who momentarily forget their mundane problems in the realm of art. There is no doubt but that Hesse continually contrasted the validity of the rare and happy experience induced by art with the everyday hum-drum existence. There is a hint of this memorable experience right in the preface written by the editor of Haller's manuscripts when he describes the Steppenwolf listening to Baroque music during a concert. Haller himself reports about the same event later in the book. The Magic Theater is supposed to drive the lesson home that reality and the play element in the immortal magic must carefully be kept separated from one another. However, Hesse did not feel that this was the final solution, and it is most probable that he did not want it to be taken as his own interpretation and solution of Haller's case. He indicated as much in *The Journey to the East* in 1932, which once again treated the division between reality and imagination. The pilgrims here were both fictional characters and real creatures of the twentieth century. It is quite clear: the lessons of Pablo and Mozart did not contain the final recipe for solving existential problems. As an expert on German romanticism, Hermann Hesse had in this respect—despite Schopenhauer's views on this subject—no illusions, for it had already been demonstrated by E. T. A. Hoffmann in *The Golden Pot* that life in Atlantis, in the world of immortal poetry, could cover up the misery in the daily routine of life in Dresden only for brief moments. At the most, then, Haller could hope for the same fate as Hoffmann's student Anselmus or the musician Kreisler. Actually, his situation is worse, for in the twentieth-century world and in the middle realm between two world wars, the separation of reality and the Magic Theater could only contribute to an intensification of the crisis. If Haller really carried out the teachings of Mozart and Pablo, then he would only be helping to prepare new and even more difficult crises for future Steppenwolves.

Hesse apparently intended to leave the ending of the book an open question, and one should, therefore, avoid reading the closing pages as though they contained a "solution." The *Treatise on the Steppenwolf* substantiates this point. It is an unusual and bold piece which, moreover, gave a startling impression because of the special type used in the first edition and because it was bound into the book as a small pamphlet with the title and the closing pages in bright yellow. The weird contrast of the words *Treatise* and *Steppenwolf* as well as the absurd arabesques on the title page made it seem like a carnival, a ballad, and a book of devotions. This undoubtedly heightened the contrast between the carnival without and the scientific analysis within, which was detached and highly learned. One could sense this contrast in reading the very first words of the *Treatise on the Steppenwolf,* for they actually begin a psychological and sociological examination in which life and crisis and death are compressed into a scientific subject, and oddly enough the traditional formula of a fairy tale is selected for the beginning. "Once upon a time there was a man named Harry, who was called the Steppenwolf." Once upon a time. The beginning of a fairy tale and a scientific analysis. Once again—as is so often the case with Hesse—we have both actual science and a playing with science. A treatise in Spinoza's sense and a treatise in the sense of a book of devotions.

Even in the reading of the *Treatise on the Steppenwolf,* one must be cautious. Not merely because it is supposed to be written "for madmen only," *"Nur für verrückte,"* which should be read as *ver-rückt* (to have lost one's place). More important is the realization that the solution to Haller's case cannot be found in the treatise or in the final scene of the Magic Theater. They contradict one another and are intended to do so. In addition, the treatise contradicts Haller's own notebooks and his own poem about the Steppenwolf as well. The treatise seems to base its analysis on objectivity, yet it hardly renders an interpretation of the affair which would allow the reader to classify Haller's case. Whom should one believe? The immortals who took ideas from Schopenhauer and gnosticism to emphasize the separation of reality and Magic Theater, or the treatise which looks upon the same ideas merely as paradoxical documents of intellectual history? Haller shows strong romantic traits in his struggle to return "home," to his childhood, to the simple forms of existence, and the Magic Theater even helps bring out these traits in him. In contrast, the *Treatise on the Steppenwolf* does not speak about steppenwolves as special types but plays down their uniqueness, the very thing they pride themselves on. The pamphlet wants to understand these types as "those who feel guilty because of their individualism, those souls whose goal no longer appears to be the development and perfection of themselves, but the dissolution of the self, the return to the mother, to God, to the All."

However, this romantic regression is no longer possible. Moreover, Hesse is not to be regarded as a romantic. The Steppenwolf Harry Haller is to be understood as a product of the modern bourgeois society. Even worse, with all his yearning for the bourgeois life and in spite of his lone wolf traits, he is actually used to fortify the world of the bourgeois. "In this way he always recognized and affirmed with one half of his nature and behavior that which his other half fought against and denied."

If the bourgeoisie, which the treatise depicts as culturally unproductive, could nevertheless expand, then it is to the treatise we must also turn for an explanation: "The answer: it is because of the steppenwolves." Here again we have the contrast between the artist and the bourgeois just as Thomas Mann portrayed it twenty-five years earlier in *Tonio Kröger*. However, Hesse's answer is derived from insights based on World War I and the postwar period. The steppenwolf type helped to consolidate the gains made by the bourgeois world mainly because of the dualism of its animal and human nature. Here is the parallel between the chain of thought in the treatise and the visions of the wolfish nature of bourgeois civilization in the Magic Theater. Even the world of the bourgeois proves to have steppenwolf tendencies.

The treatise goes even further: it expressly ridicules the formulation "Steppenwolf," considering it to be an expression of an obsolete anthropology: "We need not be astonished that such an intelligent and educated man as Harry should take himself to be a steppenwolf and believe that he can reduce the rich and complicated system of his life to such a slick, brutal, and primitive formula." The question does not concern the contrast of his animal and human nature, nor is it correct to assume that Harry—like Faust—has two souls in his breast. "Harry does not have two souls, but a hundred, a thousand." In this regard, he corresponds to the pluralism of a society which continually alienates the individual from his own self and transforms him into a mere instrument with numerous functions. The bourgeois world as it is described in the novel makes it impossible for Harry to become a whole person, an "individuality," as the treatise expresses it at one point. Steppenwolf would like to affirm his unique identity vis à vis society and its tendency to alienate. Many steppenwolves would like to do this, but it is because of this very desire that they accelerate the alienation process which leads to depersonalization. The result? Magic Theater with the continual loss of individuality. Perhaps one should go one step further than the treatise and add: depersonalization as a consequence of playing too often with the Magic Theater.

The treatise does not go this far. It maintains that there can be no return at all, neither to the wolf, nor to the child. In the beginning of all things, there is no innocence and simplicity. Every created thing, even the simplest, is already guilty, already complex, and is thrown into the muddy stream of becoming, and can never swim against the stream and return to its source. "The way to innocence, to the uncreated, to God, does not lead back to the wolf or the child but forward to the great depths of guilt, further and further into human evolution." This is not romantic regression but a step forward. The treatise considers individuality possible but only in the form of a future process which would mean that the coming evolution would naturally be understood as "guilt." It is in this passage that the most important thesis of the treatise is propounded, and it is here that we also have the sharpest contradiction to Haller's own notes. Everything remains an open question in this unusual book. Hesse presents the contradictions much more poignantly and directly than he did later in *The Glass-Bead Game*. In both cases we are presented mainly with an analysis, a warning, not a solution. Neither Castalia nor the Magic Theater is a solution. We are left with an alarming book written especially for the German intellectuals, who did not heed the alarm. A book about a personal crisis, the crisis of the artist, a social crisis.

Robert Musil: A Remembrance
of Things Past

So, Törless sat there, completely still and quiet. He kept staring at Basini and was thoroughly immersed in the crazy rumblings within him. Time and again the one question came to his mind: What is this special quality I possess?

ROBERT MUSIL, *Young Törless*

Among the fascinating stories told by the philosopher Ernst Bloch, there is one about an episode that occurred about 1908. At that time he was living as a private tutor in Garmisch, and the Bavarian composer and conductor Richard Strauss was also in the vicinity. Every now and then, Strauss had the young Dr. Bloch over for dinner. At that time Bloch had already commenced work on the musical-philosophical parts of his first book *Geist der Utopie* (*The Spirit of Utopia*), which contained the following about Strauss: "It is difficult to form a clear opinion about him. He is an ordinary man, and one recognizes in him that enterprising person who knows how to take life and enjoy it. It is actually because of this and in spite of this that Strauss is extremely good company." Upon one of the dinner occasions, Dr. Bloch discussed the nuances and questionable features of the *Salome* partitur from a philosophical point of view. The host sat there and meditated deeply without understanding a thing.

At times he said, "Yes, yes," but it was apparent that he was not paying attention. Gradually the young philosopher became angry, wished to himself that the insensitive fool would go to hell, but then quickly remembered with a shudder—"that guy there was the one who composed the work."

It was difficult to form a clear opinion about that man at the table who had nonetheless composed a work which challenged the mind of this astute philosopher. It was not much different at times with Thomas Mann, who was quite well-educated and sophisticated, and grew up in the cosmopolitan seaport of Lübeck. He held both an honorary doctorate and honorary professorship, was most polite and well-informed. It was a joy to talk to him because he knew so much and understood the art of giving praise. Naturally there were those moments during a conversation when his bright eyes suddenly and dangerously lit up, moments which one had to overlook. He was photographing. He felt it would be a sin—as a writer addicted to reality—to let anything go by. Yet, there was always the question: was he really one and the same with the author of *The Magic Mountain* and *Doctor Faustus*?

Whoever chanced to meet Robert Musil could rest assured about his identity as a writer. In his case one always knew that one was being confronted with the author of *Young Törless* (*Die Verwirrungen des Zöglings Törless*) and *The Man Without Qualities* (*Der Mann ohne Eigenschaften*). It is true, whether we like it or not, that our recollections are modified and sometimes falsified by our present knowledge of a person when recalling the past. So, "now" and "then" are mixed in a conglomeration, reality experienced in the past and information gathered today. As soon as a person dies, our relationship to him has changed. Sartre speaks about this in *The Words*. It is easy to deal with a dead person, for we know how and when he died, and we possess his works—the published ones and even the fragments, providing that the scholars have done their job well. Because of this we are prevented from recapturing any of the past moments in the dead person's life the way it had been lived. This is true even for those moments one might have experienced with him. Here, too, the memory is handicapped by those two determinants which have been passed on by the dead person: the manner of his death and the balance of his works.

Whenever I think about Musil, whom I first encountered on September 3, 1940, in a small house near Geneva and last saw in March of 1942, a few weeks before his death, it becomes most difficult to discard my present knowledge of him, namely, all the posthumous information. The result is that the actual dimension of our meetings cannot be entirely illuminated.

Perhaps it is really wrong to proceed this way. Today it has become much easier to decipher the attitudes and particular reactions from his statements which I *now* remember were crucial for the man and writer Robert Musil and which, in spite of the lapse of time, I think, belonged to his "qualities."

Musil was exhausting. I cannot find a better word to describe him when I recall my encounters with him. Exhausting in conversation, in every confrontation. This was part of his greatness; it was what he in his doctrines demanded from the writer, particularly himself: the creation of original material at every moment. In other words, the impossible.

So it was always highly likely that he would develop rather remarkable observations in conversation concerning the structure of psychological phenomena. Just before his death the source books on Gestalt psychology had the prominent place on his desk. It seemed that the situation of his voluminous novel demanded this specialized study. The diary of his last years bears this out. Furthermore, Musil was always on familiar ground when it came to psychology.

At that time he expressed some new and startling ideas—perhaps in connection with the research of Hans Kelsen on the ethnological and anthropological basis of natural law among primitive peoples. It was impossible to stay with him while he was speaking. One just listened, attempted to see everything clearly, and answered politely, as is always the case when a young person meets and talks with a great man who is much older. One agreed with everything and said: "Why naturally, certainly." In those days this was considered to be an elegant reply. However, Musil would immediately sweep you off your feet by retorting: "What do you mean 'naturally'? That's not at all natural." And he would proceed to present a series of arguments which questioned the ideas he had just developed. So he would force one to forgo all the usual mechanisms of conversation and convention, all the stopgap measures.

He certainly was exhausting. That was all part of the substance. Many years later Ernst Rowohlt recalled in Hamburg how his entire publishing house (Rowohlt Verlag, which was located in Berlin during the late 1920's and early 1930's) would become uneasy when the news spread that Dr. Robert Musil would shortly be arriving from Vienna to look into matters concerning his books.

Here there was a connection: the man and his work. Actually there was only his work. Musil liked to draw special attention in conversations to his achievements as an athlete, especially to his technique as a freestyle swimmer, and he was also not too modest in commenting about his success with women. One really would have difficulty believing all this, though it was true. Even toward the end of his life, Musil appeared quite slim and athletic. In spite of the aggravating kidney disease, one had a sense of the strength and dynamicism of the man. So the reason for doubt did not lie here. It was mainly in the suspicion that Musil understood all life, every single moment of the young as well as the aging man, all the mathematics and techniques, ballistics and love, to have but one meaning—material for his work.

In connection with this, however, one must take every passage of his work much more specifically as part of a particular event and experience in the author's life than one may be accustomed to do with other important writers, at least in this century. Of course, Thomas Mann also transformed himself into his characters. He made himself into both Hanno and Thomas Buddenbrook, into Castorp and the patriarch Jacob, cloaked himself in Goethe's dressing gown, and toward the end of his life used his own nature to create the identity of Adrian Leverkühn and Serenus Zeitblom. It was always autobiography. In spite of this, Mann knew how to objectify the autobiographical material in such a manner that the figures took on an epic dimension which he himself respected. Leverkühn had to deal with many of

Thomas Mann's experiences and problems along his way, but he was not Thomas Mann. Insofar as Franz Kafka transformed all experience into parable during his nocturnal writing sprees in an attempt to elude psychology, he could afford to endow his protagonists with his own initial K, without ever crossing the border which irrevocably separates life from literature.

This is not to say that Musil did this. Even he respected this borderline between reality and fiction. However, the realities are different in his works, even more questionable than in the works of Thomas Mann and Kafka. Musil was familiar with one predominant theme: himself. What is so fascinating about his peculiar situation is that this theme with which he was so familiar constantly eludes him. Thomas Mann and Franz Kafka, who are so different from one another, are similar in that they are convinced that they know the causes of their sufferings, and they project them into their narrative fiction with their own special and specific literary techniques. Musil does not have this certainty at all. Like his young hero Törless, he continually asks himself: What is this special quality I possess? Here in his very first work we have the key word "quality"—used to express how conscious he is of his helplessness.

There is no doubt but that Musil is quite different from all those other important writers whose works and creative methods we think we understand because of our knowledge of their death and their posthumous papers. Musil is another story. Each moment in his life was simultaneously an essential part of his work —long before the author even made the attempt to objectify this moment through reflection and conception. It was for this reason that he made the titanic and impossible effort to live every moment in such a dynamic manner that it might immediately take on a literary form in the process. This is also the reason why he demanded originality—he not only demanded it from himself as a writer but also from the social and active individual Robert Musil. Each moment experienced with him was in the process of becoming his work, material for writing, a tentative formulation.

It is evident today that the novel *Young Törless* is related to *The Man Without Qualities* as Joyce's *Portrait of an Artist* is to

Ulysses. The author of *Törless* intended this from the beginning. In this famous novel of a prep school boy there are numerous passages which imply that we are not only hearing the story of an adolescent but that the narrator is already thinking of portraying a sequel to deal with the further development of *Young Törless.* There are phrases like: "Törless' inability to relate to philosophy and literature influenced his later development in a bad way and caused him many an unhappy hour." Or, "Törless' preference for certain moods was the first sign which was to reveal itself as a talent for being amazed."

Then the book continues in this manner: "Later on he was completely ruled by a peculiar ability. Frequently he was obliged to experience events, people, things, and even himself in such a way that he had a feeling of infinite incomprehensibility as well as an inexplicable relatedness never fully justified. They all appeared to him as things which could be understood and within his grasp, and yet, never allowed themselves to be reduced to words and thoughts. Between the events and his ego, even between his own feelings and some kind of inner ego which desired understanding, there was always a dividing line like a horizon which retreated before his yearning the closer he came."

Actually Ulrich's situation is the one being described here— the man without qualities. Musil did not want to, nor could he portray anything else except his own search for self-assurance and inner development. For this reason he needed all experiences for his work "if it was to continue." And it was for this reason also that he was in such a condition of restlessness and perplexity when I met him toward the end of his life in Geneva. To be sure, part of this was due to the way he had to live, but one could also sense that the misery of his outer life had endangered his work. His existence was frustrated and thereby threatened the continuation of the great novel. The work could not develop because his life was stagnating. Musil found it impossible to sustain himself as Ulrich, nor could he tell the story as a recollection of a period of confusion as in the case of *Young Törless.* Somehow an awesome simultaneousness between the lives of Ulrich and Musil had developed even though the action in this extraordinary novel took place before World War I. Furthermore, he had planned the ending—as though it depended on that—to coincide with the outbreak of the war in 1914. In this respect everything was plain and clear. Musil even wrote in his diary: "Chief idea from the beginning of volume II onwards: War." On the surface, it seemed that there was a time differential between Ulrich's life in the days before World War I and Musil's during World War II. Yet, in reality they were the same. If the novel was to proceed, then Musil would have to portray Ulrich's experience by adding material to his own life. This was, indeed, difficult in that little house on Chemin des Clochettes. He could not go on with Ulrich. Even his books on Gestalt psychology could not help him.

What caused this depletion of life? How could it be explained? Naturally, a great deal depended on the working conditions. It was a life in exile. The Swiss emigration police did not exactly look after the emigrants with great, loving care. During the early part of the war, the quick victories of Hitler had made a great impression on the Swiss. The emigrants were considered a hindrance to official Swiss-German relations. The authorities in Bern breathed a sigh of relief when Thomas Mann left his house in Küsnacht on the Lake of Zurich in order to become an American professor. However, they were less kind to Romain Rolland in Villeneuve on the Lake of Geneva: he was ordered to leave the country. Musil, too, received nice requests on a regular basis which asked him to think about making travel plans to leave his "temporary" home in Switzerland. As one can imagine, each time he received one of these letters, he became quite depressed.

In such misery, it was impossible to think of compromises, or of compromising with this misery. I remember one visit with him. It must have been during 1940. Musil had once again received a summons from Bern. He had already explored the possibility of emigrating to the United Sates, but his wife's family was apparently not in a position to provide the affidavit and financial support necessary for the granting of the visas. The question of the visas was the subject of our tea conversation on that afternoon. Right now my memory would like to make it seem as though we always talked chiefly about the problems of emigration and literature during my visits on the Chemin des

Clochettes. I was of the opinion that he should try to acquire a visa for South America. At that time some friends of mine had received without any difficulty permission to emigrate to Colombia. Musil was a Christian—this is the way I argued my case —a so-called Aryan, even a member of the nobility. He looked at me disapprovingly and then merely said: "Stefan Zweig is in South America."

This was by no means a simple witty remark. Though a great ironic writer, Musil was not a witty conversationalist. He meant it in all seriousness. Stefan Zweig, Emil Ludwig, and, most of all, Thomas Mann belonged to that hated species of "popular writers." And, if Stefan Zweig was living somewhere in South America, then Musil had no use for the entire continent.

In the meantime the Musils had practically nothing in their small house outside the gates of Geneva. They depended on refugee help. The minister Robert Lejeune from Bern proved to be Musil's most loyal and almost only supporter. He had become aware of Musil through a young Austrian emigrant, Fritz Wotruba, who admired Musil and who was also to become famous later on as a sculptor. Wotruba thought it an honor to be able to help a man like Musil. On the other hand the Swiss literary world did not pay him an iota of attention. On one visit I found Musil sad and troubled. He had been invited by a literary society to give a reading somewhere in the German part of Switzerland, and he had read some unpublished material from *The Man Without Qualities* to a very small audience. None of the society's officers were present. They had even forgotten about the small reception which usually followed the main affair. A secretary came to him and handed him an envelope with the honorarium. Musil's bitter remarks received a cool response from the secretary, who implied that the whole affair was nothing more than an act of charity.

Weeks after this degrading experience, we met once again in Geneva, but he had not gotten over it. He took all this seriously. Incidents of this kind formed the substance of his life instead of more eventful experiences which should have been material for his book. Later when I returned to Geneva more than twenty years after Musil's death and talked about these emigration episodes with the historian Carl J. Burckhardt, who had a great respect for Musil, he told me about another unfortunate incident. As a matter of fact it was the cause of Burckhardt's first meeting with Musil. At that time there was a society for German language and literature in Geneva. As usual it was headed by the professor who held the chair for German at the University of Geneva. To become a member of this society one had simply to submit an application. Dr. Robert Musil took the view—and he was not entirely wrong—that he, too, could have a place in this society, but the president appeared to be of another opinion: the professor did not want to admit the Viennese emigrant. Robert Musil turned to Burckhardt with the request that he speak to the professor on his behalf. Musil's diary reveals just how extremely serious he was about his academic adversary, even if his use of initials instead of names seems to make the gravity of this small war less tense today than it was.

What a ridiculous and tortuous pattern. Robert Musil and Carl J. Burckhardt as claimants to membership in a literary society. Generally speaking, it is assumed that the amount of energy expended in a given situation will be reduced if the causes are minimal. However, the opposite is more often the case. Balzac knew that. In *The Minister from Tours*, two members of the clergy fight over a furnished room, and it is like a battle for a kingdom. Musil, too, fought in such cases as though his life depended on it.

His life did depend on it. All this had to do with the process of finding the self, with the dominating leitmotif of his creative work: the whimsical incongruity between his desire for success in life and for the creation of great literature. There is no doubt that this writer knew who he was and what the world would have to say about him one day. On September 24, 1939, he wrote the following to the minister Robert Lejeune about his Swiss "benefactors": "They are solid in their judgments and always remain true to the dead whether it be Keller, Meyer, Rilke, or Hofmannsthal. To a certain extent, I, too, feel certain that they will look upon my stay in Switzerland in a favorable light. But to wait first until one is dead in order to live is truly quite an ontological trick!"

Three years before this, Musil had brought out a collection of stories and reflections in a small Zurich publishing house under the title *Nachlass zu Lebzeiten* (*Posthumous Papers of a Living Author*). It contained one short piece called *Eine Kulturfrage* (*A Cultural Question*), which deals with the same subject that Musil had analyzed shortly after the outbreak of the war. This time it concerns himself and asks the question Musil never tired of asking: What is a great writer? His answer points out that genuine failure is part of great writing, but that numerous non-writers and opportunists knew how to live off great writers even during their lifetime, generally postmortem. "I estimate that there are about a dozen of these great writers left in the world. Whether they can continue to live while others live off them is uncertain. Some are probably in a position to do this; others not. Everything is up in the air as far as this is concerned. If one would desire to compare this to a similar situation, one could say that numerous people live off fish and chickens. But the fish and the chickens do not live off them. Just the opposite. They die because of the relationship. One might also add that our fish and chickens even live for a while because of the very fact that they must die. Yet, this comparison falls apart because one knows what these creatures are, that they actually exist, and that they do not disturb the fish foundaries and chicken farms. In contrast, a writer can most definitely disturb those businesses which make a living off literature."

The period of misery in Geneva took on the meaning of self-affirmation for Musil. It had to take this course since he seemed to belong to the breed of great writers who were vanishing at that time. And it has become evident that he was right. Robert Musil's work today affords vast opportunities for master's theses as well as doctoral dissertations. There are also research grants available for Musil specialists. Some scholars travel across the world to look at his manuscripts. Musil has become one of those great writers for posterity. What was important for him was that he would no longer be assigned this place "as a living author." That was all that mattered. As a living author he remained a troublemaker and a charity case. Everything went according to plan. But it was still an extraordinary ontological trick.

Of course, there was something much more to all of this. The genuine artist and the popular writer were considered opposites. There was no getting around this. Here Musil's opinion of his contemporaries was influenced by this basic doctrine: popular success in almost every case must speak against the authenticity of the popular writer. I always had the impression that Musil's relationship with me was hindered somewhat by my high regard for Thomas Mann, which I did not conceal. Thomas Mann. Musil was unfair to him and was later surprised (even moved) to learn that Mann had helped his Austrian colleague to obtain financial support from an American foundation. Mann was one of the first writers—and he also wrote about this—to feel that Musil's off-beat, grandiose manner deserved respect, at the very least, even if one could not admire him. In contrast, Musil did not think highly of the writer Mann. Actually, when I think about it, there were only two writers about whom Musil talked with respect: Kafka and Rilke. The only thing Musil held against Rilke was that he was the darling of the aristocrats, and he even mentioned this in his funeral oration. Nevertheless, respect. Kafka was Musil's very own, for he was not a "popular writer." It should be remembered at this point that it was impossible for Musil during those days in Geneva to predict the Kafka boom which followed World War II. Rilke and Kafka. Only those two. Karl Kraus?—dismissed with the wave of a hand. You couldn't take him seriously. Mann?—a "popular writer." Hofmannsthal?—a shrug of the shoulders. After this came Ludwig and Zweig, both of whom he intensely disdained and disrespected. Here it was actually difficult to ascertain whether the disdain outweighed the disrespect. All of this sounds rather cruel, yet it must be understood as the portrait of a complex person. He was, in fact, most difficult. Difficult and exhausting.

All of this was incorporated in his works. The hate and the disrespect for the "popular writers" and their literary bacchanalia —whether valid or invalid—became productive for Musil. The young woman Alpha in the comedy *Vinzenz und die Freundin bedeutender Männer* (*Vinzenz and the Girl Friend of Important Men*) is a bluestocking, a comic, somewhat exaggerated version of Alma Mahler-Werfel, who sets up her own literary and political salon. Today she gives the impression of a fictional character created from a feeling for revenge, as well as from the artist's basic need for human props when he turned to his theme: artistic self-discovery and nonartistic popular literature. This theme is emphasized and treated in all of Musil's works—in the *Vinzenz* play, in *Die Schwärmer* (*The Fanatics*), and finally in *The Man Without Qualities,* where Ulrich's highly ambivalent relationship with Diotima becomes the definitive and final product of the earlier sketch of the young woman Alpha.

Ulrich and Diotima. Diotima and Arnheim. This coordinate system is once again superbly connected by Musil in the novel with the contrast between the genuine writer and the popular writer. It is well known that Arnheim, the great writer, was supposed to be a portrait of the politician Walther Rathenau. I remember asking Musil whether Rathenau, who was quite large, would actually place his arm around a person's shoulders or on the shoulders of his guest as they say he did in order to protect them. Musil suddenly became limpid from anger and said: "Yes, and just think, he also did it to me." Although this had happened a long time ago, and Rathenau had been murdered in 1922, Musil remembered everything in a flash when I asked the question, and he felt the humiliating manner of the great writer Arnheim-Rathenau all over again.

Despite all the misery of his daily routine, Robert Musil might have been able to exist comfortably as a writer in this area of conflicts and constellations before and after his emigration if there had not been another high voltage area: Musil knew who he was. He never in the least doubted the worthlessness of his more successful contemporaries. However, the difficulty was that Musil intensely desired—and he even admitted this in conversations—the very superficial success which he believed to be unsuitable for him and not worth the effort. Though it went against his principles, there were occasions when he would point out how his chances for success had been sabotaged at various points in his career only by a series of unfortunate and adverse circumstances. He argued that *Young Törless* had been a genuine success and that his long-awaited, monumental novel had been advertised later under highly favorable conditions. In fact, the

first volume of *The Man Without Qualities* had been published
with all the signs of future success. Only the advent of the Hitler
regime had caused the quick decline of this auspicious beginning.

Musil deluded himself with such talk, and yet was quite aware
of it. Every success he had during his lifetime was actually minimal and cannot at all be compared with the glory and money
gained by the popular writers. He talked this way in order to
console himself in moments of despair while looking back on
his career as a writer. In the meantime he could not smash the
illusion. The immense contrast between his outer life as a failure
and the awareness of his unusual talent was connected to his
concern about the progress of his great novel, which thrived on
this tension but was always in danger of being stifled.

It was during this period of his life that Musil was going
through a creative crisis which he never overcame. Death ended
it abruptly for him. There had been very little time for him to
test his surroundings. Vinzenz had asserted himself against the
background of Alpha and the "important" men in her salon.
Törless stood in that highly explosive field between Basini and
Beineberg. Kakania = Austria belonged to Ulrich: the abundance of social and historical qualities corresponded to the lack
of qualities. However, there was nothing like this in Geneva.
Kakania was not there, nor was it possible to experience a new
world. *The Man Without Qualities* could not be completed in
exile. As long as there was nothing like Kakania as the world of
contrast in any form or shape, then the eternal question concerning his own special quality as writer was the only one which
could be effectively incorporated in the novel. In Geneva life
was dominated by the misery of the daily routine, which caused
many problems. These were mainly financial ones that could be
counted on an adding machine and did not require the special
gifts of Musil the mathematician. Only here one must be careful
not to confuse these problems with the earlier, more stimulating
ones. In Geneva the difficulty arose from a lack of real conflicts.
Musil could not force his writing by reading books. He was
thrown back to his prime experience as young Törless: What
is this special quality I possess?

Actually the question has two parts to it. First, it concerns the quality which both Törless and Ulrich possess as it affects society. In other words, the man with his qualities in relationship to his surroundings, or the artist in relation to success, his contemporaries, and posterity. Musil was always able to answer this first part of the question most impressively in his work. This is the problem between the writer and society. However, the supplementary question is posed by Törless himself in an attempt to know himself. Here Musil is asking, What actually happens inside me when I write? Is it possible to trace the creative process with exactitude without losing spontaneity by being exact?

The sculptor Fritz Wotruba remembers several conversations he had with Musil during his last years that constantly revolved around the theme of the creative act. The questions put to the young artist were insistent. Wotruba had the impression in retrospect that one could almost call them indecent. Musil the writer, scientist, and psychologist was overcome by the prurient desire to know how it actually happened: the inspiration followed by the act of making a sculpture. Since he himself had not been able to become entirely conscious of the actual creative process after many years of literary activity, he attempted to obtain exact information about the enigmatic condition from a young and apparently brilliant representative of the fine arts who had a great deal in common with Musil.

The German poet Gottfried Benn, who used to speak about the "compulsion for expression" (*Ausdruckszwang*) and about the "delineated ego" (*das gezeichnete Ich*), often tried to portray how the originality of an individual forces him to take on a double life: here it was the daily routine of a doctor of dermatology on the one hand, and on the other, "the drunken déluge." With Thomas Mann it was the split between exactitude and ecstasy, between the daily role-playing as a great writer and magic. Musil felt that this idea of a "pure" split was an impossibility and a simplification. The double life was nothing but a rationalization. The story of Ulrich as the man without qualities becomes feasible only because Musil never allows for such double-talk.

The major theme of this unfinished novel is directly linked to the interminable question about the essence of the creative process. In the novel, the narrator speaks about a condition which he calls "the other state" (*der andere Zustand*). Time and again one comes across passages in those final sections of the novel that Musil was able to compose in final form which are modified formulations of the aspired-to synthesis of exactitude and ecstasy. Moonlight, moonbeams during the day, sweet breath of a summer day. It is the persistent attempt to determine "the other state" more exactly in the mutual condition of the brother and sister Ulrich and Agathe, who are closely attached to one another, and this attempt is also supposed to be a simultaneous self-declaration and self-discovery, a pure, ecstatic condition and conscious experience of this very process. Moonbeams during the day. In Heribert Brosthaus' remarkable study of the most important sections of this great novel, there is a most incisive comment about the characters Ulrich and Agathe: "The way to that great moment of fulfillment is also a way into the clarity of sunlight." Brosthaus quite perceptively points out that the narrator Musil is connected to his characters in this search for "the other state" in a way that could be called incestuous. "The characters Ulrich and Agathe, the narrator as actor and essayist, are only different aspects which move from different points of the periphery into the same center."

The search of the brother and sister and their author for "the other state" is secretly determined by Musil's unremitting attempt to comprehend the creative drive in himself. That remoteness which had separated Törless from his comrades is finally supposed to be bridged: this is Ulrich's aspiration as protagonist in the novel and Musil's as author of the novel. As a creative artist Musil felt himself continually threatened by the "irrational," which was to be overcome as rationally as possible. He hoped to make new and important discoveries in the field of human behavior that would have implications far beyond the realm of intellectual creation.

Musil recognized that this strange creative process, which one generally characterized as "being brilliant" and which Goethe sought to explain to himself with the term *demonic,* revealed highly remarkable affinities with religious ecstasy, mystical rapture, initiation rituals of primitive peoples, and modern phenomenological forms of mass hysteria. On September 3, 1940, after my first talk with him, he mentioned in his diary that we had spoken about Hans Kelsen's research on the mentality of primitive peoples, and he predicted that Kelsen's analyses might also be valid for certain phenomena in the animal world. Here Musil's observation anticipated discoveries made by modern science in behavioral research.

All this concerned him primarily as a novelist. Every conversation had the secret purpose for him of contributing to the completion of the novel that was running dry. This accounts for the clumsy and comical attempt on his part to give me the Christian names "Hans Ulrich" in the diary entry of September 3, 1940, when I happened to be his conversation partner. I have nothing to do with the name Ulrich, but this was how Musil called his man without qualities, as is well known. Actually we had talked a great deal about his novel on that afternoon. Our discussion centered entirely on Ulrich and the completion of the novel.

It had become impossible to resolve the intimate relationship of the brother and sister pair Ulrich and Agathe, the mutual search for "the other state" by bringing about a banal ending to the affair through incest. Though he desired somehow to unify the irreconcilables, he had also become too aware of the creative act to force an answer. Musil scholars have recently established that there is nothing in the present authorized text which would indicate that a physical union of the brother and sister took place. Brosthaus has demonstrated that all the passages in the novel which concern Ulrich and Agathe have no hint of "sensuality that is governed by passions and would lead to a sexual relationship." I remember asking Musil whether it would end in incest. He answered that he had originally intended to develop the novel along that line but had felt the need to change the concept. "It's not what the characters want." I can still hear the sound of his words in my ears.

It was in fact true: the characters did not want it that way. Many of the confusing contradictions in the first posthumous edition of the unfinished novel can be explained by the fact that various drafts which belong to the original concept were mixed with the ones based on his new altered concept. This is the reason that the fundamental nature of the novel had to contradict all interpretations which sought to understand Ulrich's relationship with Agathe along physical lines. The scandal of this incident would not have disturbed Musil. However, the characters just would not put up with this trivial solution. It was not so easy to achieve "the other state." Ulrich would have stopped being the man without qualities in the moment of fulfillment. Then the balance of the novel would have been written out of necessity like this: what Bonadea could not give him, Ulrich received from Agathe. In other words, a great literary effort wasted by a trivial ending.

But Musil did not plan the novel to develop this way when he experienced himself and Ulrich as men with great possibilities who thrived on a confrontation of customary realities inside and outside of Kakania. Ulrich (and Agathe as well) was characterized by a certain lack of reality. It showed profound distrust of those realities they were offered. Albert Schöne has demonstrated that the basic feature of the novel and its protagonist is expressed in the language by the preferential use of the subjunctive mood. The subjunctive is necessary here because reality is distrusted and because the two leading protagonists are seeking the possibility behind all reality. However, Musil wrote his last pages, under the heading "The Fresh Air of a Summer Day," in the indicative.

It was quite evident when conversing with Musil that he was serious about making a synthesis out of reality and possibility and the exact description of a "mysticism bright as day." He endured a great deal of suffering because of *The Man Without Qualities*. He wanted to get it off his back, and in the course of his work, he arrived at a point where he decided not only to change the basic concept of the novel but to reduce its size. The ending was still planned to occur at the outbreak of the war in 1914. The irony in portraying all the organized "parallel actions" consisted in the fact that the reader knew from the very beginning how the account, both the historical and the fictional, would have to end. The narrator had no difficulties here. However, Ulrich had to be led—with or without Agathe—to that experience which would allow for a more exact determination of the quality of lacking qualities. The man who is characterized by his lack of qualities had to be socially "integrated," as one would say today.

Sometimes Musil would try to enjoy a feeling of relief which might come from the completion of his novel by talking about his work on a new project—a philosophical investigation, a type of theology without God, an irreligious concern with religion. He hinted at his new plans for work, and it was already clear that the books on Gestalt psychology and the mentality of primitive peoples that were on his desk were part of this plan. But they were also connected to "the other state." The new project, which was conceived to help him recuperate from the novel, proved to be a secret and integral part of it. Nothing worked anymore. There was nothing in sight that could lead to the exact determination of Ulrich's lack of qualities and thereby transform everything into a quality.

What was actually meant by the formulation of the title *The Man Without Qualities*? When we talked about the translation of the title, Musil gave a most remarkable explanation. In the romance languages and English as well, the novel is always associated with the term *qualitas. Der Mann ohne Eigenschaften* has become *The Man Without Qualities* in translation.* When plans were being made to translate the book into French, the publishers wanted to translate the title as *L'Homme sans caractères*, "the man without characteristics." Musil discussed this matter with André Gide in Paris. Gide's German was not very good, but he had an astonishing flair for words. He advised Musil against the translation *L'Homme sans caractères* and suggested that the French version should bear the title *L'Homme disponible*, "the disposable man."

Musil was delighted with the idea. Ulrich was, in fact, disposable in his condition without qualities. Yet, this very disposability of the hero (and his author) prevented the spiritual completion of the novel. This vast disposability and the moment of fulfillment excluded one from the other. Ulrich, the man of great possibilities, on the same path as Doctor Faustus. Musil

---

* *Translator's note:* The word *Eigenschaft* can have several implications. It has the meaning of trait, property, attribute, feature, character, quality, and condition. Hence, the problem in translation.

clearly went to great pains to characterize his hero. We come to know Ulrich better as we continue to read and are even able to predict some of his reactions along with the narrator if certain factors in a situation are known. Yet none of these characteristics contradict the condition of lacking qualities. Ulrich is never consumed by an experience, never becomes at one with an incident. Desire in the pleasure, as is the case with Faust. This is why Ernst Fischer's analysis, which covers Musil's entire canon in great detail, is wrong. Fischer argues that *"The Man Without Qualities* has too much character—and what is more, it is conditioned by class. The ironic mood does not contain this, but the emphasis on pathos does bring it out. The protagonist who allows himself a year 'to learn' and seek form and substance remains a *character* without development. After numerous physical and mental adventures he does not take on a new human consistency but only a new intellectual awareness. The sceptical and amoral individualist achieves the realization that one cannot live without morals and that individual solutions can only be found within the social ones."

Of course Fischer also recognizes the degree to which the remarks in the novel about the central protagonist must be understood as the author's disclosures about himself. Yet, his conclusion here, too, does not tally: "Musil identifies with Ulrich, endows him with his ideas and many of his own traits—and yet, he overlooks the most crucial point. In contrast to his creator, a disciplined, productive writer absorbed in a great work, Ulrich is a do-nothing, a troublemaker, and an anonymity, and because of this, everything about him is wrong, distorted, and unpleasant."

This antithesis—the hard-working Musil and the parasitical Ulrich—misses the mark. Fischer is wrong about the novel's protagonist. Musil's affinity with his literary alter ego is much closer. One should not question the seriousness and the solidity of Ulrich's undertakings, otherwise the narrative will be misunderstood. The tone of the narration set by the apparent ironic distancing of the author from his hero concerns only the manner of portrayal, not the incidents as they are portrayed. Ulrich is not a dilettante and gossip but rather a serious person who merely cannot finish anything in spite of all his talents and good will. At one point in the second volume of the novel Musil says this about him: "A believer who simply believed nothing." Ernst Fischer is sceptical about the way Ulrich conducts his life. Musil is sceptical about the possibility of results when one conducts one's life seriously. The unsuccessful Ulrich is, no doubt, inferior to the industrious and enterprising Arnheim in the opinion of the author, and he cannot match the frenetic attempts at bourgeois respectability made by his friend Walter. These are the advantages and disadvantages of disposability.

Nonetheless, it is this very principle of disposability in particular that is supposed to be discovered behind all the experiments that go awry. In this respect the principle is dialectical, since it is never satisfied with any one condition but allows one immediately to see an abundance of different possibilities in every creature (*Sein*). This is where Ulrich enters the race with time, for he would like to determine all possibilities in advance. Hence, the dialectic degenerates into a paradox for him. Possibility is supposed to be included in reality. The disposability appears as an obvious element of reality. In "the other state," a mystical process is not only supposed to be experienced rationally but is also to be described this way. Ulrich, the man with great possibilities, tried to experience possibility as an element of reality that is conceivable only if one does not at the same time demand solid and valid insights. But this is just what Ulrich did. He wanted to concoct the formula for living and even being productive in Kakania, for performing meaningful work, and for remaining dissatisfied all at the same time. All-around disposability.

That could not succeed. Musil did not have a new social experience that would have liberated him from this paradox and saved the ending of the novel. *The Man Without Qualities* did not remain unfinished because Musil had wanted it that way. On the contrary, the author believed in the possibility of its completion in his contest with the devil—something he had accepted as in the case of Faust with Mephistopheles: to find that moment of fulfillment and to describe it without restricting the condition of disposability from continuing as it always was. Yet, if the novel had reached such an end, then the disposability would have really stopped and the "man without qualities" would have been a man with qualities. In this case, then, Ernst Fischer's thesis might be right, and Musil's novel, which has no comparison in modern literature, would be like all other novels of development in the tradition of Goethe's *Wilhelm Meister*. This would also have meant a sinking to triviality, similar to ending the Ulrich-Agathe relationship in incest. Musil recognized the impossibility of such a physical union in time. Was this also the impossibility of completing the novel under the conditions which he imposed upon himself? Here one is tempted to answer the basic question in Musil's novel and all his works with his own words: "It's not what the characters want."

Bertolt Brecht
and the Tradition

This is precisely the strength of great characters: they do not choose but are completely and naturally just what they want and achieve . . . . On the contrary, their fame is to have done what they really have done. The worst that could be said about such a hero would be to imply that he acted out of innocence. Great characters have the honor of being guilty.

HEGEL, "The Concrete Development of Dramatic Poetry and its Types" in *Lectures on Aesthetics*

Another essential element of *The Street Scene* is that our demonstrator derives his characters completely from their actions. He imitates their actions and consequently allows inferences to be drawn about them. A theater which follows him in doing this will depart greatly from the course of the traditional theater that bases the action on the characters and thereby removes the action from the criticism that it makes the characters who perform it seem an unavoidable consequence of natural law.

BRECHT, "The Street Scene" in *Dialectics in the Theater*

Change—Transformation

The word Brecht preferred most during the last years of his life was *dialectics*. He constantly worked on understanding the different demonstrations of the dialectical method in the works of Hegel, in Marx's *Das Kapital,* and in Lenin's studies on Hegel. Shortly after his return from exile his expert knowledge of this field was brought to bear in a seminar at the University of Leipzig that undertook the task of interpreting Hegel's *Phenomenology of the Spirit.* While participating in this study group, Brecht suggested that exact minutes of the meetings be kept so that one could go back, examine, and possibly correct the results of the work. And this was done the way he suggested.

Aside from the thesis concerning the unity of contradictions, he was particularly attracted to the element of constant changeability in dialectical thinking and found that it could have productive results. Toward the end of his life he came to believe that the original term *epic theater* was too formal, and he indicated this in his essay *Dialectics in the Theater:* "Epic theater is certainly the prerequisite for these contributions; however, it does not of itself imply that productivity and changeability of society from which they must draw for the major part of the enjoyment. Therefore, the term must be designated as inadequate without it being possible to propose a new one." Productivity and changeability of society. They had not received their due in the original thesis on epic theater, not even in *A Short Organum for the Theater.* The antithesis to the previous bourgeois aesthetic, this "heirloom of a class, which has become depraved and parasitical" (*Short Organum*), was overemphasized. The opposition to Aristotle was the important point. Up till then, the theory seemed to be one of negation. The transition to a negation of the negation, even in the sphere of ideas, was not an easy one. Dialectical understanding was to make the doctrine of changeability productive of real changes. This is what Brecht stressed time and again toward the end of his life, and it had always been one of his basic tenets. While he was in exile he had written that one should be impatient with patience. This idea was now repeated in a letter written to the 1955 Darmstadt Conference of Dramaturges, which was concerned with the question of whether the theater can reproduce the present-day world on stage. The first draft of the letter was not sufficient for such an extremely important question. Brecht's final answer on the question about the possibilities of the theater in a changeable world is not only more thorough than the first version but also more dialectical in its treatment of all the factors. Changeability demands *human action* (*menschliches Tun*). Mere confirmation of changes and alterations cannot be sufficient in dialectics: "From the standpoint of a billiard ball it is difficult to conceive of the laws of motion."

The expressionists had already made a great deal out of "change." One of Ernst Toller's typical dramas even had this term as its title, and Rilke's sundry songs of praise celebrated change. Just change alone. The question was never asked about what was being changed and how it happened. The Orpheus sonnet sufficed: "Desire change. O be enthused about the flame/ Wherein a thing eludes you that boasts of transformations" (*Sonnet 12,* Second Part). This cult of transformation without direction and purpose was torture for Brecht, just as mere spiritual revival was like the call for the new man with a "new spirit" which the German expressionists considered their "cause." When the dramatist Friedrich Wolf (who, though a member of the Communist Party, had secretly remained true to his early expressionist tenets) remarked to Brecht in a conversation recorded in 1949 that he did not see the inner transformation of Mother Courage, the learning through suffering, the new realization, he was answered by Brecht rather disdainfully: "Even if Courage doesn't learn anything more, I believe that the audience can still learn something, simply by watching her."

Change understood as transformation, as action. A change of conditions, not merely spiritual revival. Brecht strives for openness to change in his thinking. Only the dialectical transformation of theory into practice can do justice to the historical changes. We derive our heritage from this. Our tradition.

Brecht never worshipped the cult of change. In his early period he quickly distinguished himself from Rilke and the expressionists. And yet his attitude and relationship to the phenomenon of change was changed rather decisively.

In the beginning it was somewhat of an obsession with the impermanence in nature and in society. As a young man, Brecht looked skeptically at man's illusions about the permanence of the edifices in the big cities and the dreams of immortality of the poets. He had misgivings when his beloved Horace, whom he also found amusing, praised his own volume of poetry: "Exegi monumentum aere perennius" ("I have created a monument for all times"). Whereas Rilke fell victim to the cult of change, the continual flow, just like the expressionists, the young Brecht began a type of anticult, that of impermanence. He envisioned decline in all changes, a sinking. This was one of the hidden leitmotifs of *Die Hauspostille* (*Domestic Breviary*), his first book of poems. A four-line poem written in 1927 deals with this:

THE CITIES

Under them are the gutters.
In them, nothing. Over them, soot.
We were in them and enjoyed them.
We did not last. And they ahe also going gradually.

DIE STÄDTE

Unter ihnen sind Gossen.
In ihnen ist nichts. Und über ihnen ist Rauch.
Wir waren drinnen. Und haben sie genossen.
Wir vergingen rasch. Und langsam vergehen sie auch.

One year earlier (1926) one could have read the following poem by Brecht in Stefan Grossmann's magazine *Das Tagebuch*:

ASSERTION

I.
Shut up.
What do you think changes more easily,
A stone or your attitude toward it?
I have always been the same.

II.
What does a photograph say?
Some great words
That one can prove to anyone?
Perhaps I have not become better
But
I have always remained the same.

III.
You can say:
Previously I used to eat my beef
Or I used to
Be quicker in taking the wrong path.
But it is good old ignorance
Which perishes and
I have always remained the same.

IV.
How much does a great rain weigh?
Some thoughts more or less.
Not many feelings or none at all.
Where everything does not suffice
Nothing is sufficient.
I have always been the same.

BEHAUPTUNG

I.
Schweig.
Was, meinst du, ändert sich leichter
Ein Stein oder deine Ansicht darüber?
Ich bin immer gleich gewesen.

II.
Was besagt eine Photographie?
Einige große Worte
Die man jedem nachweisen kann?
Ich bin vielleicht nicht besser geworden
Aber
Ich bin immer gleich geblieben.

III.
Du kannst sagen:
Ich habe früher mein Rindfleisch gegessen
Oder ich bin
Auf falschen Wegen schneller gegangen.
Auf die gute Unvernunft ist die,
Welche vergeht und
Ich bin immer gleich geblieben.

IV.
Was wiegt ein großer Regen?
Ein paar Gedanken mehr oder weniger
Wenige Gefühle oder gar keine
Wo alles nicht genügt
Ist nichts genügend.
Ich bin immer gleich gewesen.

The structure of the poem was determined by the dialectical tension between the subjective yearning for permanence and the objective incessant change. However, the anticult of impermanence held sway. The fascination in mortality and decline. The poem about the mortality of "poor Bidi" gives an idea of how this anticult originated.

Brecht overcame this situation. The poem "Einst" takes a retrospective view of the problem:

Once, living in the cold, this seemed wonderful to me.
And the freshness touched and refreshed me.
And I enjoyed the bitterness, and it seemed to me
As if I would remain the choosy one,
As if darkness invited me alone to dine.

From the cold fount I gathered cheerfulness
And nothingness gave this plenty of room.
Rare brightness separated itself exquisitely
From natural darkness. For long? Hardly.
But I, my friend, was the faster.

Einst schien dies in Kälte leben wunderbar mir
Und belebend rührte mich die Frische
Und das Bittre schmeckte, und es war mir
Als verbliebe ich der Wählerische
Lud die Finsternis mich selbst zu Tische.

Frohsinn schöpfte ich aus kalter Quelle
Und das Nichts gab diesen weiten Raum.
Köstlich sonderte sich seltne Helle
Aus natürlich Dunklem. Lange? Kaum.
Aber ich, Gevatter, war der Schnelle.

Two of Brecht's Keuner stories also show how he went about confronting the phenomenon of change. This time it is Brecht the dialectical thinker who plans and conceptualizes everything. It is the writer and dramatist of those persistent *Versuche** who determines the message here.

ON MEETING AGAIN
A man, whom Mr. K. had not seen in a long time, greeted him with the words: "My, you haven't changed a bit." "Oh!" said Mr. K., turning pale.

There is also this counterversion:

THE TRIBULATIONS OF THE BEST PEOPLE
Mr. K. was once asked: "What are you working on?" He replied: "I'm having a great deal of difficulty. I'm preparing my next mistake."

The Negated Tradition Established

All connection to a humanist tradition depends in each case on what one thinks about history in the making and history as it passes. The cult of change, and whatever is connected to it in the way of pure spiritual revival, the primacy of the intellect, the mere desire to be good, all this is intricately bound up with Platonism, the doctrine of ideas. It is the counterposition to Brecht, and he attacked it relentlessly with the intention of devastating Kant's categorical imperative, the ineffectual goodness, the desire to be good which was placed ahead of the social requisites necessary for the love of humanity. This became one of the major motifs in his plays after the 1930's. St. Joan of the stockyards dies renouncing this ineffectual goodness. The three

* *Translator's note:* In 1930 Brecht began to publish his works in gray brochures under the title of Versuche, which connotes "essays," "projects," "drafts," and "experiments." Most of the volumes of the Versuche contain more than one work by Brecht. They are numbered consecutively according to the date of composition. There were seven issues between 1930 and 1933. Publication was resumed again in 1949, with volume fifteen published shortly before Brecht died.

children of Mother Courage are ruined because of their "good" qualities: Eilif because of his boldness, Schweizerkas because of his honesty, the dumb mute Kattrin because of her motherliness. Shen-te as the good woman of Setzuan must perish when she devotes herself only to being good to the exclusion of everything else. The much too docile Kantianer Pätus in Brecht's adaptation of J. M. R. Lenz's *Der Hofmeister* becomes the very model of a humbled philistine who actually has a lust for following commands and luxuriates in it.

The anticult of impermanence led either to inactivity or to mere tolerance, or secretly became tied again to philosophical idealism as though it were a thing to conceal. This produced a kind of delight in impermanence, and at the same time, in the creation of static poems.

Even though he strongly opposed this position, the early Brecht had some affinity with it. His later dialectical thinking, however, had to view tradition in a different way. It was from Hegel that he borrowed the dialectical term *Aufhebung*, "negation." The German word *Aufheben* has three meanings: "to conserve," "to end," "to elevate." A basic understanding of the changeability of the world, of the necessary correspondence between recognition and changing practice also determines the relationship to tradition. The great productions of the past are not, as has been assumed, beyond time and without history. They are, as they always were, part of a process, part of the constantly changing relationship of a changing subject in the present to the likewise dynamic works of the past. Three things must be achieved simultaneously with all works of tradition: conservation, annihilation, renovation. Brecht's constant preoccupation with reworking his productions and those of other writers—which accounts for the essential and perhaps the decisive part of his work and consequently led to a new art of acting and audience participation— can be explained only by this dialectical relationship to tradition. For Brecht as writer and theoretician, tradition always meant negated tradition.

However, it did not stay that way. Brecht distrusted the term *genius,* especially the idealistic concept of the poet, and here he showed himself to be an opponent of the expressionists. As far as we know, Bertolt Brecht never referred to himself as a "poet" (in the German sense of the word *Dichter*).* His opposition to such a concept can be recognized in his formulation of the term *playwright,* in German *Stückeschreiber,* "the writer of plays or *pièces.*" He did not opt for ingenuity and inspiration, but rather for good craftsmanship, literature of practicability. Not ineffectual goodness, but friendliness.

He was not only a playwright but also a *teacher.* Käthe Rülicke, one of his closest collaborators in the Berliner Ensemble, has commented: "One time when I wrote an article on Brecht for a magazine, I asked him somewhat helplessly what I should write about him. 'Describe me simply as I am,' he said, 'as a teacher.'" This, too, is a leitmotif in his life and work. Beginning with his adaptation of Maksim Gorki's *Mother* to his adaptation of Lenz's *Der Hofmeister* (*The Private Tutor*) his plays are filled with teacher figures. There are also the *Lehrstücke* ("didactic plays") and themes in his poetry about teaching without pupils. The origination of the book of Tao te ching is presented as the origination of the *Lehrgedicht* ("didactic poem"), and then there is the Lehrgedicht "Erziehung der Hirse" ("The Education of the Millet"). In 1953 when Brecht was to write a few lines in honor of Arnold Zweig's sixty-sixth birthday, he quite naturally began it this way: "It has always seemed to me that there was a great deal to learn from Zweig's novels since he himself has learned so much."

Along with all the dialectics of negation, Brecht conducts himself in regard to tradition as one who intends to learn because he wants to teach. One should learn from tradition since it is important to establish a tradition. Brecht's relationship to tradition is simultaneously a negated and established tradition. The changes in his relationship to classicism, especially to German classicism, make this evident.

Newspapers often circulate questionnaires which have an air of "eternal solemnity" about them, as Alfred Kerr has remarked. The questions about the function of the modern theater and

---

* *Translator's note:* In German, a distinction is made between the "great writer," or *Dichter* (also "poet"), and the *Schriftsteller,* or "popular writer," whose reputation varies with the times.

about adequate staging methods were not asked for the first time at the 1955 Darmstadt Conference of Dramaturges. Almost thirty years before this, during Christmas of 1926, the *Berliner Börsen-Courier* began taking a poll that was similar in nature. It was Herbert Ihering* who had formulated the circular. The leading theater and literary personalities were chosen as the usual easy and cheap way out, and they were asked to give their opinion on the following questions: "Does it seem possible to maintain a classical repertoire in the contemporary theater? What fundamental rule should be used if classical plays are to be changed? Where does free choice begin? What role does the change in the composition of audience constituency play in influencing the production of a play, or the regrouping of the old repertoire?" Brecht's response, which had as its title *How Should the Classics Be Played Today? (Wie soll man heute Klassiker spielen?)*, was printed in the Christmas edition along with other answers. It was not filled with the Yuletide spirit.

Brecht boasts in this piece that his plays and productions have helped influence a portion of the audience so that "they can no longer enjoy the range of subject matter of the prerevolutionary theater nor its well-defined psychology and attitude toward the world." He is in complete agreement with Erwin Piscator, and he quotes a statement made by Piscator which presumably summarized Piscator's intention in his new stage production of Schiller's *The Robbers*: "The people realized upon leaving the theater that 150 years are no small matter." Due to the dissatisfaction with the entire traditional repertoire felt by many actors and small circles of the audience, "meaningless experiments" have erupted. Inventions have been contrived that have simply served to worsen the situation. Brecht is forced to smile at this. "But these inventions are rather interesting since they're being made on branches that droop. People on drooping branches generally invent more and more saws. They may rack their brains about what they want, but in the end, it has always been a saw."

---

* *Translator's note:* Ihering was one of the leading theater critics and dramaturges of the time. He has published numerous books on the theater and presently resides in East Germany, where he was *Chefdramaturg* of the Deutsches Theater for a time.

The inference here is that the old classical repertoire has shown itself to be "sufficiently full of holes and broken down." It can no longer be presented to "mature newspaper readers" as originally conceived. The only thing one can use is the material of the classical works, and with certain dramas of the past "whose pure material worth is not adequate," not even that. This is an extremely rough interpretation of the predialectical Brecht's tradition and its negation. The restructuring of such material, however, demands new viewpoints—a modern way of looking at the world. Only "by utilizing a political point of view could one make more out of a classical play than a bath of luxuriating memories." Brecht concludes his article this way: "To be quite frank, I believe that it doesn't make any difference at all to produce a play by Shakespeare until the theater is able to make the contemporary works more effective. There is no getting around this. Also it would be foolish to think that one could purely cull out the viewpoints from modern plays in order to apply them to the old ones. They will not be easy to find. I see a dim future for a theater that wants to elude the hard demands of an impatient time."

There are certain fundamental principles in this essay which the playwright never disavowed. Just two years later *The Threepenny Opera* was conceived as an attempt to put the theory into practice. Afterward Brecht produced *Antigone* and *Coriolanus,* Molière's *Don Juan* and Lenz's *Der Hofmeister.* Old material presented then from "new viewpoints." Brecht also tried the opposite: the contemporary material of *The Resistible Rise of Arturo Ui* in the form of an Elizabethan drama and *The Communist Manifesto* as a Lehrgedicht in hexameters.

It is impossible to deny the continuity. However, Brecht's essay *Intimidation by Classicalism** (*Einschüchterung durch die Klassizität*), written in 1954, had the effect first of a recantation of the doctrines of 1926. When first published in the magazine

---

* *Translator's note:* John Willett has translated this essay with the title *Classical Status as an Inhibiting Factor* in *Brecht on Theatre.* Generally I have followed his translations of titles, but I have deviated here because his English title does not convey the sense of this essay.

Sinn und Form, it combined a short theoretical essay with an analysis of the Berliner Ensemble's production of Molière's *Don Juan.* This latter part of the article was appended to the collection of his plays quite appropriately as a commentary on his adaptations. Both parts were given the common title of *Essays on Theater Practice (Aufsätze zur Theaterpraxis).* When Brecht as the young playwright and reformer of the theater had looked at the classical theater with a jaundiced eye, his attitude had been that of a member of the opposition who had occasionally had his plays performed and had even been allowed to direct some but had been kept from holding great responsibility for a theater, scheduling plays, and determining the style of production. However, in 1954, the man who took over the responsibility for the Berliner Ensemble is speaking. It is also a person who has changed his political habitat. .

The doctrines of 1926 took the offensive and were provocative. The title of the 1954 essay points to a defensive strategy. Classicalism intimidating? Brecht on the defensive? At first he repeats his early attacks against the late bourgeois experimentation with classical works: "The formalist 'revival' of classical works is the answer to a straightjacket tradition, and it is the wrong one." Here, too, Brecht has a shocking image at hand which he intuitively selects from the culinary sphere: "It is as though some preserved meat had become putrid and could only be made tasty again by dosing it with some sharp spices and sauces." Then, however, he moves on to points of another kind.

The difference between the observations of 1926 and 1954 in regard to the tradition of classical works in the contemporary theater resulted from Brecht's transitional move from social opposition to social representation. During the Weimar epoch his aggressiveness stemmed from his tendency to consider classicism simply as an object of material evaluation. This time his questions are more precise and have more depth. "We must bring out the original ideas of the work and grasp the play's national and international significance. For this purpose we must study the historical situation during the period of composition as well as the classical author's special peculiarities and his position in regard to his times." Of course, in doing this one should not become intimidated by classicalism, that is, by a superficial understanding of it.

Both should be rejected: the senseless formalist experimentation of the Weimar epoch and the spectacular productions of the court theaters and later those of the Third Reich. Ideals were confused with idealization, solemnity with pomposity, genuine pathos with false pathos. "Goethe's wonderful sense of humor in his *Urfaust* does not fit the overly dignified Olympian gestures attributed to the classics—as if humor and genuine dignity were opposites! The magnificently conceived plots were used only to contrive effective declamations. In other words, they were completely neglected." The deeper social meaning of great works can be made relevant to modern man, but not by a theater of pomposity and sensationalism nor by mere superficial sets and staging innovations. The theater, that is, the Brechtian theater, cannot be intimidated by the greatness of the works themselves nor by fashionable staging if it is to reach its goal.

There are contradictions here between the theories of 1926 and 1954. Are the classics mere subject matter or do they have an intrinsic value of their own? Brecht decided that they did have intrinsic value—that what was necessary was a new conception of classical substance, new performances which also demonstrate their function. During the 1920's Brecht was fighting either Max Reinhardt or Leopold Jessner—in 1929 Herbert Ihering published his controversial book *Reinhardt, Jessner, Piscator or the Death of the Classics? (Reinhardt, Jessner, Piscator oder Klassikertod?)*—and he thought the only use of the classics from Shakespeare to Schiller was to demonstrate to contemporary audiences that these plays could at the most deal with "characters who have outlived their times." However, the older Brecht, the man responsible for the repertoire and style of the Berliner Ensemble, talks about grasping "the national and international significance" of a classical work in a production and demonstrating it on stage. Here we can even see another contradiction. One has the impression that the dialectician Brecht was making the effort in his adaptations of classical plays to ignore the real substance of a play in order "to set its inherent content free." Later it will be necessary to discuss how he used this new conception about the national and international function of classical works basically to bring about a "reutilization" (*Umfunktionierung*) of the classics.

Brecht's theoretical writings are like his plays in that they have been thought out in detail and have been continually reworked. There is no flowery language. Every sentence means something and is supposed to mean something. It would be misleading if we took Brecht's concern about the national and international significance of classicism as a comment on the actual political situation of his day. This is positively precluded by a doctrine he put forth in 1951.

It is well known that Bertolt Brecht never felt the call to become a public speaker. In the same year that he wrote *Intimidation by Classicalism* (1954) he participated in the International Congress of the PEN Club in Amsterdam. From there he was to travel to Paris, where some of his plays were being produced. A French journalist at the congress who spoke perfect German interviewed him and remarked that he had heard that Brecht would most likely be giving a talk about his concept of the theater while in Paris. The playwright, shuddering at the thought, answered quite curtly: "That is something I definitely won't do!" Five years before this in 1949, Brecht had made an appearance in the large lecture hall at the University of Leipzig in order to answer some questions by the students. He could not be persuaded to take the rostrum but took a stool and sat himself down in front of the first row of the overflowing lecture hall. From there he answered the questions: sometimes he was irritated and snapped his answers from behind, over his shoulders; other times he was most interested and gave detailed answers while facing the person who asked the question.

We do not possess many texts of Bertolt Brecht's speeches. The last volume of his Versuche, number fifteen, which was published posthumously but had been edited by Brecht himself, contains three speeches from the years 1935, 1937, and 1955. There is a fourth speech, which was delivered in the Kongresshalle of Leipzig in May of 1951 during a cultural congress in which intellectuals from both parts of Germany participated. Brecht thought that this short programmatic speech was so important that he placed it at the beginning of the volume *Theater Work* (*Theaterarbeit*), which he helped edit and which was supposed to report on the first six productions of the Berliner Ensemble.

This 1951 speech also deals with the style of the theater and classicism. Once again we have the arguments against false pathos and blind experimentation. Brecht is especially bitter about the interest at that time in the "spectacular technique" of the theater in the Third Reich—"as if such a technique could be adopted now that the Nazi spectacle itself was over, and it didn't matter what its function was. As though a technique which served to veil causality could now be used to uncover it!" In the course of this speech he conceives the ideas which later were to form the heart of his essay *Intimidation by Classicalism*: "Poetry had stooped to declamation, art to artificiality. Superficiality and pretentious profundity had triumphed. Instead of the exemplary, we had mere representation, instead of passion, we had temperament. A whole generation of actors had been selected from the wrong point of view and trained according to wrong doctrines." As Brecht continues his chain of thought, he connects his critical observations on past productions and reproductions with new tasks. Negated tradition is in itself understood here as a new tradition which is to be established. Brecht asks "how to found a dramatics of contradictions and dialectical processes—a dramaturgy, not an objective theory. How should the new positive critical attitude of the new audience be induced by the producers?" The dialectician Brecht had already glimpsed the answer by posing the question in the right way. It is the negated tradition which must be established. "Insufficient in itself as theater, it must strive to change its surroundings." However, the surroundings then went by the name of Germany. Social renovation in Germany was a task which was also to serve the interest of the theater in its relation to classicalism.

At the end of his speech, Brecht addresses the West German visitors at the conference. He implies that all these efforts may have to remain fruitless "without like efforts in other parts of Germany." The final sentence of the Leipzig talk is also an anticipation of the later ideas on the national and international significance of German classicism. It reads: "It is still worth the effort to find a solution to classicism: either we shall build a national theater or none at all . . . ."

It now becomes apparent that Brecht's relation to tradition itself can be seen as the continuation of a great tradition. It is not merely a new stage in his debate with the products of an artistic classicism but a continuation of the classical stream of thought. In that Bertolt Brecht speaks here about classicism and classicalism, *he himself is thinking like a German classicist.* And in complete awareness of the fact. In an appeal for German classicism. "We shall build a German national theater or none at all." This is Lessing's Hamburg dramaturgy. Schiller's Mannheim dramaturgy with the question about the stage as a moral podium. Schiller as the man who imported and carried on the ideas of the Frenchman Sébastien Mercier. German Sturm und Drang in close connection with that world of ideas which made the storming of the Bastille possible, also the destruction of Zwing-Uri in Schiller's *Wilhelm Tell.* Goethe's new intellectual starting point right in the middle of the European revolution (1795) serving as the basis of the essay *Literarischer Sansculottismus,* which tied the question about a national author and a national theater with the question of classicalism as Brecht did in 1951: "When and where does a classical national author emerge?"

Goethe's formulation of the question is also unmistakenly in contrast to Brecht's stream of thought from 1951 to 1954. Goethe states as if hesitating: "Let us not wish for the upheaval that could prepare the way for classical works in Germany." Brecht, on the other hand, sees the function of the national theater and the classicists that he is demanding in this way: "From now on it could hope to shape the images of the world only if it helped to shape the world itself." The playwright and the dramaturge Brecht's insistence on a dialectical attitude toward tradition is itself a tradition.

Augsburg—The Influence
of His Native Town

Brecht never cared for Thomas Mann. The feeling was mutual. By the end of the 1920's Thomas Mann had already entered into an argument with Brecht by responding to Brecht's deprecating remarks about Klaus Mann's literary sins of his youth. The feud lasted for decades. Brecht included sarcastic "Magic Mountain" stanzas in his poetry while Mann shook his head about the politician Brecht. Brecht placed the twelve-volume edition of Thomas Mann's collected works which appeared in 1955 low down and out of reach on his bookshelves. It certainly never would have occurred to him, as it had to Thomas Mann in 1926 on the occasion of the seven hundredth centennial of Lübeck, to speak on the "intrinsic form of life" in his home city Augsburg even if this imperial city on the River Lech had called upon its son, the great poet—something highly unlikely—to speak to its "beloved citizens." In spite of this, one cannot think of Brecht without thinking of Augsburg. He retained vivid impressions of his childhood there. He never dismissed this realm of experience in *Die Hauspostille*. Later, in a commentary to the play *The Resistible Rise of Arturo Ui (Der aufhaltsame Aufstieg des Arturo Ui)*, Brecht used recollections from his childhood in his argument as a matter of course: "I never heard the philistines of my native town speak with anything but devotion and enthusiasm about a mass murderer by the name of Kneisel, so I have remembered his name to this very day. And it was never considered necessary to attribute to him the usual acts of kindness to poor old mothers. His murders sufficed."

It must have been during the early fifties that a young West German student appeared one afternoon at Brecht's home to obtain information for a dissertation on the young Brecht. The person to be interviewed was irritable from the very beginning and did not take kindly to the completely legitimate questions put forward by the young scholar of Germanic studies who asked about Brecht's early connection with expressionism, anarchy in the drama, Freud, and even the surrealists. Brecht continually replied as if he had memorized a refrain: "Didn't exist then in Augsburg." He wanted to own up only to the influences of Karl Valentin and Frank Wedekind. Naturally it is rather easy to dispute this statement by pointing to the unmistakable parallels in his work to Baudelaire and Rimbaud, Villon and Kipling, Shakespeare and Büchner, who generally speaking cannot be said not to have existed at that time in Augsburg. Nevertheless, early in his career Brecht quite clearly prepared for Augsburg to become his "instrinsic form of life" in his own way. The settings in his first play *Baal* are from Augsburg. The folk scenes from this drama, as well as the speech of the people in *Drums in the Night (Trommeln in der Nacht)*, and even much of the background of the play *In the Jungle of Cities (Im Dickicht der Städte)* can be traced back to his native town on the Lech and its inhabitants. With Brecht there is no father complex or family tragedy, which is often so inspiring in literature. His home life and literary works were devoid of the father-son conflicts notable in the lives of Walter Hasenclever, Johannes R. Becher, Franz Kafka, or Arnolt Bronnen, where the conflicts developed first as a real family drama and continued to have an effect as an expressionist literary style. Brecht must have felt lonely in Augsburg early in his life, but the theme of authority and tradition, or rather, that of anarchy and the lack of tradition which was a trademark in his first works was not a result of his home life but of the greater Augsburg environment.

Arnolt Bronnen has left us with an outsider's view of Brecht's home in Augsburg, where Bronnen lived in the fall of 1922, sleeping in Brecht's room while the latter was in Munich. Though Bronnen wrote his recollection some years later, he knew how to preserve his impressions and transmit them. As a young man, Brecht always lived with his father in Augsburg. His mother Sophie had died in 1920 at the age of forty-nine. Bronnen recalls: "In addition to the dry, squeaky tone of the widower, there was a housekeeper who grumbled about in the gloomy puritan home. The only one who was really alive was Bert's younger brother, who slavishly admired him and shared many of his views. These views were opposed by the father, who on his part did not have a high regard for his sons."

Views which contradicted the authority of the father—this is highly likely. But there was still no conflict as there was in Bronnen's own home or in his play *Vatermord (Patricide)*. In addition, this puritanical feature of Brecht's home became ingrained in his attitude toward life no matter how he may have stylized it. It was common knowledge in his family and the immediate vicinity that Brecht preferred to eat only Augsburg cooking to the end of his life. His surroundings did not upset him. The conflicts that are most accurately reflected in Brecht's early dramas had more to do with social rootlessness than with the generation conflict. The early Brecht was not about to lose himself in the cisterns of illusory problems such as the father-son conflict, the battle between the sexes, the struggle between raw power and the intellect. He opts neither for Strindberg nor for Heinrich Mann. The very first conflicts that this writer wants to formulate are clearly social ones. They deal with the relation of the individual to the world around him, his dislocation or conformity. Actually, they concern the strange situation of an outsider who strives for any kind of a compromise with his environment. In regard to this question, Baal and Andreas Kragler, Brecht's first heroes, are not at all opposites. The asocial genius Baal, who wanted only to consume people and conditions, dies in a "wooden hut in the forest" yearning for attachment and a place in the community. Andreas Kragler renounces his position among the group of one-sided revolutionaries, who want to raid the newspaper district in Berlin. Yet, their raid is essentially their attempt to become part of the real community of citizens who remain home, place emphasis on security and enjoyment, want to have their peace and quiet through brotherly love. These revolutionaries are nothing but romantic outsiders who gape and want to bring about the new man and the new spirit by yearning. Here we have the state of the outsider and conformity as early basic themes. This is directly connected to the early form of life in Augsburg. Brecht must have been aware of his potential when he was quite young. Some of his more characteristic poems written in 1913–1914, when he was fifteen and sixteen, as well as stories, critiques, and essayistic sketches reveal how conscious and disciplined he was as a writer during his Gymnasium years. H. O. Münsterer has passed on this significant diary entry to us: "I can write. I can write plays better than Hebbel, wilder than Wedekind." However, this awareness also served to isolate Brecht. He stylized his Augsburg circle of friends, George Pflanzelt (to whom he dedicated *Baal*), Müllereisert, and Caspar Neher for his own needs. Baal among the pirates. Brecht providing himself with a threefold connection to the world around him: that of the lonely outsider with a tendency toward conformity; that with the group of outsiders who seek to provoke (as with the pirates) and who likewise have a tendency toward conformity, as can be seen when the group of men depart for Mahagonny; lastly, that of the individual who attempts complete conformity to deny the expressionist cry, protest, and revolt.

Now that we can look back in history it is easy to recognize the tensions in Brecht's plays stemming from his Augsburg period. There is also an autobiographical statement which almost vanished and which sheds a great deal of light on the situation. Since Brecht liked to stylize himself and wrote poems with roles for Bert Brecht, who was not to be confused with the real Bert Brecht and continually avoided making blunt autobiographical pronouncements, the small column of memoirs which the Berlin *Film-Kurier* published on November 9, 1928, celebrating the tenth year of the November Revolution, is especially important. This time—with the revolution as the focal point—Andreas Kragler is not the center of attention but rather the twenty-year-old Brecht, whom the thirty-year-old Brecht describes in this way: "At that time I was a counselor for soldiers in an Augsburg hospital, and I became this only because of the urgent pleas of some friends who maintained that they had an interest in this. (As it turned out, it was impossible for me to change conditions in a way that would benefit them.) We all suffered from a lack of political conviction, and especially me, since I also had to contend with my old lack of enthusiasm. They threw a ton of work at me. Half a year before this, the high military command had failed to send me into combat. Blessed with a little luck, I had learned how to impede my military training. After six months I still didn't know how to salute and was considered too sloppy even for conditions at that time, which had become quite lax for the army. It did not take me long after that to get my discharge. To sum it all up: I didn't differ much from the overwhelming majority of the soldiers who had had enough of the war, yet were not capable of thinking politically. It's for this reason I don't like to think about it."

A loner as chosen representative of a body of men, a counselor of soldiers. A man without strong political convictions who nevertheless is aware of this. A soldier who ostensibly was not different from other soldiers, but who secretly knew he was. A tense, tortuous situation. "It's for this reason that I don't like to think about it." This indecision can be traced in Brecht's first differences with the tradition of classical literature. They were initially determined by his environment in Augsburg and the conditions in the local theater. Bertolt Brecht's theater reviews between 1919 and 1920 are still extant. A theater critic, twenty-two years old, who reviewed for the newspaper *Volkswille,* the daily organ of the Independent Social Democratic Party (USPD) in Swabia and Neuburg. Naturally there were arguments with the director of the state theater in Augsburg and the personnel: an open letter written by the company and Brecht's published reply. There were good reasons for this quarrel. Brecht wrote his review of the play *Der Graf von Gleichen* by Wilhelm Schmidtbonn in doggerel and closed it this way:

> The play itself teaches: only a dead man
> 'tis who can bear more than a woman.

> Ihr seht am Stück, daß nur ein toter Mann
> Noch mehr als eine Frau ertragen kann.

He began a review of *Alt-Heidelberg* in October 1920 with these friendly words: "In this rotten play there is a scene which is too putrid to describe in words." In the course of the argument, which became public, the critic was ready to make concessions three weeks later: "A few compromises can be made in my choice of words. Instead of rotten play (*Saustück*), one can write stinking little play (*Schweinstückchen*)." Now all this was permissible

in a sense with writers like Schmidtbonn and Meyer-Förster. But
how did Brecht review the classical repertoire? With Goethe's
Tasso he speaks out against the play itself. He is also angry about
the direction and design. With Schiller's *The Robbers* he is apparently in agreement about the choice of the play itself, but not
at all with the Augsburg production. "I protest against this
manner of introducing Schiller to the young." One actor pleases
Brecht so much that he demands: "He must play Wallenstein."
This was obviously to be understood as praise. The real argument
with the German classics which was to take place later, especially
with Schiller's plays after the Sturm und Drang period, can be
gleaned in Brecht's review of the Augsburg production of *Don
Carlos* (April 15, 1920): "God only knows how long I have loved
Don Carlos. However, recently I've been reading Sinclair's *The
Jungle,* the story of a worker who starves to death in the stockyards of Chicago. It deals with simple starvation, cold, and sickness which bring about a man's downfall in such a controlled
fashion as though God had ordained it. One time this man has a
vision of freedom, but then he is clubbed down. His freedom
doesn't have the least thing to do with Don Carlos' freedom. I
know that. But I can no longer take Carlos' servitude too seriously. Also, Schiller always has his characters demand their freedom in distinctly beautiful arias. I admit that it is good they are
there, but they could also be sung by some other characters and
not just Posa and Carlos and Philip, opera singers, who sing for
nothing. Otherwise *Don Carlos* is a beautiful opera."

These early reports about Brecht's life and his own early writings contradict only seemingly his later statement that the styles
of the expressionists, surrealists, or other renovators of literature
and art did not exist "at that time" in Augsburg. Naturally
Brecht's answer to the student doing research on his doctoral
thesis was also a joke. The truth is that Brecht began quite early,
in elementary school, to write poetry and criticism. He read
classical as well as modern literature. If *Baal* was actually written
as an answer to Hanns Johst's play about Grabbe, *Der Einsame
(The Loner)*, then Brecht must have known a good deal about
his subject matter. However, the intellectual world of young
Brecht was not stamped by the great literary and political currents

of the war years and postwar years but by Augsburg and its provincial world.

This has nothing to do with lack of knowledge and information but with conscious seclusion. Brecht knew all about the work of the expressionists and the literary styles which were being discussed in the big cities. After all, Augsburg is not far from Munich. The young Brecht knew Frank Wedekind and knew him quite well, but he did not join him. Like his Andreas Kragler, he left the front of the literary revolutionaries. He renounced the expressionist storming of the theater that was protected by the bastions of the bourgeoisie. He rejected the revolt of the sons against the fathers. For Brecht, it was *retreat to the Augsburg province as against the expressionist twilight of mankind.* The other things did not exist in Augsburg because Brecht did not want to have them. The indecision remained—in the political as well as in the literary diatribes. Brecht knew first what he did not want to have: the bland stage schemes of writers like Toller, Unruh, and Hasenclever—with Georg Kaiser it was different; the divine but imprecise language. The ignorance about life which these intellectual revivalists all revealed.

Brecht was still unclear about his relationship to the poetic tradition. *Don Carlos* is indeed a beautiful opera which no longer sounds so beautiful when one reads Upton Sinclair's *The Jungle* shortly before hearing it. This is, by the way, the first place where Chicago emerges—the world of the meat markets, later the setting for *St. Joan of the Stockyards* (*Die Heilige Johanna der Schlachthöfe*). The antithesis of Schiller and Chicago was first conceived in the Augsburg theater reviews of 1920. And this in a time when the young expressionists all looked, even physically, like flaming young Schillers: Unruh, Toller, Hasenclever, Wolf. Their dramas sought to revive the Schiller pathos by emphasizing the spiritual transformation of guilt and atonement. Hence, these beginnings in Augsburg are significant not only because they shed light on the contrast between Schiller and Chicago but because they explain the reasons for the altercation between Bertolt Brecht and Friedrich Wolf about guilt and atonement in regard to the camp follower Anna Fierling, otherwise known as Mother Courage.

Karl Valentin

Frank Wedekind and Karl Valentin* did not live or work in Augsburg. However, Brecht did not want to deny their influence. Wedekind probably had a greater effect on Brecht the poet who wrote *Die Hauspostille* than on Brecht the dramatist. Many of the motifs in Wedekind's poetry and ballads were picked up by Brecht. On the other hand Karl Valentin was more important for Brecht as a playwright. There is a famous photograph with the young Brecht wearing what one called at that time a "hustler's cap" in front of a stand at the annual fair. Valentin's group was about to do a musical routine. Brecht is a member of the woodwind section of a band, and a performance is about to begin under the direction of the conductor Liesl Karlstadt, assisted by Karl Valentin in the brass section. However, this group was bound to fall apart due to the constant disputes between Valentin and Karlstadt. This is where Brecht began to participate, where he learned. In acknowledging his debt to Valentin he was acknowledging an allegiance to tradition, to the experiences and customs of the Munich folk comedy.

In his memoirs concerning Karl Valentin, the actor Kurt Horwitz has given an account of how the young actors, directors, and dramaturges Brecht, Erich Engel, Albert Steinrück, and Horwitz himself came to Valentin in the early twenties because of their high regard for him. The young Brecht was one of Valentin's assistants. Yet the unpredictable and shy Valentin rewarded him, as Horwitz recalls, in an astonishing way. It was known that Valentin used to go to the theater only once a year. This was on All Souls' Day when the wonderful play *Der Müller*

---

* *Translator's note:* Valentin (1882–1948) was one of the leading comedians in Germany. He wrote most of his own material, generally farces with folk characters, in the Bavarian dialect. In 1911 he met Liesl Karlstadt, who teamed with him to write sketches and act in them. Valentin's reputation in Germany is comparable to Charlie Chaplin's, but the fact that he wrote his skits in dialect has limited his appeal outside the German-speaking world. Valentin's influence on Brecht was great and can be traced in Brecht's humor and his theory of *Gestik* (gesture).

und sein Kind (*The Miller and His Child*) was performed in the *Volkstheater*. Well, the unexpected happened. Karl Valentin appeared with Liesl Karlstadt in the Munich Kammerspiele to see a performance of *Drums in the Night*. Horwitz relates: "We met in the restaurant named 'Malkasten' on the Augustenstrasse after the performance. There was a great deal of dancing and talking. Brecht, always the polite one, did not ask [Valentin's opinion], nor did we in the least dare to. Valentin was silent, and Karlstadt smiled out of embarrassment. A long silence! In order to break this impasse, we ordered more drinks and food than was necessary. Whatever we could afford. Again there was a long silence! Finally Valentin said 'D'you know—with these here modern plays, someone's got to come to the people at the end of the performance, take them by the arm, and say to them: Hey, you—it's the end!' "

Everyone present, Brecht included, understood immediately that this was anything but crass narrow-mindedness. Valentin hit upon the weak point of the play—the ending. Brecht was never able to change it to his satisfaction, as he has revealed in his preface to *On Scanning My First Plays* (*Bei Durchsicht meiner ersten Stücke,* 1955). The question concerned the irremediable dilemma. The negativity of the closing statement does not allow for productive results. To be sure, the revolution is renounced, and a pact with the bourgeoisie is in the offing, but this can only come about with a guilty conscience. So Brecht must have, in spite of the pithy remark, felt understood by Valentin on this evening. The Munich folk actor who wrote his own scripts had a great deal in common with Brecht. Even Valentin's contact with the world around him had been disturbed —due to many reasons—though the causes here were more psychological than social as in the case of Brecht. This condition of being an outsider was, however, transcribed in Valentin's skits and dialogues into dialectics that wander off the track and conversations which fall apart. It was impossible to communicate and to be understood. In one of Valentin's skits, his partner asks a question which is impossible to work out: Is it remarkable that a bicycle rider happens to come by just as he (Valentin) is thinking about a bicycle rider? Valentin replies with a sigh that his friend just has a different way of looking at things. There is a great deal here that today must be considered as an anticipation of Brecht's later dialogues.

Conversations that fall apart were also characteristic of Büchner's figures. In *Woyzeck* there is no understanding, just monologues that parallel one another. Wedekind borrowed this device —for example, in the isolated monologues (disguised as dialogues) of Keith and Scholz in his *Marquis of Keith*—and most likely passed it on to Brecht. Valentin used this constantly to make it impossible for his central character to understand his surroundings or to make himself understood even with great effort. Here he anticipates much of modern literature. The master bookbinder Wanninger resembles a Munich craftsman who, like Kafka's Joseph K., falls into the machinery of bureaucracy and hierarchy. The individual whose everyday familiar routine no longer appears familiar and whose words are no longer understood by the people with whom he talks. The conflict between the familiar and alien worlds is prevalent in all the sketches of the great Munich actor and writer. From the very beginning Brecht had in common with Valentin more than just the tense relationship of the outsider to the world around him. They also shared the same tendency to think in contradictions, and they refused to accept the daily and familiar routine without question.

The Unliterary Tradition: Mystery Novels, Sports, and Techniques

The contradiction between the outsider and the conformist, the negation of the expressionist dramas, the rejection of the bourgeois world that was restored in a makeshift way—these were not the only factors which determined the structure of the early plays. For a long time Brecht tried to solve his personal conflict as an artist by breaking it down into different literary genres: poetry for the outsider, drama as the means to find his place in modern society. He indicated this in a conversation he had with the French journalist Bernard Guillemin. It was published in the

Literarische Welt on July 30, 1926, under the title *What Are You Working On?* The interviewer admits that he has intentionally translated the statements of the dramatist from the "Brechtian slang" into a "language workable in traditional terms." Today we know that something essential is lost in this process of translation, that Brecht's thinking cannot be separated from his language. In spite of it, we can still reconstruct his artistic position of that time on the basis of the conversation. Guillemin maintains at one point that Brecht is apparently poet and dramatist at the same time, and he receives the following response: "My poetry has more of a private character. It should be accompanied by the banjo and piano and should be recited mimetically. In a drama, on the other hand, I do not present my private mood but the mood of the world as it were. In other words, a matter that has been viewed objectively, the opposite of mood in its usual poetical meaning." This appears at first to contradict Brecht's increasingly conscious use of poetry in the dialogue that he wants to maintain between writer and reader. Later Brecht allows certain concluding lines in his poems to stand in an unfinished form because the understanding reader himself is supposed to create; he makes evident breaks in the lines, causing contradictions to be visible so that the reader can think about them. It would seem that the Brecht of 1926 was far from doing something like this.

Not entirely. When Guillemin complained that Brecht did not make the dramatic events comprehensible, he replied: "I present merely what happens in order to let the audience itself think. That's the reason I need an attentive audience that knows how to observe and enjoys having its intellect challenged as in a game." This is already a step in the direction of Brecht's later plays. The only thing that is missing here is the particular new substance for the new function of a dialogue between the playwright and his critical spectator who thinks along with him. Brecht's vision of a new art of staging and a new art of audience participation appears in its own way to be another art for art's sake. The intellectual enjoyment "in itself" could be likened to the artistry of the struggle for the sake of struggle in some of his early plays, for instance, *In the Jungle of Cities*. Yet, Brecht had

already intuited that it would be necessary to create new substance for the reciprocal action between the new drama and the
new spectator. Since he posed the question from the point of view
of the spectator and made it dependent on outside factors, it was
at first impossible to gain new substance. Therefore, Brecht's
answer to Guillemin about the audience he was writing for
could only amount to this: "For those people who go to the
theater for their own enjoyment, not for those who pose in line
with their hats on." Once again the answer is lodged in negative
terms. To be sure, it is the perfect complement to his essay in
1926 of how one should or should not play the classics, but it falls
apart, as did his reply to Herbert Ihering's questionnaire, because of its own negativity.

Since Brecht sensed this, he tried to overcome the negation in
two ways. In one case he endeavored to make the form into
content. The outward behavior, that is, the kind of dress and
manners, was to be a characteristic trait for the substance of the
new audience. However, after this, he sought the new substance
in areas of society which one looked upon in 1926 as most unliterary, if not antiliterary. Since Brecht had not tied his dramas
and dramaturgy to certain social classes in society and had instinctively distrusted mere form, he made the attempt now to
proceed with *new themes and areas* for a while. The way to the
plebeian tradition began with an avowal of the unliterary tradition.

The upholders of bourgeois literary history and contemporary
cultural journals had insisted up to this point upon a strict
separation of great and trivial literature. Brecht now attempted
to make the contents and techniques of certain areas of trivial
literature yield results for his own works. He was not the only
one among his contemporaries who made this endeavor. Georg
Kaiser, whom Brecht greatly admired and even considered as
his mentor, had already written a "comedy with a prelude and
three acts twenty years after" in 1924 with the title *Kolportage
(Sensational Rubbish)*. Brecht was not actually looking for
"sensational literature" as much as for the rich potential of
mystery and adventure novels. And even these works in their
entirety were too literary for him, so he searched for new ma-

terial related to sports and techniques of presentation and production. When Bernard Guillemin wanted to know what Brecht was working on then in 1926, the play *A Man's a Man (Mann ist Mann)* was referred to only as being of secondary importance. His prime concern was the work on the biography about the German heavyweight boxer Paul Samson-Körner, who was world famous at that time. Brecht answered the question in such a way that the readers of *Die literarische Welt* would appreciate it: "Samson-Körner is a splendid and significant type. I wanted to get him down on paper for myself. The simplest method was to let him tell me his life story. I've a great regard for reality. Quite frankly though, you can count such realities like Samson-Körner on your fingers. He's one in a million. The first thing that attracted me to Samson was that he appeared to box according to a principle that was un-German. He boxed nonchalantly. There's a great charm to such plasticity. For instance, it's absolutely impossible to imitate Samson stuffing a simple train ticket into his pocket. That's why he's also such a remarkable film actor." Brecht even reveals his method of work in this interview: "It's more pleasure than work. I ask him to talk to me, and his views are what count most for me. People's views interest me more than their feelings. Their views generally produce their feelings, which just simply follow suit. On the other hand, the views are decisive. Only experience can sometimes be ranked higher. But we all know that our views do not always come from experience."

Nothing ever came of this biography of a boxer. The readers of the newspaper had the delightful privilege of viewing a photograph of Samson-Körner preparing to hit the smiling and pensive Brecht with a left uppercut while Brecht tipped his head backward. Fragments of this life story were printed, yet only the beginnings of this story have remained extant. It was to open like this: "I want to remark at the very beginning that I was born in Beaver, Utah, in the U.S.A., in the Mormon area right near the Great Salt Lake. I can also point out why I was born there: it's because Beaver, Utah, is not on any of the railroad lines in the US.A. You can marry twelve women there, but you have to walk if you want to look at the place where I was born.—On the other hand, I was born in Zwickau, Saxony, because that's where I came into the world. I lived in Zwickau about thirteen years and spent most of my time in the Hotel Deutscher Kaiser. An uncle of mine owned it. That's where I learned the game of opening doors, carrying valises, and polishing shoes. I occasionally found this useful, like the time I was in England and was about to go under. But I managed to get a job in the Hotel Cardiff because of my training. When you come down to it, everything's about the same wherever you go. There's not much of a difference between London and Hamburg. . . ." *Die literarische Welt* did not overlook the opportunity to give its readers a view from the other side, and it subsequently printed a second interview, this time with Paul Samson-Körner about Brecht. The boxer, who was, by the way, a truly fantastic fighter, an extraordinary person, reported that he liked to read technical books and also had recently finished reading Robert Louis Stevenson's *South Sea Tales,* which he enjoyed immensely. Then he was asked whether he liked to read the classics. Samson-Körner replied: "No. I'm working with Mr. Brecht on a book. A good guy, that Brecht." Did he like to go to the theater? "Yes, but not to those things which make me sad. I like operettas. What I like best is the vaudeville. I'd pay anything to go to one of those shows." A man after Brecht's own heart.

The key word *Stevenson* leads us further. Brecht had already published *Commentaries to Stevenson* in the form of a review on May 19, 1925, in the *Berliner Börsen-Courier.* He praises the translator of *South Sea Tales* for "anglicizing the German language." Brecht's own Anglomania, which can be traced up through *Mahagonny* by studying the way he uses English fragments and terms, also belongs to the unliterary tradition. On the other hand, Brecht manages to maintain a critical perspective while admiring the new techniques and forms of life at that time. He praises Stevenson as a narrator for using cinematic techniques long before the discovery of the film. "From a purely linguistic standpoint, the regrouping around the visual viewpoint had begun in Europe some time ago. For instance, Rimbaud sees things purely from a visual viewpoint." Whoever might have expected Brecht to call upon his contemporaries to follow the course of cinema technology also learns the lesson here that the film itself is part of a literary tradition. The *Commentaries to Stevenson* closes with some praise for a story by the Scottish novelist because it presents "an extraordinary example of an adventure novel in which the sympathy of the reader for the hero himself (on which the success of all adventure novels depends) must be achieved only by a great effort." Most likely it was Brecht who infected his friend Samson-Körner with this enthusiasm for Stevenson and the *South Sea Tales*.

New themes, new material, new functions. Everything far from being actual literature. Sports becomes subject matter, but it is not merely sports for the writer, but sports as a technical model for the writer. At the beginning of the same year Brecht's essay *More Good Sporting Events (Mehr guten Sport)* had appeared. It was a dramatist's programmatic challenge to the theater and the theater audience. The primary purpose of the essay is not to win over the theater audience—the consumers of great literature up to that time—to sports stadiums, as the title might lead one to believe. On the contrary, the sports fans are to be won for the theater. The very first sentence calls for this: "We pin our hopes on the sports fans." The theater has lost contact with the audience and no longer interests anyone. The artist must move with the times, for one cannot sail "without the wind or with tomorrow's wind." The wind that is blowing right now whisks through the sports arenas, as anyone can tell by simply glancing at the attendance figures. If the theater wants to win an audience again, then it, too, must provide for "good sporting events" on the stage. "If we come along and say that we and the audience had imagined things differently, that we're in favor, for instance, of elegance, levity, sharpness, and objectivity, then the theater will naïvely reply: those things which you passionately desire, my dear sir, are not suitable for any man's dinner jacket. As if one could commit patricide in an elegant, objective, and classically rounded way, as it were." Sports represents for Brecht both a new area of concentration and a new technique.

It was not by chance that he brought his friend the boxer the stories of Robert Louis Stevenson. Brecht felt Stevenson's narrative technique in the adventure stories to be the complement

and counterpart to the technical elegance found in different types
of sports. And what was considered good in the adventure novel
also had to be acknowledged as good in the mystery novel. As
a theorist, Brecht continually concerned himself with the technical side of the mystery novel. He was caught up in this until
the last years of his life. During a trip in 1949 he saw the backs
of some American pocketbooks on a bookshelf and rushed to
them with a cry of delight: "Oh, mystery novels!" He took a few
from the shelf, read the titles, and then put them down disap-
pointedly: "Damn, just regular literature!" In his posthumous
papers there are numerous drafts of studies which deal with the
technique of the followers of Arthur Conan Doyle. A fragment
entitled "On the Popularity of the Mystery Novel" ("Über die
Popularität des Kriminalromans"), apparently written in 1926,
praises the mystery novel because it demands logical thinking,
not psychological empathy, on the part of the reader. The American pulp writers in the field are given the edge over the English
mystery writers because of the schemes they conceive. "The decisive factor here is that the characters grow out of the action,
not the action out of the characters. One sees the people act. In
parts. We are left in the dark about their motives, and yet, they
must be connected logically." Mystery novels befit a scientific age,
for they center "almost exclusively on material interests." These
products are popular because they allow for the enjoyment in
watching people act and in following the tracks people leave
behind them. Brecht makes the perfectly correct observation that
readers get vicarious pleasure from mystery novels because they
are provided with substitute action. Brecht expresses it this way:
"Adventurers in our society are criminal." Wherever this is the
case, where it becomes less and less possible to act in reality,
then it is bound to be a pleasure to experience the criminal
adventures in a book, to see people in action.

Even with all the economic differences and all the murders
committed for personal profit (without which it would be impossible to imagine an average mystery novel), Brecht believed
he could establish that both the detective and the reader within
the sphere of the mystery novel lived "in an extraordinary atmosphere free from conventions." "The crafty baron as well as the

loyal servant or even the seventy-year-old aunt *can* be the murderer. Not even a cabinet minister is free from suspicion." Brecht evidently wants to imply that the reader's pleasure is determined by this "equality before the law." Along with the vicarious satisfaction we have the fiction of social harmony. It is here that Brecht's notes, which were clearly fragmentary, break off, just where Brecht tries to show the reverse, namely that the apparent social harmony in the dialectics of the mystery novel definitely underscores the material inequality. "It is solely the social conditions that make crime possible or necessary: they rape character just as they build it." In a sketch written later and dealing with the same theme, Brecht as analyst emphasizes the fact that we are accustomed by our lives to make catastrophes out of our experiences. "This basic situation, in which intellectuals find themselves objects and not the subjects of history, molds a type of thinking which they can discover to their own enjoyment confirmed in the mystery novel. *Existence depends on unknown factors.* 'Something must have happened,' 'something is coming to a head,' 'a situation has arisen'—they feel this, and the intellect goes on watch."

The year 1926 marks the high point of Brecht's efforts to build an unliterary tradition. When the magazine *Tagebuch* sent a questionnaire at the end of the year to Brecht asking for a personal list of the best books of the year, he selected a Lenin biography, a book about America by the architect Eric Mendelsohn, the biography of the Swedish champion swimmer Arne Borg, and finally, a *History of the Great American Fortunes,* which he recommended to all "lovers of crime stories." In addition, he mentions *War Against War* which he calls "that horrendous picture book consisting of documentary photographs that succeed in rendering a portrait of mankind."

The quintessence of all Brecht's collected ideas, that is, the application of all the techniques and fine points, can be found in the comedy *A Man's a Man.* The preface of April 1927 summarizes everything and, at the same time, indicates a turning point. Much of what is in this preface still recalls Brecht's earlier orgiastic delight in impermanence. He thinks back on a human order and a type of man that has now come to an end. "Whatever such a perishing class may do, it will no longer be of any consequence for the doings of the people." Those people who belong to a perishing social class can no longer produce art nor consume it. Even their monuments and traditions cannot prevent the decline. "These people have had their great epoch. They have erected their monuments which have remained, but even these remnants are no longer a cause for great enthusiasm. The huge buildings in the city of New York and the great electrical inventions do not by themselves increase mankind's feeling of triumph." Brecht is of the opinion that a new type of man is in the making and everything depends on him from now on. "This new type of man will not be the one the old type of man imagined. I believe that he will not let himself be changed by machines but that he will change the machines. And no matter how he may look, he will above all look like a real human being." Old and new motifs permeate one another: motifs from the imagistic world of *Die Hauspostille* are coupled with Brecht's visions of new technicized inhabitants of the city who regard everything with great detachment. Also apparent are the first traces of Marxist thinking about the change of consciousness through social being (*Sein*) and about the primacy of revolutionary practice.

How does all this apply to the comedy *A Man's a Man*? The packer Galy Gay, whose usual trip to the market to buy a fish turns out to have unforeseeable consequences one day, appears to be "a new type." It may even be that he is a "progenitor of this new type of man" that Brecht mentions at the beginning of his preface. The conclusion of this preface tells us that one thing is certain: "This Galy Gay is not harmed in the least, but rather he profits from all this. And a person who takes such an attitude must win in the end." At least, this is the way Bertolt Brecht would regard the matter. Perhaps the spectator might view it differently? "I would not object to this in the least." One could interpret this last sentence to read that the author deems it dialectically possible to hold a completely opposite view. However, this is actually not the case, for Brecht takes the doctrines of this play quite seriously, in spite of all the comic antics. The interlude, in particular, is the turning point of the play. The widow Leokadja Begbick, one of Brecht's monumental female characters (whom he loved so much that he also worked her into the *Mahagonny* opera), announces to the spectators that there is to be no conciliation.

Mr. Bertolt Brecht claims man is man.
And this is something anyone can claim.
But then Mr. Bertolt Brecht also proves
That one can do a lot with a man.
This very evening someone is taken apart like a car,
And he doesn't lose anything in the process.

. . . . .

Mr. Bertolt Brecht hopes that you'll see the ground you're standing on
Disappear right from under you like snow
And that you'll notice as in the case of the packer Galy Gay
That life on earth is most dangerous.

Herr Bertolt Brecht behauptet: Mann ist Mann.
Und das ist etwas, was jeder behaupten kann.
Aber Herr Bertolt Brecht beweist auch dann
Dass man mit einem Menschen beliebig viel machen kann.
Hier wird heute abend ein Mensch wie ein Auto ummontiert
Ohne dass er irgend etwas dabei verliert.

. . . . .

Herr Bertolt Brecht hofft, Sie werden Boden, auf dem Sie stehen
Wie Schnee unter Ihren Füssen vergehen sehen
Und werden schon merken bei dem Packer Galy Gay
Dass das Leben auf Erden gefährlich sei.

The reassembling of the packer Galy Gay does not weaken him. It makes him strong. Galy Gay is for Brecht the incarnation of the new hero with roots in the unliterary tradition, the hero for whom Brecht so desperately yearned after his earlier period of negativity and negation. Aside from this, the preface and the play also reveal a new stream of thought: the contrast between the decline of one type of man and the rise of another is not regarded in crude, antithetical, basically aesthetic terms that are set up according to sympathy and antipathy. It is now considered in historical and dialectical terms. So, we have here a climax and turning point.

The magazine *Simplicissimus* published a poem two years later, on February 11, 1929, that can be regarded as an ironical swan song for this creative period and can in turn be designated as part of the antiliterary tradition. As concerns his earlier Anglomania, cult of technique, and provocative attitude stemming from his hostility to literature, the lines here give rise to a "negation" just as the poem "Einst" had given rise to a swan song that meant the end of all poetry which centered on impermanence.

700 Intellectuals Pray to an Oil Tank

Without invitation
We have come
Seven hundred (and more are on the way)
From everywhere,
Where the wind no longer blows,
From the mills which slowly tread, and
From the ovens where it is said
That dogs no longer come out from under them.

And we have seen you
Suddenly overnight,
Oil Tank.

Yesterday you weren't there,
But today
You alone are left.

Hurry here, all of you,
Who saw off the branch on which you sit.
Workers!
God has returned
In the form of an oil tank.

You ugly one,
You are the most beautiful!

Do not harm us,
You objectivist!

Dissolve our ego!
Make us collective!

For we don't want it our way,
But the way you want it.

You're not made out of ivory and ebony wood
   but out of
Iron.
Wonderful, wonderful, wonderful!
You Invisible One!

You are not a phantom,
Nor are you Infinite!
But seven meters tall.
There is no secret in you,
Just oil.

And you proceed with us
Not by how you think it would be good, not without research,
But by calculation.

What is grass for you?
You sit upon it.
Where before there was grass,
That's where you sit, oil tank,
And there is a feeling about you
Nothing.

Therefore, hear us
And save us from the evil of the intellect
In the name of electrocution,
Ratio, and statistics!

700 INTELLEKTUELLE BETEN EINEN ÖLTANK AN

Ohne Einladung
Sind wir gekommen
Siebenhundert (und viele sind noch unterwegs)
Überall her,
Wo kein Wind mehr weht,
Von den Mühlen, die langsam mahlen, und
Von den Öfen, hinter denen es heisst.
Dass kein Hund mehr vorkommt.

Und haben Dich gesehen
Plötzlich über Nacht,
Öltank.

Gestern warst Du noch nicht da,
Aber heute
Bist nur Du mehr.

Eilet herbei, alle,
Die ihr absägt den Ast, auf dem ihr sitzet.
Werktätige!
Gott ist wiedergekommen
In Gestalt eines Öltanks.

Du Hässlicher,
Du bist der Schönste!

Tue uns Gewalt an,
Du Sachlicher!

Lösche aus unser Ich!
Mache uns kollektiv!
Denn nicht wie wir wollen,
Sondern wie Du willst.

Du bist nicht gemacht aus Elfenbein und Ebenholz,
    sondern aus
Eisen.
Herrlich, herrlich, herrlich!
Du Unscheinbarer!

Du bist kein Unsichtbarer,
Nicht unendlich bist Du!
Sondern sieben Meter hoch.
In Dir ist kein Geheimnis,
Sondern Öl.

Und du verfährst mit uns
Nicht nach Gutdünken, noch unerforschlich,
Sondern nach Berechnung.

Was ist für dich ein Gras?
Du sitzest darauf.
Wo ehedem ein Gras war,
Da sitzest jetzt Du, Öltank,
Und vor Dir ist ein Gefühl
Nichts.

Darum erhöre uns
Und erlöse uns von dem Übel des Geistes.
Im Namen der Elektrifizierung,
Der Ratio und der Statistik!

At that time the literary fashion of the day was still *Neue Sachlichkeit*.* Brecht was actually one of the forerunners of this movement; yet, even though he agreed with its doctrines and creative methods, he could not bring himself to expand his interest and join the writers of this movement. Brecht never became an integral part of Neue Sachlichkeit, just as he earlier could not become part of expressionism. His sardonic attitude toward the seven hundred *neusachlich* oil-tank fanatics had been prepared two years before this by the vote he cast against four hundred poets of the expressionist or "Rilkean" school. *Die literarische Welt* had asked Brecht to be one of the jury in a poetry contest. He cast his vote under the title *A Short Report on 400 (Four Hundred) Young Poets (Kurzer Bericht über 400 (vierhundert) junge Lyriker)*—as though he were writing a check and had to spell out the digits. There had been more than a thousand poems, and Brecht actually did not find one to his liking. "I've always known naturally that every halfway decent German can write a poem and also that this proves nothing about every other German. But what is worse is that I've become acquainted here with an assortment of young people whose acquaintance I would have been better off without." The world of the large cities appears to resist "the new blood of the bourgeoisie" in poetry. Everything is imitation from the period of im-pressionism and ex-pressionism. It is, as Brecht says, merely an "im-print" *(Druck-kunst)*, and its days are numbered. Moreover, since he does not think highly of the poems by Rilke, George, and Werfel, he is completely unqualified to "judge these sorts of products or related ones in any way." Then he lets loose with some bitter words about the poets: "Here we have

* *Translator's note:* This term has generally been translated as "new objectivity." The movement itself lasted from 1925 to 1933. It was a trend in the arts which roughly corresponds to the current trend toward the documentary as an art form.

again those silent, fine dreamy people, the sensitive part of the depleted bourgeoisie, and I want nothing to do with them." Brecht's vote: a rejection of all the solicited poems coupled with the suggestion that Hannes Küpper's poem "He, He! The Iron Man!" be printed. This poem had appeared in a sports newspaper on bicycle racing and had been dedicated to the six-day bicycle racer Reggie MacNamara. Brecht believed that he had found a documentary value here which he had not discovered in the poems that had been submitted. The basic purpose a poem should have was realized here, or at least, implied: the "original gesture [Geste] of communication of a thought or feeling which is also beneficial for strangers." This is almost doctrinaire: "All great poems have a value as documents."

He dismisses Rilke, George, and Werfel as poets. For Rilke there is at least a friendly addendum—he is "in other ways a really fine person." George does not get off that easy. Brecht writes in Die literarische Welt (July 13, 1928) that George's influence on the young people in literature appears to be insignificant. His views are incidental and of no consequence. This must be taken as an extremely sharp rejection in view of Brecht's insistence that only the opinions of a poet in a poem are interesting. He feels that George's poetry is "retirement poetry" (Rentenpoesie) and poetry written for retired people. "The pedestal which this saint has chosen for himself has been chosen with too much cleverness. It rests on a spot that is too densely populated with people and offers a view that is much too picturesque. . . ." Neither Werfel's expressionistic ecstasy nor George's picturesque loneliness nor the lyrical world of Rilke's Duino Elegies will do. Still, Brecht's early poetry remained closely bound to the late bourgeois conception of literature—even with all his antiliterary tendencies.

Brecht looks for views and experiences in a poem, not feelings. It should not be forgotten here that seventeen years before Brecht cast his vote in the poetry contest, Rilke had written in The Notebooks of Malte Laurids Brigge: "Poems are not feelings as people assume they are—one has these early enough. Poems are experiences." Despite this statement, Rilke and Brecht share only a common rejection of subjective expression in a poem.

They mean basically different things when they talk about experience. Rilke classifies experience under his central term "the world within" (*Weltinnenraum*). He isolates the outer event experienced by the lyrical "I" from the crystallizing process of "subjectivication." On the one hand there is the outer world that transmits experiences, on the other the transported or transformed result of the experience. The thinking of *Malte Laurids Brigge* is fundamentally idealistic. The subject-object relationship became disturbed. Rilke's world within excluded dialectics.

In contrast, the early Brecht frequently exaggerated the relation between outer experience and the experiencing poet to the disadvantage of the poet himself. He would like to transmit the outer events in a pure way as it were—without the unnecessary emotional accouterments of the subject who is registering everything. His antisubjectivism sometimes goes beyond the borderline between the human and the inhuman. This is the reason why the structure of Brecht's early poems is conceived mainly in epic images, reports, and chronicles. Even when a poem is not expressly composed as a chronicle, Brecht prefers to use certain phrases that provide distance such as "we hear," "thought I," "I asked myself." Here, too, real dialectics is excluded. It seems that there is only an object without a subject.

Brecht was also not very clear in outlining his position in regard to the prominent dramatists of that epoch. To be sure, there is his contribution to Shaw's seventieth birthday, "Ovation for Shaw," written in 1926, but one year later he uses another one of those inane newspaper questionnaires as an opportunity to retouch his statements. Some paper wanted to know how often he had laughed in his life and what the causes had been. Brecht's answer (which appeared in *Film-Kurier* on July 11, 1927) focused on five occasions. A short laugh "when I heard that Shaw was a socialist." Resounding laughter when learning that Thomas Mann remarked that the difference between his generation and Brecht's was not very great. Incredulous laughter upon listening to someone compare the collected works of Friederike Kempner and Alfred (Kempner) Kerr. "Interminable frenetic laughter as part of a final tribute when I heard the great German comedian Karl Valentin, the only true revolutionary figure in the contemporary theater, respond to the question why he wore glasses without lenses. He said to wit: it's better than nothing. When he said that I immediately associated this with the new developments in the theater." Finally, irritated laughter "at the thought that one might believe after reading this answer that I laugh the entire day only about literature." The foolish editor in charge of the *Film-Kurier*'s questionnaire added in his sparkling manner that Brecht had apparently forgotten to laugh about himself "in a hearty and self-knowing manner."

At that time the hard-boiled journalists in Berlin and Vienna considered Brecht a fool with fool's privileges, and they asked him the most ridiculous questions with the expectation that he would be ready with an impudent reply. Brecht assumed this role with great pleasure, answered all the questionnaires, and simultaneously played Karl Valentin and the brave soldier Schweik. The only thing that mattered to him was making the enemy visible at each occasion. He was against Thomas Mann, against the expressionist poets and playwrights. He dismissed Rilke and George. Shaw's Fabian socialism could only make him laugh. The German members of the PEN-Club—once again in an answer to a questionnaire in 1926—are characterized as "absolutely hopeless, superfluous, harmful." Georg Kaiser is one of the few who comes away looking better. Brecht's congratulatory message on his fiftieth birthday, which appeared in the *Berliner Börsen-Courier* on November 24, 1928, is quite friendly: "Asked whether I believe that the dramas of Georg Kaiser are important and have decisively changed the situation of European theater, my answer would be yes. *Without* the knowledge of the changes he has brought about, no dramatist can produce a play that will yield results. His style is not simply a personal style like the others. Moreover his rather bold basic doctrine of idealism must definitely be discussed, and this discussion must lead to a decision."

It is evident that the tone here is much different from that of his answers to the questions about George, Mann, Kerr, and the majority of the derivative writers. Kaiser is especially important as the subject of a discussion. His importance derives from the fact that one should not follow him. The philosophical idealism of the dramatist who wrote *Die Bürger von Calais* should be discussed and, apparently, should be rejected. Kaiser was a Platonist, Brecht, not at all. Nor was he an Aristotelian. The unliterary tradition rooted in mystery and adventure novels, the views and experiences of technicians and athletes, the sports public, and the modern world of the machine, was continued in the field of literature by Brecht's opposition to all those poetical and philosophical currents which he at that time felt—sometimes justifiably so, other times not—to be expressions of a bourgeoisie which was depleted and which he wanted nothing to do with. In spite of this, Brecht could not join the proud apostles of Neue Sachlichkeit with all their brutality, worldly experience, and cleverness. This, too, was still a literary fashion of a perishing social class. It was like wearing your heart on your sleeve.

Laxity and Intellectual Property

The Threepenny Opera is an engrossing, ambivalent work because it did not manage to bring about a balance between Brecht's old and new positions, and he was to become preoccupied by it time and again until the end of his life. During his later period he once said with a sigh that he would go down in literary history as the man who wrote the lines: "Most important is eating, then comes morality." The lessons of his songs were enjoyed like fine cooking instead of being critically regarded. The "yearnings" of underworld figures for the bourgeois life, that is, the bourgeois rules of the game set up by a seemingly unbourgeois trade, became obvious enough indeed, but this same bourgeois underworld brought forth accusations, and it had no right to do this. Brecht sought the connection to the plebeian tradition but had yet to encounter the right plebeians. He turned back to John Gay, and this proved fruitful. Yet, the reutilization was not sufficient. There was a real problem hidden behind the famous and grotesque story of plagiarism. One could not object to the fact that Brecht borrowed a great deal from tradition for *The Threepenny Opera,* as Alfred Kerr and Kurt Tucholsky asserted. The main objection stemmed from the fact that all his remodeling of the beggar's opera into the threepenny opera, his resetting the English events of the early eighteenth century into the world of capitalism failed despite the dramatic and musical splendor.

The ridiculous charge against Brecht that he plagiarized twenty-five lines of K. L. Ammers' translation of Villon and incorporated them as part of the hundreds of lines in *The Threepenny Opera* touched upon Brecht's relation to tradition and "intellectual property." Brecht was not without tradition but set tradition against tradition. For instance, he took a term of intellectual originality which had taken on its authoritative meaning only since the end of the eighteenth century, since the advent of bourgeois individualism and the rise of a literature of confession and self-portrayal, and against this term he set another one, an early bourgeois, partly prebourgeois, concept of art that regarded the substance and forms at hand as material for the handicraft of later writers. It is well known that Bach and Handel (the same Handel who had been attacked in *The Beggar's Opera*) had also treated the scores of other composers in this manner. *The Threepenny Opera* was not the first public occasion where Brecht was pressed to announce his concept of the material value of a literature that already bore someone else's imprint. The art critic Herwarth Walden had already spoken about plagiarism in the play *In the Jungle of Cities.* Brecht had answered in an article entitled *An Established Fact (Eine Feststellung)*, which appeared in the *Berliner Börsen-Courier* on November 4, 1924: "One of the characters in my drama *In the Jungle* quotes lines from Rimbaud and Verlaine in several places. In the text these passages are marked as quotes with quotation marks. Ostensibly the theater has yet to develop a technique to express quotation marks. If it did, then it would make a large number of popular plays suit the taste of philologists perhaps, but audiences in general would find them rather unbearable. The people who are concerned with the production of plays in our time will not have time either now or in the next ten years, I'm afraid, to think about this without disturbance due to the difficulties of their craft. Therefore, those interested parties from philological circles must be requested to call up again in approximately eleven years. (It is all right to reveal to you now that the drama, if it is to make progress at all, will proceed in any case with composure over the corpses of the philologists.)"

When *The Threepenny Opera* gradually became an international success despite all the negative prognostications of the critic Kerr, an attempt was made to liquidate Brecht as a literary figure by using the twenty-five lines of verse by Ammers against him. Brecht answered as he had always answered: he was this one time "lax" concerning the question of intellectual property. By this, he meant that his conception of the intellectual tradition differed fundamentally from the bourgeois tradition of possession. His meaning of tradition was both prebourgeois and postbourgeois.

Karl Kraus grasped this immediately. He was not at all ready to go along with Brecht, but he had recognized Brecht's talent rather early. Above and beyond this, Kraus took the side of the alleged plagiarist with great relish because the question of plagiarism was raised by his arch enemy Kerr. During World War I, Kerr had praised a miserable piece of chauvinistic poetry of his own, written under his pseudonym Gottlieb. Kraus had pointed this out in his magazine *Die Fackel*. Now again in *Die Fackel* (Nos. 811-819) he made the sarcastic comment: "The only thing left to say would be that he was more unfortunate than Brecht in so far as it has never occurred to anyone that he did not write the Gottlieb poems." Kraus judged Brecht's case like this: "It is highly improbable that an intellectual existence would be successful if it attempted to succeed only by borrowing someone else's verse, and it is downright idiotic to want to make us believe that this particular, talented clever author would find it necessary and think it possible to smuggle lines as though they were like movable sets and characters to be used for a dramatic purpose and also to steal the credits as though they were like literary contraband stolen from an author whose rights were to be neglected." This is still the final word on the subject.

Brecht never forgot Kraus's support. When the editor of *Die Fackel* kept quiet in 1933 because he could "think of nothing" to say about Hitler, and when he was attacked by all sides because of this, Brecht wrote a poem in celebration of the Viennese satirist's sixtieth birthday. The title was "On the Significance of the Ten-line Poem in the 888th Number of *Die Fackel* (October 1933)," and it closed this way:

> When the said person apologized
> For not raising his voice,
> Silence appeared before the judge,
> Removed the mask from its visage,
> And as witness made itself known.

> Als der Beredte sich entschuldigte
> dass seine Stimme versage
> trat das Schweigen vor den Richtertisch
> nahm das Tuch von Antlitz und
> gab sich zu erkennen als Zeuge.

The discussion about laxity and intellectual property was brought to an end not by the dramatist Brecht but by the poet, and in a cunning way. In 1930 the Kiepenheuer Publishing Company in Berlin printed a new edition of the Ammers' translation of Villon's poetry. Brecht contributed a poem as introduction called "Sonnet on the New Edition of François Villon's Poetry":

> Here you have taken from old yellow paper
>   his testament printed again
>   in which he bestows upon all he knows—dirt.
>   And as for the distribution: please yell, "Here!"

> Where is the spit you have spewed on him?
>   Where is he himself whom you have disdained?
>   His song has lasted longest of all.
>   Yet how much longer will it last, his song?

> Here instead of your smoking ten cigars,
>   you can have for the same price this book again,
>   (and now you can learn what you were to him . . .)

> When have you ever received something more acid for just 3
>   marks?
>   Everyone should take from this just what he needs.
>   Even I have taken something for myself.

Hier habt ihr aus verfallendem Papier
noch einmal adgedruckt sein Testament,
in dem er Dreck schenkt allen, die er kennt—
wenn's ans Verteilen geht: schreit, bitte, "hier!"

Wo ist euer Speichel, den ihr auf ihn spiet?
Wo ist er selbst, dem eure Buckel galten?
Sein Lied hat noch am längsten ausgehalten,
doch wie lang hält es wohl noch aus, sein Lied?

Hier, anstatt dass ihr zehn Zigarren raucht,
könnt ihr zum gleichen Preis es nochmal lesen
(und so erfahren, was ihr ihm gewesen . . .)

Wo habt ihr Saures für drei Mark bekommen?
Nehm jeder sich heraus, was er grad braucht!
Ich selber hab mir was herausgenommen . . .

Basically, tradition was being set against tradition here. It was the same attitude Brecht had taken as he cast his vote on the four hundred poets of the bourgeois "experience poetry" (*Erlebnis-Dichtung*). Brecht's reaction to the accusation of plagiarism corresponded to the statements he had made on that kind of poetry. The real complaint one could make about him, one that he himself made, had nothing to do with the incorporation of practical verse in the form of movable sets but with his lack of consistency in the arrangement, in the rearrangement. In contrast to the situation of Galy Gay, the reutilization of Mackie Messer and his gang was not successful. Werner Hecht compared *The Beggar's Opera* and *The Threepenny Opera* and drew this conclusion: "The incorporation of material that has already been shaped cannot redeem the lack of inventiveness or creativeness. Rather it is a differing with the past. It is here in this process that creativeness must prove itself. In *The Threepenny Opera*, Brecht did not limit himself by following his original model too closely, and this was to his advantage." One might add: he has continually limited himself too much by following his model too closely, and this to his disadvantage.

"You're going to laugh—the Bible."

During the period in which he wrote *The Threepenny Opera,*
Brecht wrote another answer to a questionnaire submitted by
the Berlin magazine *Die Dame* (similar to *Ladies' Home Journal*).
It was a good name for this publication, which was one of the
favorites of the people from the fancy Tiergarten and Grune-
wald sections of Berlin. It even carried a special section "Die
losen Blätter" ("The Loose Sheets") which had a teasing ambivalence to it. Once again prominent people were being solicited
for another questionnaire, and evidently Brecht belonged to this
select group. "Der stärkste Eindruck" ("The Strongest Impression")—this was the heading and theme of the questionnaire.
Brecht wrote only one sentence as his answer, which appeared
on October 1, 1928: "You're going to laugh—the Bible." The
sentence has two parts to it which were meant to provide a strong
contrast. The dash was the turning point. "You're going to laugh"
was at that time slang in the west section of Berlin and in the
corresponding social classes in other German cities. It had the
tone of a literary cabaret. Numerous jokes had this as their
punch line. A married man suddenly returns from a trip and
discovers a strange man in his bathroom without any clothes.
When asked what he is doing there, the stranger replies: "You're
going to laugh. I'm waiting for a streetcar." Brecht borrows this
formula. No doubt the readers of *Die Dame* and its "Loose
Sheets" were familiar with this line. However, what follows is
something totally unexpected: the Bible. No matter what their
attitude was toward religion, the readers of *Die Dame* were not
accustomed to discussing the Bible. If anything, they would
sooner talk about *The Threepenny Opera.* "You're going to
laugh"—a contrast between the familiar and the totally unfa-
miliar. Brecht must have carefully edited the formula so that
it would have effect.

On the surface it seems to smack of blasphemy, like the title
and structure of *Die Hauspostille,* published the year before in
1927, like the worship of the oil tank, written in February 1929,
which wickedly rearranged several parts of the Lord's Prayer in

a neusachlich formulation. Nevertheless, Brecht's answer concerning his "strongest impression" cannot be simply dismissed with the word *blasphemy*. *Die Hauspostille* does not merely play with recollections from a book of devotions but is among other things a reutilized theology. The poem about the oil tank is a nasty critique of religion but within the framework of Brecht's greater social criticism. It is not blasphemy. And Brecht's answer to the readers of *Die Dame* was not blasphemy: it told the truth.

Of course, one thing immediately strikes our attention. Brecht's range of themes in his plays and adaptations is extensive: Greek and Roman antiquity with *Antigone* and *Coriolanus*; Roman history with *Lucullus*; *Edward II* from England; *Mother Courage* and *Galileo*; German misery* at the end of the eighteenth century represented by the Hofmeister Läuffer; a luminous China and a fictitious Caucasia; the Paris Commune and the history of St. Joan—three times in order to prepare the necessary groundwork; the American Revolution in the adaptation of Farquhar's *The Recruiting Officer* (with the title *Drums and Trumpets*) and the Spanish Civil War in *Die Gewehren der Frau Carrar* (*The Rifles of Señora Carrar*). Biblical subject matter is not included.

At the beginning of his career, Brecht had apparently wanted to treat a biblical theme and had developed it quite extensively, if one can believe a report of a friend at that time. H. O. Münsterer, in his memoirs that deal with Brecht's 1919 Augsburg period, recalls two dramas that were near completion: "One of these plays had the title 'David, or the Messenger of God' at first and was later changed to 'Absalom and Bathsheba.' The material was taken from the Bible. As is well known, Brecht constantly read the Bible and imitated its style in numerous works. David is God's man with all his recognizable immortal traits taken from the Holy Scriptures. The entrance scene shows Absalom in the courtyard of the fortress telling notorious stories to the soldiers about the sly ways of the aging king. Then David

---

* *Translator's note:* Heine coined the term *deutsche Misere* to indicate the wretchedness and poverty of German conditions. Both Marx and Engels made use of this phrase to point to the limitations of a people who are oppressed.

appears on the top of the wall, a gigantic silhouette. 'I want to settle accounts with my son Absalom!' An uneasy silence, curtain. It was an opening which Brecht could not have written more effectively in his great years." In spite of this, the project was evidently discarded by the author. He did not conceive a new biblical theme after this. Still, Münsterer is right to have stressed the importance of the Bible for the young Brecht (and this has been completely substantiated by Brecht's own answer to the readers of *Die Dame*). Quotations from the Bible appear everywhere in his works. Reinhold Grimm has documented this fact in a significant study. Generally speaking, the familiar biblical quotation in a passage of one of the plays or in *The Threepenny Novel* is simultaneously supposed to produce an ironical reminder and dialectical tension between the original situation in the Bible and the situation at hand. The packer Galy Gay uses the same words of the Apostle Peter who betrays Christ: "I know not this elephant." Mackie Messer gives an account in prison of how he behaved to the pernicious policeman Brown: "And that wants to become police chief. It was a good thing that I didn't yell at him. That's what I first thought of. But then I considered in the nick of time that a long, punishing stare would make him more uneasy. That did it. I stared at him, and soon he was crying bitter tears. I learned this trick from the Bible." Naturally, there is more to this than just the pun that is determined by the quotation. Grimm sees in most of these biblical quotations an application of the alienation principle, a dialectical inflammable relationship between the origination and the actualization of the biblical word. In Scene Six of *Galileo* there is an important dialogue between the protagonist of the play and Cardinal Barberini, consisting just of biblical quotations. It reaches a point where both characters base their arguments on sayings from Solomon. Of course, here in this Galileo play the Bible belongs thematically and substantially to "the heart of the matter." The tension is twofold: on the one hand, it exists between the contrasting use of the biblical sayings by the scientist and the cardinal; on the other, it is provided by the contrast between the original biblical situation and the present.

Blasphemy, puns, alienation. There is more. Brecht rejected, to be sure, the message of the Bible "without compromise." Grimm has proven this most convincingly. In the process of adaptation we are left with biblical forms, especially the melodious language of Luther's translation of the Bible. Brecht always wanted to test this rich language in his own work. The "Four Psalms," published posthumously, gains its power from the use of the form and language of the psalms to express a lack of faith. Cry from the bottom of your soul but not above to just any "O Lord." Many of Brecht's sincere poetical lines employ the linguistic harmony of Luther's translation for the intensification or catharsis of emotions. In his poem "Die Nachtlager" ("The Night's Lodgings"), the first line of the third stanza, which is so important as a synthesis (in a poem which basically deals with the contrast between social reform and social revolution), begins with: "Do not put that book down, thou who dost read, man." ("Leg das Buch nicht nieder, der du das liesest, Mensch.")

The biblical harmony can just as well serve to denounce a false sincerity. This is echoed in the wedding song of Polly and Mackie:

> The plate from which thou eatest thy bread,
> Do not stare at it for long, throw it away!
>
> Der Teller, von welchem du issest dein Brot
> Schau ihn nicht lang an, wirf ihn fort!

Brecht's fascination with the Bible, which lasted well into his late period, led him to develop a biblical theme even greater than it had been when first intoned in *Mother Courage*. In Scene Three of the chronicle about the Thirty Years War, the army chaplain sings a seasonal hymn about Christ's passion. South German folk idiom, Bavarian and Swabian, cross rhymes, folk ballads. When Brecht was requested in 1949 by the Austrian composer Gottfried von Einem to write the text for a choral cantata, he returned to the seasonal hymn, which he lengthened into an actual passion cantata. New stanzas were included in the

account of the passion, and it was all crowned with a reflective
epilogue, as it were, with these words:

> Look, now he's stuck him through!
> Look how strong the torturer is!
> Look, he's told the truth!
> Serves him right! Serves him right!

> Schaut's, jetzt hat er ihn derstoch'n!
> Schaut's, der starke Folterknecht!
> Schaut's, er hat die Wahrheit g'sproch'n!
> G'schieht ihm recht! G'schieht ihm recht!

This is not the standpoint of the evangelist as in the *St.
Matthew Passion*. It is also not a sympathetic account. The passion is observed from the outside, from the viewpoint of the
crowd that luxuriates in a horrendous admiration for the torturer
and also manages to show some scornful sympathy for the victim.
It is a picture similar to Grünewald's Munich account of the
mocking of Christ. However, at the same time, there is an element of dialectical tension. It "serves him right" because he
told the truth. This is a familiar Brecht motif and can be found
in the poem written during the emigration period "Chased Out
for Good Reasons" ("Verjagt mit gutem Grund"). Also in the
"Solomon Song" from *The Threepenny Opera,* and above all,
in *Mother Courage*. Always with the same refrain: "You're
better off without it all." Caesar's boldness, Socrates' honesty,
St. Martin's altruism, and in an additional stanza, the thirst for
knowledge of Brecht "thirsting for knowledge." Is this really the
case? Even the text of the passion cantata is composed in such a
way to make it possible for the composer to renounce through
the music the position which the Turbae take before the passion
and thereby to fulfill the task of a passion cantata. Once again,
Brecht offers alienation. The passion poem of Brecht the poet
from Augsburg in the Augsburg intonation remains a non-
Christian poem, but it is far from being blasphemous or provocative. So the readers of *Die Dame* received an honest answer
after all.

German Classicism Reutilized

Brecht's reliance on the language of Luther indicated first and foremost a negation. Like his endeavor to return to and go beyond the era of bourgeois individualism, as well as beyond German classicism, with his conception of intellectual property, his regression to Luther must be understood as a direct affront to the language of Schiller and Goethe. The young Brecht proceeded here only with great hesitation at first. Later he directed his attack, which became quite sharp at times, against the language, concerns, substance, and function of German classicism. This began with assaults on the language and verse and led almost immediately to assaults on the classical dramaturgy. The essay *On Form and Subject Matter (Über Stoffe und Formen)*, which appeared in the *Berliner Börsen-Courier* on March 31, 1929, had already focused on this question: "Can we speak of money in the form of iambics? The mark, quoted at fifty dollars the day before yesterday and today already at one hundred dollars, tomorrow beyond this, etc.—Is that right? Gasoline resists the five-act form. Today's catastrophes do not proceed in a straight line but take the form of cyclical crises. Heroes change with the individual phases, are interchangeable, etc. The graph of actions is complicated by abortive actions. Fate is no longer a single coherent power but more like a power plant with currents flowing in opposite directions. The power groups move not only against themselves but also in themselves, etc., etc. Just to dramatize a simple newspaper report, one needs much more than the dramatic technique of a Hebbel and an Ibsen. This is not said with a sense of triumph. It is a sad statement of fact."

Brecht held this opinion to the very end. His work manual on *Arturo Ui* notes on April 12, 1941: "Aside from the fact that blank verse never gets along harmoniously with the German language—just look at the horrendous parts of *Tasso*—there is also something anachronistic about it, something annoyingly feudalistic." This was the reason why Brecht approached the works of German classicism for decades largely as mere superstructures in the service of exploiters. However, the Marxist

Brecht's analysis was wrong here. He misunderstood German classicism as feudal ideology in the service of the deceiving social ideas of harmony. Actually these works beginning with *The Robbers* up to *Wilhelm Tell*, from *Götz von Berlichingen* to *Faust*, were all bourgeois and antifeudal in nature. German classicism would have been anachronistic only if it really had wanted to preserve the declining feudalism and to legitimize it along intellectual lines. No matter how ambivalent the relationship of Schiller and Goethe may have been to the bourgeois revolution, they were not anachronistic writers but bourgeois artists. This was something that Brecht was to realize later.

In spite of the misinterpretation, everything still depends on his initial approach. The classical quotations have a much more defined job in his works than the biblical ones. The classical pathos is woven into embarrassing life situations so that the quotation inadvertently has a comical effect and takes the opposite meaning of its original intention. Here again Reinhold Grimm has assembled a fine selection from Brecht's best quotations from Schiller, Goethe, Hölderlin, and others, as he did with the biblical echoes. Next to *Arturo Ui*, which remodels the garden scene from *Faust* and famous scenes from *Richard the Third*, there is *St. Joan of the Stockyards*, which shows Brecht at his best in his use of classical words and situations for the purpose of parody and contrast. This play has become well known not only because of the quotations but because the central figure is intended to be a repudiation of Schiller's romantic tragedy. The classical language is expressly used as the language of the exploiters. Mauler speaks with a Schiller intonation, Joan in Brechtian verse forms. In a later production of *The Caucasian Chalk Circle* (*Der kaukasische Kreidekreis*) by the Berliner Ensemble, the director Brecht simply gave masks to all the rulers and their known accomplices instead of allowing them to use their bare faces. The only characters who had faces were Grusche, Simon, Azdak, and the poor people. Mauler speaks like a German classicist, leads discussions in classical blank verse, yet acts like one who is familiar with all the economic complexities and ties. The structure of the play—this has been demonstrated by Käthe Rülicke—follows Karl Marx's discussion of the cyclical crisis in

Das Kapital with great exactitude. The small speculators, on the other hand, are idealistic and unsuspecting. Idealism and agnosticism correspond to their social situation.

> Woe! The eternal laws
> Are eternally opaque
> For the human economic system!
> Without warning
> The volcano erupts to devastate the area!

> Wehe! Ewig undurchsichtig
> Sind die ewigen Gesetze
> Der menschlichen Wirtschaft!
> Ohne Warnung
> Öffnet sich der Vulkan und verwüstet die Gegend!

Eight sonnets that Brecht wrote about 1940 and later included in the eleventh volume of Versuche under the title "Studies" form the high point of Brecht's negative and largely pseudo-Marxist evaluation of German classicism and its historical role. Even by this time Brecht had already modified his standpoint. In the preface he explained: "These sonnets of social criticism are not, of course, intended to kill one's enjoyment of classical works but rather to make this enjoyment more pure." This is not the way the playwright would have formulated it twenty years earlier when he had Schiller and Chicago confronting one another, nor would the author of *Arturo Ui* have thought this way. *Mother Courage* can also be dated back to J. J. C. von Grimmelshausen if necessary, that is, to the preclassical period. The new phase in Brecht's relation to German classicism—this should be designated as "reutilization" (*Umfunktionierung*)—becomes evident by his work on *Der Hofmeister.* Both works, by the way, belong to the Sturm und Drang period and not to the period of real German classicism.

Brecht's *Hofmeister* sonnet begins this way:

> Here you have a Figaro on this side of the Rhine!
> The people teach the nobility a thing or two.
> Over there they win power, here honor.
> So over there it becomes a comedy, not here.

Hier habt ihr Figaro diesseits des Rheins!
Der Adel geht beim Pöbel in die Lehre,
Der drüben Macht gewinnt und hüben Ehre:
So wirds ein Lustspiel drüben und hier keins.

In the title of the sonnet Brecht places great value on classifying the play *Der Hofmeister* by J. M. R. Lenz a *bourgeois tragedy*. The poem is supposed to show just how the tragic nature requires a social decision in advance: what would have been a comedy in France degenerates in Germany into tragedy. For Lenz and his times, the private tutor Läuffer was a tragic figure.

He snivels and grumbles and slanders and castrates himself.
The poet's voice breaks when he talks about it.

Er flennt und murrt und lästert und entmannt sich.
Des Dichters Stimme bricht, wenn er's erzählt.

For Brecht he is no longer tragic. His most important concern when he prepared a production of the play by the Berliner Ensemble in the spring of 1950 was to draw out the comedy which was hidden under and behind the original bourgeois tragedy. One of Brecht's letters (March 25, 1950) written in conjunction with *Der Hofmeister* production deals with the change of genres that is to be understood as a social decision. "That is where German classicism fails us. Here where it voluntarily takes its place as one of the great bourgeois caryatids which become petrified like salt pillars in the face of the revolutionary Sodom. The important beginnings of realism must be re-established. One must reveal how Lenz has been suppressed in literary history. The theater must return to this point if it is to progress, that is, if it is to work out a realistic style from great subject matter. We have carried on a great style just for idealistic works! Then there is the problem of the tutor in *Der Hofmeister* which is part of the German misery, and perhaps it might be necessary to explain the metaphorical meaning of the castration story. Of course, the story is not purely symbolical: the castration of the intellectuals who were all forced to join the 'caste' of tutors about this time is portrayed with great realism as a live flesh and blood example. (As a matter of fact there was a real horrible incident in East Prussia that served as the basis of the play.) In other words, the physical self-castration is not to be taken only for an intellectual self-castration but is itself portrayed as the grotesque solution to Läuffer's social situation. Furthermore, the play is really a *comedy*, and it is thoroughly in keeping with the character of the classical writers that they did not cultivate this genre! (*The Broken Jug* is perhaps an exception, but even here this play belongs to the realistic work of Kleist and has rather interestingly the same metaphorical character of *Der Hofmeister*)."

If the comedy is drawn out from under the bourgeois tragedy, then the adapter must contradict both his original model and its author. Where Lenz reports with a breaking voice, Brecht shows himself to be cheerful and calm. This is only possible, of course, if the adapter breaks his agreement with the social postulates of the original Sturm und Drang playwright. Brecht's adaptation does not intend to return to the tragedy of Lenz in its basic conception or to limit the adaptation to mere refinement while adhering to the contemporary dictums of the theater. Brecht's adaptation of Lenz's play becomes a critique of Lenz. The adapter remains an adversary in those places where Lenz already was an adversary. However, he also becomes an adversary in those places where Lenz had sought to make friends.

Lenz's *Der Hofmeister* was derived from his struggle to point out particularly flagrant social inequalities through the theater and to cause vibrations that might improve the situation. Yet, Brecht is not at all correct, formally speaking, when he allows *Der Hofmeister* to figure in the title of his sonnet as bourgeois tragedy. The first edition of Lenz's play, which was published in 1774 by the Weygand Book Company in Leipzig, had the following title: *Der Hofmeister oder Vorteile der Privaterziehung. Eine Komödie.* (*The Private Tutor, or The Advantages of a Private Education. A Comedy.*) *The Soldiers* (*Die Soldaten*), published two years later in 1776, was also classified as a comedy. In spite of this fact, Brecht the adapter is right. Lenz's designation of the play as comedy says only that *Der Hofmeister* story does not end on a tragic note, and that the stage is not covered with corpses when the final curtain is drawn. The affair itself was undoubtedly felt by Lenz to be a human tragedy. Not by Brecht.

Lenz mocked the life and conditions of a private tutor. He was a proponent of the general education of the people and also of the sons of the aristocracy. His play is intended to promote reforms and represent the Enlightenment, shows a familiarity with Rousseau, and has affinity with Pestalozzi's ideas on education. This is why the privy councillor von Berg is also the author's mouthpiece in Lenz's drama—he is the *raisonneur* and enlightened, philanthropic aristocrat. In Brecht's play he no longer has this role. Whereas Lenz selected the privy councillor to be the confidant of the private tutor and the speaker against the other narrow-minded members of the aristocratic clique, Brecht makes him into an especially cunning specimen of the aristocratic class. Like so many German bourgeois artists and reformers, Lenz strove to achieve a bourgeois-feudalistic compromise. In his play the privy councillor as the aristocratic man of the Enlightenment also represented the bourgeois demands. Brecht criticizes this position of the Sturm und Drang taken by Lenz as an expression of the crippled German conditions, as "part of the German misery." The self-castration of Läuffer is for him just as much socially determined as the seemingly enlightened speech for freedom by the privy councillor. Brecht criticizes with Lenz and criticizes Lenz.

This twofold criticism occurs in the adaptation with great subtlety. The text of the original play seems to have been followed in large sections; only sometimes are there large deviations. Yet in actuality the text that appears to be the same has been completely reutilized. Since Brecht usually regarded the productions of his plays as an integral part of the works, the performance of *Der Hofmeister* had to serve as the final step in the process of reutilization in those places where the text had been too cautious or ambivalent. In Act Two of Lenz's play the privy councillor instructs the father and the pastor Läuffer and warns about the state and condition of being a private tutor: "The best hours of his day are spent sitting with a young man who doesn't want to learn a thing and with whom he dare not quarrel. The remainder of his day is concerned with the preservation of his life, sanctified by eating and drinking, sighed away in chains. He runs at the slightest sign from the esteemed mistress; he gets to know every line on his master's face; he eats when he's full and fasts when he's hungry; he drinks punch when he would like to piss and plays cards when he has better things to do. Without freedom life goes downhill in a backward way. Freedom is the natural element of mankind as water is to a fish, and a man who renounces his freedom poisons the most noble spirit of his blood, cuts off his sweetest pleasures at the stem, and murders himself." A comparison here with Scene Eight of the Brecht adaptation reveals that Brecht seems to have made only some minor cuts from the original text. However, the figure of the privy councillor has been endowed with an entirely different function. The humane pathos which Lenz means quite seriously is transformed into empty phrases and high-sounding talk by Brecht, and this talk is only supposed to prevent any further reduction of the private tutor's salary. During the rehearsals Brecht as director endeavored relentlessly to move the actor playing the privy councillor to give the little speeches on freedom in a well-intentioned way that lacked sincerity and conviction. The figure of the *raisonneur* and man of enlightenment was reutilized to criticize the bourgeois German Enlightenment and the wretchedness of German Rousseauism. The play by a bourgeois artist became an occasion for Brecht to present the critical history of bourgeois literature in Germany on the stage.

While working on the production of Goethe's *Urfaust* with the Berliner Ensemble, Brecht proceeded in similar fashion. This time Brecht had less to do with the adaptation of the text. He played more of a decisive role as director of the performance. In this capacity he carefully eliminated all the traces of the charlatan from the character of Faust. The self-reliant individualist and Sturm und Drang protagonist, whom the young Goethe had conceived, was changed back into the real arch magician of the *Volksbuch* and puppet play in large stretches of the play. Under Brecht's direction the prebourgeois elements come out in a dialectical manner. Yet, no matter what Brecht wanted to say, the *Urfaust* tended in the direction of Thomas Mann's novel *Doctor*

Faustus. Brecht, like Mann, intended to renounce Goethe's *Faust*. It was actually not the express intention, but the following passage from *Intimidation by Classicalism* reveals what Brecht had in mind: "The process of falsification and depletion went so far that—to take another example from *Urfaust*—such important incidents in the play as the great humanist's pact with the devil (which is after all of great significance for the Gretchen tragedy, since it would have had a different outcome or not happened at all if it had been omitted) were simply 'played out of the play.' One presumably held the view that a hero can only act heroically in a classical play. It is self-evident that *Faust* and also *Urfaust* can only be produced knowing that Faust will be changed and purified at the end of Part II. It is the Faust who defeats the devil and moves from an unproductive life concerned only with pleasure provided by the devil to a more productive life. But what remains of this magnificent transformation if the beginning stages are skipped?" It should be added, by the way, that the pact had not been incorporated into *Urfaust*. Therefore, Brecht was forced to fill this gap in his production, and this could be made visible largely only through age-old hocus-pocus.

Since a production of *Urfaust* was not able to achieve the re-utilization of the Faust figure that had ostensibly been the goal, Brecht became even more interested than before, after 1952, in the plan for an opera, to be called *Johann Faustus,* that his friend and collaborator the musician Hanns Eisler was writing. Eisler had his text published in 1952 and encountered strong criticism. Brecht quickly came to the defense of the composer and librettist. In a letter to the author of this book, dated February 22, 1953, he wrote: "Considering the justifiable desire to have positive heroes, one should not dismiss the attempt to shape great figures like Faust, whose effect can likewise be positive in a social sense. Literature shows that even tragedy can take care of some of the functions of comedy. By this I mean a certain social extraction." The question was raised by the critics as to whether "each new shaping of the Faust figure, if it is to be completely new, must damage Goethe's figure simply because it is so deeply ingrained in the consciousness of the people, and hence, everything new must be related to it," and Brecht replied: "But what about the works of Euripides, who reshaped the figures of Aischylos and Sophokles and generally in a most critical vein?"

The principle which underlies Brecht's reutilization of German classicism becomes most clear at this point. In *Der Hofmeister* Brecht had drawn out the virtual comic aspects from under the real tragedy. With *Faust* he wanted to transplant certain functions in his new version of the tragedy—above all, those which result from the "social extraction" that he would otherwise keep in reserve, predominantly for comedy. He himself sees his relationship to German classicism as a relationship to tradition. The process should be similar to that of Euripides, who wrote an *Orestes* without consideration for his predecessors Aischylos and Sophokles. When Brecht had his adaptation of Molière's *Don Juan* presented in the theater at Schiffbauerdamm—toward the end of his life he was greatly concerned with introducing Germans to Molière—a Frenchman complained rather hesitatingly that the performance departed somewhat sharply from the real Molière. Brecht supposedly replied: "It's Molière adapted by Brecht."

With this, we can see a change in his old deprecating attitude to the great literature of the bourgeoisie. This attitude is largely overcome. Of course, Brecht never really reconciled himself to Schiller. In particular, he hated the Kantian side of him. Brecht always fought alongside Hegel against Kant. Other than this, Brecht essentially gave up reducing German classicism to its supposed exploitative and deceiving function. In his programmatic poem "Literature Will Be Investigated" ("Die Literatur wird durchforscht werden"), which was a formulation of Brecht's avowal of the plebeian tradition and was dedicated to Martin Andersen Nexö, he asserts that the following people should be lauded in future times:

> Those who told about the sufferings of the oppressed
> Those who told about the deeds of the fighters
> Artistically, in noble speech
> Which formerly had been reserved
> To glorify the kings.

Die von den Leiden der Niedrigen berichteten
Die von den Taten der Kämpfer berichteten
Kunstvoll. In der edlen Sprache
Vordem reserviert
Der Verherrlichung der Könige.

This means not destruction but reutilization of the linguistic
and artistic forms. Here, too, the "negated" tradition. Brecht himself does not simply found a new heritage but places himself in
the line of the heritage. Euripides and his predecessors. Molière
adapted by Brecht. As late as July 1, 1955, Max Frisch wrote an
essay on the publication of the first four volumes of Brecht's
collected plays with the intention of demonstrating the real
dimensions of the great playwright to readers in West Germany
and Switzerland. The title alone, *Brecht as a Classical Writer,*
was obviously meant to be ironical.

The irony was misplaced. Brecht actually felt himself to be a
classical writer, but not a classicist. From the very beginning he
endeavored to embody the classical term "writer" (*Dichter*) in
his works with a new social attitude. The age of Goethe recognized the writer—"the classical national author," as Goethe
phrased it—by his genius and especially by his ability to achieve
the remarkable in all the genres of literature with great ease. This
principle lasted well into the nineteenth century. Not only in the
field of literature but in other fields of the arts as well. When
Robert Schumann moved from the work of his youth, which was
exclusively devoted to the piano, and took up other types of in-
strumental and vocal music with the desire to master them and
show that he was truly a master in terms of the old school, he
was acting out of a stubborn tradition of artistic continuity that
was widespread in his day. Johannes Brahms and Friedrich
Hebbel took exactly the same position in relation to the works
of the classical heritage. However, the twentieth century no
longer recognized this catchall term (*Dichter*) of the great master.
It was the *poet* Rilke, the *novelists* Thomas Mann and Franz
Kafka, the *lyricist* and *essayist* Gottfried Benn. Stefan George
made a doctrine out of his meager talents: poetry is identical with

lyrical poetry; everything else is impure. Of course, the classicality of Hofmannsthal would correspond to the demand for total versatility by the classical authors.

From the very beginning Brecht set this goal of versatility for himself. Poetry and drama are simply parts of an all-encompassing totality for the early Brecht. His *theater work* was also a necessary addition to the totality in the beginning. Brecht never accepted poetical substance without caring about its function. The unity of theory and practice might have taken a different form in the various stages of his development, but it was always present as a basic concept. He also never tolerated a separation of literary criticism and belles lettres in a narrow sense. Nor did he care for the favorite German game of placing the *Dichter* against the *Schriftsteller*. As far as we know, Brecht never labeled himself a *Dichter*. The division of his collected works into plays, poems, and prose took for its precedent the inherited genres. In addition, Brecht liked to imagine that part of the mission of the classical writer was to provide a connection between literature and related artistic fields and to act as a catalytic agent. Even in his early phase the poetry was accompanied by music. The songs as well as the projections were part of the dramas. The goal here was not a romantic, total art work but the opposite. *The Magic Flute* rather than *Tristan und Isolde*. The all-encompassing artistic vision of a man of the Enlightenment, a dialectician, and a classical writer, not the culinary, delirious totality of the romantics. Brecht as a classical writer. In a much deeper, all-encompassing sense of the word. This was more than Max Frisch—even with his good intentions—could possibly have surmised.

Marx and Lenin as Classical Writers

The expression *classical writer* is one which is also used by Brecht. A chronicle poem with the title "The Takeover of the Great Metro by the Moscow Working Class on April 27, 1935" ("Inbesitznahme der grossen Metro durch die Moskauer Arbeiterschaft am 27. April 1935") which originated that same year closes with the following lines:

> When we saw them driving in their cars,
> The work of their hands, we knew:
> This is the great picture that the classical
> Writers foresaw at one time
> Trembling.

> Als wir sie fahren sahen in ihren Wagen
> Den Werken ihrer Hände, wussten wir:
> Dies ist das grosse Bild, das die Klassiker einstmals
> Erschüttert voraussahen.

The classical writers are the classical writers of socialism, of the proletarian revolution. The authors of *The Communist Manifesto* and Lenin. It is not by chance that the expression *classical writer* is applied in this instance. Brecht made further use of this term with the same meaning in 1945 when he began transcribing *The Communist Manifesto* of February 1848 into hexameters in the form of a didactic poem. He never finished the poem, even though he constantly worked on it. The various drafts all began with the expression *classical writers,* which took on the same meaning as in the chronicle of 1935. Brecht followed the stream of thought in the *Manifesto.* After he transcribed the famous remarks about the specter haunting Europe into verse, he focused on an epic portrayal of the section that Marx and Engels called "Bourgeois and Proletarians." The original text reads as follows: "The history of all hitherto existing society is the history of class struggles. Free man and slave, patrician and plebeian, lord and serf, guild master and journeyman, in a word, oppressor and oppressed, stood in constant opposition to one another, carried on an uninterrupted fight sometimes hidden, sometimes open, a fight that ended each time either in a revolutionary reconstitution of the whole society or in the common collapse of the contending classes. In the earlier epochs of history we find almost everywhere a complete arrangement of society into various orders, a manifold gradation of social ranks. In ancient Rome we have patricians, knights, plebeians, slaves; in the Middle Ages, feudal lords, vassals, guild masters, journeymen, apprentices, serfs; and in almost all of these classes, again, subordinate gradations." Brecht introduces this section with his remarks on the classical writers and reworks it this way:

> You have heard a great deal about it. However, this is what the classical writers say.
> If you read history, then you read about the deeds of great persons,
> Their stars, rising and falling, about the campaigns of their armies,
> Or about the glory and destruction of kingdoms. But the classical writers
> See history first and foremost as the history of class struggles,
> For they see with great insight the people divided into classes
> And fighting. Patricians and knights, plebeians and slaves,
> Feudal lords, serfs, and craftsmen, today bourgeois and proletarian.
> Each respectively maintaining the process of the system, the production
> And distribution of the vital goods, yet at the same time
> Fighting that life and death struggle, the age-old fight for control.

> Viel davon hörtet ihr. Dies aber ist, was die Klassiker sagen.
> Lest ihre Geschichte, so lest ihr von Taten enormer Personen;
> ihrem Gestirn, sich erhebend und fallend; vom Zug ihrer Heere;
> oder von Glanz und Zerstörung der Reiche. Den Klassikern aber
> ist die Geschichte zuvörderst Geschichte der Kämpfe der Klassen.
> Denn sie sehen in Klassen geteilt und kämpfend die Völker
> in ihrem Innern. Patrizier und Ritter, Plebejer und Sklaven
> Adlige, Bauern und Handwerker, heut Proletarier und Bourgeois
> halten sie jeweils den riesigen Haushalt im Gang, der Erzeugung
> und der Verteilung der lebensnotwendigen Güter, zugleich doch
> kämpfend den Kampf bis aufs Messer, den uralten, den um die
> Herrschaft.

He retained the stream of thought. However, there was a new manner of presentation evident that is not to be explained simply by pointing to the versification. The *Manifesto* was a report written by its authors to the political party they established. Brecht's hexameters allow for a report of a report. A verse chronicle of *The Communist Manifesto*. The transformation of the *Manifesto* into an epic poem was not derived simply from the use of hexameters. The chronicler reports about the thoughts of the "classical writers," the authors of the *Manifesto*. Marx and Engels as classical writers.

Bertolt Brecht's use of language alone shows how the expression *classical writer* was connected to permanence, with an authenticity that was not ephemeral. However, the subject at hand has nothing to do with artistic durability but with scientific findings which have remained authentic. Brecht is of the opinion that this definitely allows him to set forth the knowledge that was discovered in 1848 almost a century after the discovery: the scientific findings of the past as permanent authentic knowledge presented now in artistic form. According to Brecht, it is even to be considered a *new* art form. The first publication of the *Manifesto* poem in the magazine *Sinn und Form* reproduced a sentence from Brecht's work journal in the introduction: "The *Manifesto* as pamphlet is itself a work of art. However, it seems possible to me that one can strengthen the propagandistic effect today a hundred years later by discarding the form of the pamphlet and re-enforcing it with a new authority." The art form of the pamphlet is replaced by that of the didactic poem (*Lehrgedicht*).

The term *classical* should preserve the meaning of permanent social findings, a revelation of historical laws. However, Brecht means even more than this. The lines of his 1935 chronicle talk about the foresight of the classical writers, that is, the reality on which all knowledge rests. Dialectical transformation from theory into practice. Situations have been created because the theory had established that it was possible and necessary to create them. This combination of knowing and acting is valid for Brecht's use of the terms *classical* and *classical writer*. He thought that the artistic achievements of the past from Sophokles to Shakespeare to Goethe and later Hauptmann were historical and fragmentary; they were merely ephemeral (even if extraordinary) attempts to give a form to their times that one was to develop. On the other hand, the scientific findings of the classical writers were considered to have a lasting value. They were not fragmentary.

It is for this reason that the involvement with science always ranked higher in Brecht's eyes than the involvement with art, especially with literature. Brecht's antiliterary tradition, his lust for learning and teaching, found fulfillment in the works of Marx and Lenin. In his answer to the questionnaire of 1926 asking what book had made the greatest impression on him, we noticed that Brecht gave a compilation of nonfiction: Lenin, a book about America by an architect, a sports book, the origination of America's great fortunes, and a documentation of World War I. Almost thirty years after this, in February 1955, he informed the magazine *Neue Deutsche Literatur* that "the book which made the greatest impression on me this past year was Mao Tse-tung's essay *On Contradiction*. An essay mainly on dialectics. The work of a man whose picture Brecht placed in front of him in his study. A poet, no less, whose lines about a flight over the Great Wall Brecht had imitated. Mao Tse-tung considered, then, as a classical writer. Stalin never. The decisive factor here is, however, not Brecht's personal hierarchy but the principle of selection. Brecht felt that a mastery of dialectics in dealing with social contradictions was classical.

So we have an artist who declares that only the great sociologists and social economists have contributed to the development of the classical tradition. Not poets. This contradiction is likewise genuinely dialectical, for Brecht decided to remain an artist— in spite of, or even because of, this decision—and it provides the answer to the question why Brecht found his way to the theoretical principles of Marxism after his beginnings in the Augsburg environment and in the antiliterary tradition. Brecht cannot be understood if this process is not correctly interpreted. It is time that we put an end to the fashionable and popular parlor game of the literary intelligentsia who carefully distinguish between Bertolt Brecht the "pure poet" and Brecht the Marxist. No matter what position one takes, it is impossible to analyze Brecht's works without a knowledge of Marxist thought. In like fashion, one does not have to be a Kant expert to understand Schiller, but one must have read Kant if one wants to understand Schiller's great tragedies as he himself wanted them to be understood.

In his Schiller speech of 1959 Friedrich Dürrenmatt saw in Brecht the "most extreme form of the sentimental poet" in our time and added: "Brecht's *Weltanschauung* may be painful for many people and irritating for others; yet, it should not be treated as a mere aberration or as an insignificant matter. This is an essential part of Brecht and cannot be regarded in the least as a coincidental feature of his works and their theatrical effectiveness, their poetical precision, their dramaturgical boldness, and above all, their humanity. This legitimate achievement forces us to consider Brecht's communism objectively and to reinvestigate the truth in it. We should not try to avoid this, but admit what has to be admitted." Later on Dürrenmatt states that this leads us to ask the question why "the greatest dramatist of our times took the side of a revolution in the belief that he was acting for humanity." Why did this happen? What led Brecht to Marx and Lenin?

It was hardly what one would call sympathy or a search for justice. Many former expressionists who emphasized humanity and fought to change society found their way from their idealistic rebellions to the materialist revolution: Johannes R. Becher and Friedrich Wolf are examples. Brecht was not an expressionist, nor was it the revolutionary pathos that drew him to socialism. He was fascinated mainly by the new social science. His way to Marxism was prepared by his involvement with un-literary matters. Brecht was obsessed with nonfiction and technical manuals. The *Börsen-Courier,* the Berlin newspaper that supported his literary battles, dealt largely with serious business affairs and projects that were supposed to produce income. Herbert Ihering was in charge of the cultural section and had various protégés assisting him. However, the protégé Brecht was more fascinated by the stock-exchange section of the paper than the literary. Thomas Mann may have developed a striking theme in keeping with the times by portraying the conflict between the bourgeois and the artist, but Brecht never thought of identifying himself as part of this conflict. He never wanted to become a bourgeois businessman, not on his life, and yet, he also never wanted to be outdone by any stockholder when it came to knowing the field. Therefore, he made the effort to learn from the experts how to understand the complex laws of business. To his great disappointment the capitalist businessmen failed him, and Brecht registered this disappointment.

There is an appropriate Brecht quotation in Käthe Rülicke's analysis of *St. Joan of the Stockyards*: "I wanted to use the wheat market of Chicago for the background of a certain play. I thought I could get the necessary information rather quickly by sending out some questionnaires to specialists and experienced people in the field. It turned out much differently than I thought. No one, neither the well-known economists nor the businessmen—I followed one broker who had worked his entire life on the wheat market in Chicago from Berlin to Vienna—no one could sufficiently explain to me how the process of the wheat market worked. I had the impression that the entire process was inexplicable; that is, could not be comprehended by man's intellect, that is, it was simply irrational. The way in which the wheat was distributed in the world was completely incomprehensible. No matter how you viewed it, this wheat market was clearly a quagmire. I never wrote the drama I had planned, but I did begin to read Marx. And there—only then—did I really read Marx. It was then that all my own scattered and practical experiences and impressions actually took on life." This is repeated in the *Flüchtlingsgespräche* (*Refugee Conversations*). Brecht lets the intellectual Ziffel talk about his own experiences: "It seemed that the entire civilized world had been shaken by incredible battles. No one knew why. The men who worked in the institutes for industrial research and who had a command of all the figures pertaining to the field of economic phenomena showed their heads only to shake them." This became a motif for Brecht's last, posthumous comedy about Turandot and the congress of the "whitewashing" intellectuals. Brecht's fascination with economics led him from a study of the practical operation of the currency exchanges and stock markets to the study of what Marx had called the "critique of political economy." The antiliterary tradition demanded the reading of classical works dealing with the laws of value, the cycle of crises, imperialism, and the theory of progressive deterioration. Brecht the Marxist chose the most difficult way, which led to reading the three volumes of Marx's *Das Kapital*.

Another factor which led Brecht to study the new classical writers was his old opposition to *philosophical idealism*. This idealism, he felt rather early, was to underline the difference between him and the most important expressionist playwright, Georg Kaiser. In a radio broadcast in Cologne at the end of the 1920's, which brought the station's director, the neoromantic dramatist Ernst Hardt, together with Herbert Ihering, the Marxist economist Fritz Sternberg, and Brecht (a copy of the conversation is still extant), Brecht emphasized that Georg Kaiser had developed the individualistic drama that depends on an idealistic picture of the world carried to its uttermost extreme. Hence, "this trend of his cannot be continued because the economic and sociological foundations are lacking. The development reverses itself dialectically: Kaiser developed the epic form, that is, the technique of anti-individualistic and collective drama for the bourgeois individualistic event." This anti-individualistic tradition which attracted Brecht early in his career and made him into an adversary of the expressionists and their idealistic standpoint was supported by the theories of Marx. It is the social being (*Sein*), the totality of social conditions, which determines the consciousness, not the reverse. Everything had been prepared in Brecht in such a way that he could readily accept this.

Even his love for teaching was in keeping with the postulates of a social doctrine which, ever since the publication of Marx's thesis on Feuerbach, had considered practice as of prime importance in all situations. It was primarily because Brecht wanted to be a teacher (and not one who simply hoped to bring about a change in social conditions via education) that he took the path which discarded the idealistic ethics of "pure" good will that the young Marx had already fought against in his writings on Kant, and here he hoped to create the real requirements for human goodness.

There was something else. Brecht began his study of Marxist classical writers in the middle and toward the end of the twenties. The international success of *The Threepenny Opera* occurred at the time of the Great Depression. All the positions taken by the bourgeois democracy seemed to fall apart like the efforts of social reforms. When a representative of the German workers union demanded at that time that the working class take the role of a "doctor at the sick bed of capitalism," Brecht passionately argued against this. And, as the crisis became more convulsive, banks collapsed, and millions of people were without jobs, Brecht proclaimed a totally different thesis: social revolution, not social reform.

In this connection, the poem "Die Nachtlager" is most relevant. The last stanza reads as follows:

> Do not put that book down,
> Thou who dost read, man.
> Some men have a place to lodge this night.
> They will be protected from the wind one night long.
> The snow which was meant for them will fall on the street,
> But the world will not be any different because of this.
> Relations between men will not become better because of this.
> The age of exploitation will not be shortened because of this.

> Leg das Buch nicht nieder, der du da liesest, Mensch.
> Einige Menschen haben ein Nachtlager
> Der Wind wird von ihnen eine Nacht lang abgehalten
> Der ihnen zugedachte Schnee fällt auf die Strasse.
> Aber die Welt wird dadurch nicht anders
> Die Beziehungen zwischen den Menschen bessern sich dadurch
>   nicht
> Das Zeitalter der Ausbeutung wird dadurch nicht verkürzt.

The German critic Walter Jens has given a fine interpretation of this poem: "Sure, some men have a night's lodging, but what's the use of it? The world is not going to be any better for it. On the contrary, the thesis of the *Lehrstücke* (didactic plays) is that 'Revisionism' conceals the actual conditions and plays down the need to cure the world." This and nothing else is, in fact, the main thesis of Brecht's Lehrstücke in his early phase as Marxist.

Das Badener Lehrstück vom Einverständnis (The Baden Didactic Play about Consent), which was written in 1929, is significant because of its connection with Brecht's avowal of the Marxist tradition and even more so because of its opposition to Neue Sachlichkeit. This opposition is revealed in the play in the form of an argument between Brecht and his composer of that time, Paul Hindemith. Hindemith had consented to compose a Lehrstück that followed Brecht's text. Yet, he interpreted the term *lesson* (*Lehre*) from a point of view fundamentally different from that of Brecht. Hindemith thought of a company of amateurs, a youth movement, an ephemeral collective of musicians living in a community. Everything was to be merely a pretense for a common exercise in art; beyond that there was no value in it at all. According to the view of the composer, one should be able to change the text and the music as one liked. But Brecht vehemently protested against this. He did not want a false collective of musicians but rather a genuine collective formed out of a common understanding. Therefore, "such an artificial and shallow harmony would never be able to provide a balance on a wide and vital basis even for a few minutes against the destructive forces opposed to collectives that have torn the people of our time asunder with an entirely different type of power." For Brecht, the real *lesson* was most important. Everything depended on the genuine collective of the knowers.

Idealism, goodness coupled with sympathy, and social reform were all to be rejected. The immediate decision of the people demands that the flyers who are shot down be helped. The realization that is conveyed in a dialectical sense leads to another conclusion: man does not help man. Clown scenes, once again inspired by Valentin, make this even more clear. In the *Mahagonny* opera it had not been possible to help a dead man. No one had wanted to prevent him from dying. *Das Badener Lehrstück vom Einverständnis* also affirms the thesis that man cannot help man. At any rate, not under the circumstances that count. This bitter realization must have been deeply rooted in Brecht. He enjoyed jokes immensely, but he himself seldom told any. There was, however, one story he constantly liked to tell. A father takes a walk with his son. He places the son on a wall which is somewhat elevated and demands that he jump from it. The son is afraid. The father promises him that nothing will happen, that he will catch him. The son jumps. The father does not catch him. The son falls to the ground and hurts himself. He begins to cry and the father teaches him the following lesson: "You see, you should never depend on anyone." Man does not help man. You are lucky if you have managed to free yourself from this illusion.

There is the similar anecdote in the *Flüchtlingsgespräche*

(*Refugee Conversations*) told by Kalle about the teacher Herrn-
reitter, who asks the children on the first day of school to find
seats in the classroom. One child does not find a place and receives a slap in the face from the teacher. "This teaches us all
the good lesson that we're not allowed to have bad luck."
Apparently this is a Lehrstück of the proletarian revolution:

> Agreed that everything is going to be changed
> The world and mankind
> Especially the disorder
> Of the classes of people because there are two
> Sorts of people
> The exploiters and the ignorant.

> Einverstanden, dass alles verändert wird
> Die Welt und die Menschheit
> Vor allem die Unordnung
> Der Menschenklassen, weil es zweierlei Menschen gibt
> Ausbeutung und Unkenntnis.

However, these theses cannot be corroborated. Humanity is
mixed with inhumanity. A Marxist thesis founded in Christian
thinking as it were. He who humbles himself will be exalted. He
who gives of himself will be saved. Brecht understands the new
collective that is supposed to change the world as a community of
anonymous people, the indistinguishable. His opposition toward
idealism and individualism turned into—likewise idealistic—the
abstraction of a collective.

The principle of dialectical progression is orgiastically enjoyed
to the hilt just as the principle of impermanence was enjoyed at
one time:

> If you have truthfully changed mankind completely, then
> Change changed mankind.
> Give mankind up!

> Habt ihr die Wahrheit vervollständigend die Menschheit verän-
> dert, so
> Verändert die veränderte Menschheit.
> Gebt sie auf!

In the Lehrstück called *The Measures Taken* (*Die Massnahme,*
1930) all positions are once again severed from the real dialectics,
this time almost too sharply. In a way, this Lehrstück is Brecht's
Marxist *Gesellenstück* ("play about comrades"). Here we have
once more the tendencies which led to Marxism: the old and the
new tradition in a somewhat strange mixture. But at the same
time we also have the most important doctrines of Brecht's great
exile writings. Humanity and utilitarianism as antitheses. Sympathy and social reform—or, detached objectivity and complete
change. Brecht's hatred of reformism occasionally turns into a
cult of uncompassionateness. The revolutionary struggle in this
Lehrstück appears to exclude the possibility of making tentative
and important reforms. An undialectical and un-Marxist antithesis. For Brecht, both sympathy and humanity appear to represent a danger from the standpoint of the exploited. This is why
Shen-te as the "good woman of Setzuan" and the motherly
Grusche in *The Caucasian Chalk Circle* later feel their love and
motherliness to be terrible: they know they can lead one astray
into goodness. From the standpoint of the exploiter, the relationship between humanity and inhumanity is portrayed for
Brecht as one between *the exception and the rule*. This is characterized later by *Herr Puntila*. The Lehrstück about the measures taken proclaims that it is necessary to create by being un-
sympathetic a world that will eventually make it possible to
show a sympathy that will yield real results. There would be no
other choice.

> If you could finally change the world, what
> Good would you be?
> Who are you?
> Sink in dirt
> Embrace the butcher, but
> Change the world: it needs it!
> For a long time we've been listening to you
> Not as critics anymore
> But as pupils.
>
> Könntest du die Welt endlich verändern, wofür
> Wärest du dir zu gut?

Wer bist du?
Versinke in Schmutz
Umarme den Schlächter, aber
Ändere die Welt: sie braucht es!
Lange nicht mehr hören wir euch zu als
Urteilende. Schon
Als Lernende.

The phrases already point to the great poem "To Posterity" ("An die Nachgeborenen") written later during his emigration period. Yet, there the dialectical tension between necessity and humanity is maintained, between mourning and expediency. The result in *Die Massnahme* was still a superficial radicalism with a crude antithesis. A Marxist play about comrades, not a great play.

This can be explained by Brecht's peculiar, almost unorthodox development in regard to Marxism. He was not a worker who eventually found his way to his own class. He was a son of the bourgeoisie who changed his social class. And it was not sympathy or a search for justice that helped him pave his way but the attraction of learning, just as it was later with his Galileo. The thirst for knowledge had brought him quite far, as he admitted in his "Solomon Song." The result was a Marxism that never intended to adhere to the party line. Brecht was close to the Communists, but he was never a party member. It would be rather easy to show that his theoretical concept of Marxism could never have been regarded as orthodox by the party. And it was not a coincidence that Dr. Fritz Sternberg sat next to Brecht and Ihering during that radio broadcast in Cologne. Sternberg stood outside the Communist movement. His book *Imperialism* did, indeed, represent Marx's position, but not Lenin's. Sternberg's interpretation of the imperialistic economy leaned more heavily on the ideas of Rosa Luxemburg than on those of her theoretical rival Lenin. The play *The Mother* (*Die Mutter*) was dedicated to the memory of Rosa Luxemburg, the political "champion of the German workers," and Brecht also composed a poetical epitaph to be engraved on her tombstone. He was involved with a plan to write a play about Rosa Luxemburg up to the very day of his own death. Brecht's Marxist beginnings—like those of his theoretical counterpart Georg Lukács—are connected to the thought of

Luxemburg, a theoretical and practical conception that was opposed by Lenin and the Bolsheviks long before the October Revolution. Brecht's Marxist writings still show the signs of this argument.

The intense involvement with Hegel's works, the association with the economic theoreticians influenced by Rosa Luxemburg, the rejection of party affiliation—all this had to lead the Marxist politician Brecht into a conflict with Marxist orthodoxy. Brecht's speech at The International Writers' Conference for the Defense of Culture, held in Paris during 1935, makes that especially clear. The conference was at that time part of the united front that was trying to bring together all the opponents of fascism and national socialism. It was a confederation of the Christian opposition, the bourgeois liberals, the Social Democrats, and the Communists. The purpose of the meeting was to play down the differences, the antitheses between capitalism and socialism, Christianity and dialectical materialism, social reformism and political revolution, and to establish the common features. Brecht came to Paris from his exile in Denmark and gave, for Brecht, a relatively long speech. It disturbed some people and was not received kindly by the organizers of the conference. Yet, later, when he was seriously ill, Brecht decided to include the Paris speech in one of the volumes of his Versuche, which he himself edited.

This talk is just as important for the intellectual foundation of the plays, poems, and pamphlets written by Brecht during his years in exile as it is for his political program. Actually it deals with all the points that were to distinguish Brecht from a great part of the bourgeois reformist emigration and emigration literature. In contrast to the organizers of the conference, Brecht focuses right on the differences. The false views about Hitler and his state which he opposed are essentially the views of other German writers. It is easy to link the names of certain writers with the arguments Brecht used in opposition. For instance, Thomas Mann, Alfred Kerr, and even other authors, such as Alfred Döblin, who shared some of Brecht's views. One name is mentioned expressly. "I myself do not believe in being crude just for the sake of being crude. One has to come to the defense of mankind when it is argued that man would be crude even if it weren't good business. It is a clever circumlocution on the part of my friend Feuchtwanger when he says: vulgarity precedes selfishness —but he's not right. Crudeness does not come from crudeness but from the business deals which could not be made without crudeness." For Brecht the Marxist and emigrant, there could only be the whole truth and nothing but the truth. It was impossible for Brecht to keep silent about his real knowledge of the situation for tactical reasons, as the organizers of the conference had planned. "The International Writers Conference for the Defense of Culture" was the title. Brecht answered: "Let's not speak just for culture!" And, "Culture will be saved when the people are saved." They are not to be saved by condemning their crudeness, educating them to be good, or appealing to culture, but by conquering the causes of crudeness, selfishness, and ignorance.

Toward the end of his speech, Brecht becomes uncommonly Marxistic and doctrinaire: "Comrades, let us reflect upon the roots of all evil. A great doctrine which is captivating masses of people more and more on our planet and which is still rather young says that the roots of all evil lie in our conditions of ownership. This doctrine, simple like all great doctrines, has captivated those masses of people who suffer most under the existing conditions of ownership and the barbaric methods by which the conditions are protected." This is the way Brecht closed his Paris address, and he added another sentence that was supposed to imply that he had naturally said nothing new but that it had been necessary to repeat the old at the conference even if it had to be he who did the repeating.

It was inevitable that Brecht's speech would counter the purpose of the conference and sharpen the contrast between the positions held by the Marxists and the non-Marxists, the proletariat and the bourgeoisie within the anti-Fascist movement. Here was a man who had come to Paris from Denmark to act against the political intentions worked out by the leaders of the conference. All this was predictable, and Brecht had foreseen it. Hence, he proved that his conception of Marxism and its materialization could immediately be set on a par with that of the German communist party. On the other hand, Brecht soon found ways to demonstrate that he was not against all collective and common enterprises in his essays and creative works that had a direct political bearing in relation to the trend of the times. In 1936 he showed his readiness to cooperate by joining the editorial board of the literary monthly *Das Wort*. Published in Moscow, it named Brecht, Feuchtwanger, and Willi Bredel as the editors. Bredel made his home in Moscow, Brecht in Denmark, and Feuchtwanger in southern France. Nevertheless, one cannot assert that Brecht merely placed his name as editor at the disposal of the magazine. In reality the three writers did form a common editorial board. Brecht's letters as editor to Bredel the editor reveal that the antitheses which emerged at the Paris conference had retained their validity for his conception of a literary magazine that fought against German fascism.

The disparities between the strategy and tactics of German communism and the Marxist position of Bertolt Brecht were already noticeable during the Marxist apprenticeship of the playwright, and they could not be concealed even in the middle of the common struggle against the Third Reich. To use Lenin's terminology, Brecht did not tend, as one might have assumed from his bourgeois background, toward reformism, conciliation, toward what the Bolsheviks used to call "right-wing opportunism." Brecht's position as Marxist, especially in the early Lehrstücke, is to be regarded more as that of an ultraleft radical. In Lenin's essay *"Left-Wing" Communism, An Infantile Disorder,* which was written in 1920, he sarcastically admits that the differences between the conservative Churchill, the liberal Lloyd George, and the laborite Arthur Henderson, if considered from a communist standpoint regarding the conditions in England, were "completely inconsequential and negligible from the position of a pure, that is, an abstract, that is, a practical communism which was ripe for political mass action." In contrast, the Marxist Brecht—at least in the period from 1929 to 1935—often took the side of this particular left-wing, abstract, dogmatic communism.

Occasionally one sensed that he enjoyed the position of a new convert who wanted to pass on the new teaching as fast as possible, complete, and uncompromising. Even here Brecht was in a hurry to begin teaching, though he had just finished his Marxist apprenticeship. Pedagogically speaking this was bound to lead to awkward situations. Yet there was enough of the dialectician in him that he could learn from his mistakes, and he was also patient enough to prepare himself for his next mistake. In this respect, it is interesting to read the following commentary on the Lehrstücke, written by Brecht and intended primarily for the *actors*: "The playwright continually rejected performances of *Die Massnahme* because only the actor playing the young comrade can learn from the play, and even he must play one of the agitators and sing in the *Kontrollchor* ["control chorus"] if he is to learn." This means, however, a desire to retouch the undialectical antithetics by working it out on stage.

Both Brecht's inclination toward Marxist dogmatism and his struggle against it were already apparent before the onset of the Third Reich in the juxtaposition of *St. Joan of the Stockyards* and the adaptation of Gorki's *Mother*. Here he was dealing with works that parallel one another. *The Mother* is simultaneously a continuation and a renunciation of many ideas from the play about the girl in the Salvation Army standing between the fronts of two classes. The first of Brecht's three attempts at dramatizing the figure of Joan of Arc—the other two are *The Visions of Simone Marchard* (*Die Gesichte der Simone Marchard*), written in collaboration with Feuchtwanger, and *The Trial of Joan of Arc from Rouen 1431* (*Prozess der Jeanne d'Arc zu Rouen 1431*), based on a radio play by Anna Seghers—had a dual purpose: to demonstrate the crisis cycle of monopolistic capitalism and to show in a clear-cut fashion the impotency of social reformism when confronted by the actions of the monopolists. *St. Joan of the Stockyards* belonged to Brecht's series of antireformist literature. The dying Joan Dark, the Salvation Army girl standing between the capitalists and the workers, renounces all the politics of education, all the inducements to do good deeds, all the warnings about crudeness. Here we have the basic ideas of the Paris speech from 1935 set in this play that was written five years before the speech:

For nothing will be counted good, however helpful it may seem,
And nothing considered honorable except that
Which will change this world once and for all: that's what it
   needs.

And I came to the oppressors like an answer to their prayers!
Oh, measly goodness! Feeble intentions!
I have changed nothing.
And as I depart from this fruitless world,
I say to you:
Take care that when you leave the world,
You were not only good but are leaving
A good world.

Denn nichts werde gezählt als gut, und sehe es aus wie immer, als
    was
Wirklich hilft, und nichts gelte als ehrenhaft mehr, als was
Diese Welt endgültig ändert: sie braucht es.
Wie gerufen kam ich den Unterdrückern!
O, folgenlose Güte! Unmerkliche Gesinnung!
Ich habe nichts geändert.
Schnell verschwindend aus dieser Welt ohne Frucht
Sage ich euch:
Sorgt doch, dass ihr die Welt verlassend
Nicht nur gut wart, sondern verlasst
Eine gute Welt!

There is no worthy opponent to the business magnates in the
play. The figures of the workers are shadows and phantoms.
Joan's relationship to them appears to determine their importance. They themselves serve merely as coordinating points for
the actions of the central character. The actions of the workers
that one experiences on stage are rather vile. Even Joan can reply
to these charges only with the following:

If you, Mauler, show me the wickedness
Of the poor, I'll show you
The poverty of the poor, for they live far away from you,
And that puts beyond their reach the goods they need just to live.
You cannot see these people you
Hold down in such poverty, weakened
And in such dire need of unobtainable food and warmth that they
Can be just as far away from any claim
To higher things as they are to the most vulgar gluttony and ani-
    mal habits.

Zeigest du, Mauler, mir der Armen
Schlechtigkeit, so zeige ich dir
Der Armen Armut, denn von euch entfernt
Und damit entfernt von Gütern, unentbehrlichen
Leben, nicht sichtbar mehr, solche, die ihr
In solcher Armut haltet, so geschwächt und in so dringlicher
Abhängigkeit von unerreichbarer Speis und Wärm, dass sie
Gleichermassen entfernt sein können von jedem Anspruch
Auf Höheres als gemeinste Fressgier, tieristische Gewöhnung.

This portrayal of the proletarians does not come from Brecht's questioning the power of the working class, as has often been asserted. On the contrary, Brecht endeavored to present the situation of the proletarian in as frank and unsparing a manner as possible, the proletarian who, as it were, has no Marxist understanding of his intrinsic nature. He explains this in the *Flüchtlingsgespräche,* where Ziffel, the up-and-coming intellectual from the bourgeoisie, tells the Communist worker Kalle: "Do you know that your Confucius Karl Marx was pretty low on the moral qualities of the proletarian?" Kalle protests, and Ziffel qualifies his remark: he wanted to set up an original paradox in order to provoke his partner. Otherwise, the matter was as follows: "Marx did not downgrade the workers. He proved that the bourgeoisie gave them cause to be insulted. My knowledge of Marxism is not sufficient, so you had better be careful. A colleague of mine assured me that today you can only get a halfway decent knowledge of Marxism between 20,000 and 25,000 gold marks, and that's without the trimmings. And even then, you don't get the correct thing. At the most, a kind of inferior Marxism without Hegel, or one where there is no Ricardo." In any case, the workers in *St. Joan of the Stockyards* are portrayed almost exclusively at this stage—the early phase of class consciousness. In the parable play *The Good Woman from Setzuan (Der gute Mensch von Sezuan)*, which was written approximately ten years later, it is essentially not much different. The portrayal of proletarian solidarity in the scenario *Furcht und Elend des Dritten Reiches (Fear and Misery of the Third Reich)** is an

---

* *Translator's note:* Translated as *The Private Life of the Master Race* by Eric Bentley (New York, 1944) .

exception, but it takes a step backward in regard to the treatment of the nature of bourgeois behavior. The play which truly balances this almost stereotyped description of the intrinsic nature of the workers is *The Mother*. Here Brecht presented for the first and only time the process that lets the proletarian *in himself* become a proletarian *in and for himself*: the origination of proletarian class consciousness.

This resulted from the adaptation of a famous novel by Maksim Gorki. It was written between 1930 and 1932 to honor the memory of Karl Liebknecht and, above all, Rosa Luxemburg. The first production was in Berlin on January 15, 1932. The American premiere took place in November 1935. Brecht himself thought the play important enough to be produced soon after his return to Leipzig in 1949. He even helped the director Ruth Berlau, and his friend the composer Hanns Eisler conducted the music rehearsals. Some years later on January 10, 1951, the play became part of the repertoire of the Berliner Ensemble under the direction of Brecht, assisted by Helene Weigel and Ernst Busch.

Gorki's novel was written shortly after the Russian Revolution of 1905. The recollection of the development of this unsuccessful revolution determined the attitude of the narrator, who wanted to resist the counterrevolution as well as the despondency of the defeated revolutionaries. Brecht wrote twenty years after Gorki in full knowledge of the October Revolution of 1917. Gorki depicted how a woman of the proletariat became a revolutionary. Brecht, writing during the final years of the Weimar Republic, designed a Marxist Lehrstück about conditions of ownership, atheism, and class struggle. Disregarding the structure of the novel, the playwright broke through the objective portrayal of opposing sides not only in the songs, but also in many speeches of the mother in order that he himself might say directly through Pelageya Vlasova: "Why are you only afraid of death? My son was hardly frightened of death."

> He was very much afraid of the misery
> which is right before all our eyes in our cities.
> We are horrified by the hunger and depravity

of those who feel hungry and those who cause it.
Do not be afraid of death so much as the insufficient life.

Warum fürchtet Ihr nur den Tod?
Mein Sohn fürchtete den Tod nicht so sehr.
Sehr erschrak er über das Elend
Das in unseren Städten vor aller Augen liegt.
Uns entsetzt der Hunger und die Verkommenheit
Derer, die ihn spüren, und derer, die ihn bereiten.
Fürchtet doch nicht so den Tod und mehr das unzulängliche
    Leben!

This thesis is repeated almost word for word in the poem
"Resolution der Kommundarden," which Brecht incorporated
into his play *Die Tage der Commune* (*The Days of the Commune*) in 1949 as a recurring refrain:

Considering that you will of course
Threaten us with weapons and canons,
We have decided: from now on to be more
Afraid of a life of misery than of death.

In Erwägung, dass Ihr uns dann eben
Mit Gewehren und Kanonen droht
Haben wir beschlossen: nunmehr schlechtes Leben
Mehr zu fürchten als den Tod.

Brecht worked relentlessly on the fine points of the play *The
Mother* up to the time of the Berlin production, and a comparison of the various printed versions will show this. In fact, the
work holds a most exceptional place in the canon of his dramas.
An answer to *St. Joan,* the culmination of all the Lehrstücke, the
only play which has proletarians portrayed in a manner that
depicts Marxism in action as the unification of theory and practice. For the first time in a great Brecht play, the principle of
negativity is penetrated. *The Mother* is a dramatic avowal of the
plebeian tradition. Baal, Andreas Kragler, Galy Gay, Mackie
Messer, and Paul Ackermann were not heroes, but were used in
contrast to the typical concept of the hero in bourgeois drama.

Joan Dark's actions were the opposite of what might be considered exemplary. She was to demonstrate how one should not act. Here the dramaturgical function of this figure is analogous with the way Mother Courage and Galileo conduct themselves: they serve as warnings.

In contrast, the mother Pelageya Vlasova acts in an exemplary manner. The drama here assumes the poetical task of *praising* in the plebeian tradition. The "solution" is not dialectically bypassed as in *The Good Woman of Setzuan* or in *Der Hofmeister* but demonstrated didactically and clearly in great detail. The work is still exceptional. As a matter of fact, even Maksim Gorki was never again to rework the position of his early novel so expressly and unrestrictedly in his later novels and plays. It is not worth asking why Brecht as a playwright later gave up this manner of accentuation to allow the great dramas of the 1930's to follow in the tradition of the Chicago play about St. Joan rather than along the lines established by the dramatization of the Gorki novel. Yet, it should not be forgotten that the playwright was *chased out for good reasons,* as the *Svendborger Poems* phrase it; that is, he had to leave his home country just a year after the premiere of *The Mother.* From this point on, a literature of praise in the theater seemed hopeless. From this point until his return to Germany, the plebeian heroics was to be found only in his poetry. The rest of the works, the dramas and the prose, *Die Geschäfte des Herrn Julius Caesar* (*The Business Deals of Mr. Julius Caesar*) as well as the *Kalendergeschichten* (*Calender Tales*), the parable plays, and the dramatized satires are all written in "slave language."

Texts in Slave Language

After the February Revolution of 1917 that allowed his return to Russia, Lenin could, in his own words, forgo the "damned slave language" and now express all that was necessary to say without circumlocutions and stratagems. Brecht had to learn the slave language when he fled Germany and lived in exile. It became apparent that even here the new beginning was to be understood as the *acceptance of a new tradition*. Eager to learn as he was and concerned with all forms of an intellectual heritage that had yet to be tested, Brecht set to work studying the new tradition and learning slave language.

The theoretical extract concerning these efforts is in the treatise *Five Difficulties in Writing the Truth* (1934). The ideas and phrases of this study were used almost word for word in his Paris speech of 1935. Brecht himself thought this essay so important that he placed it with *Mother Courage* in volume nine of his *Versuche*, the first to appear in Germany at the end of World War II. It was the correct thing to do: the treatise about the difficulties involved in writing the truth coupled with the chronicle about the Thirty Years War. They belong together. *Mother Courage* is the product of Brecht's reflections concerning the possibilities for a seemingly powerless emigrant to proclaim a useful truth. The treatise itself was printed illegally in the anti-Fascist magazine *Unsere Zeit,* which was published by the League for the Protection of German Writers, a group of émigrés in Paris, and smuggled into Germany. It was the same situation as that of Galileo, who makes sure that the manuscript of his *Discorsi* is smuggled out of the country so that it can be circulated.

The five difficulties arise because one must have the *courage* to write the truth. One must be *smart* enough to recognize the truth, understand the *art* of making the truth manageable as a weapon. One must have enough *discernment* to select those in whose hands the truth will become effective. One must employ *artifice* to spread the truth to many people. The treatise is not merely an avowal of Marx and Lenin, who are once again designated as "the classical writers of the proletarian revolution," nor is it to be understood merely in contrast to all the collective endeavors of his political friends whom he was to oppose in full force one year later at the Paris conference. Many of the arguments and examples, now that we can look back and survey all of Brecht's works, seem to be largely the intellectual seeds for his later, great writings. For instance, there is the sentence from the fifth paragraph of the treatise: "A complete description of all the conditions and operations a man must endure in opening

up a tobacco store can be a hard blow against the dictatorship."
The reader acquainted with Brecht's works will immediately
think about the good woman of Setzuan's tobacco store and
realize that even the parable play in its beginnings had obviously
belonged to the inner group of anti-Fascist plays.

The first four difficulties deal with themes of the general Marxist theory. They are basically a summary of Brecht's early reali-
zations and are employed here with the purpose of supporting
the fight against Hitler. The fifth difficulty is new and determined by the new situation of the emigrant. Artifice is to serve
the truth, to be sure, no longer in the Hegelian sense. It is the
artifice of the bearer of ideas. It is connected with the *form* that
has to be given to the knowledge gathered under difficult conditions. Brecht discovered the universal tradition of satire anew.
He had a thorough understanding of his models: Lucretius,
Confucius, Thomas More, Swift, Voltaire, Lenin. Great artistry
could, as Lucretius had proved, spread ideas in a cunning way
and thereby serve the intentions of the author. Whoever reads
the treatise of 1934 carefully will understand why Brecht—something for which he was often criticized later—made a great effort
to portray the Hitler dynasty in *Arturo Ui* and in *Schweyk* with
satirical devices and in a most serene manner. It was completely
in keeping with his endeavor to overcome the fifth difficulty in
writing the truth by choosing a special tone of voice for all the
works which dealt with the Third Reich. This tone is to be
found in works of such different natures as *Furcht und Elend
des Dritten Reiches* and *Mother Courage* as well as *Flüchtlingsgespräche, Die Geschäfte des Herrn Julius Caesar,* and the
play *Schweyk im zweiten Weltkrieg (Schweik in the Second
World War).* Actually Brecht makes use of the brave soldier
Schweik's intonation everywhere. Schweik's language becomes for
Brecht *pure* slave language. It is even employed in places where
there is no protagonist who acts with craft and cunning as
Schweik does when he begins to speak.

The first scene of *Mother Courage* makes that particularly
evident. The chronicle play of Mother Courage and her children
opens with the Swedish sergeant and his recruiting officer lament-
ing about conditions to one another in the spring of 1624. The

situation is bad for those who enjoy war and those who intend to make a profit from it. "You can see that these people here haven't had a good war in a long time. What's going to become of their morals, I ask you? Peace, that only makes people sloppy. You need a war if you're going to have order. Men and animals are filthy as hell around here, and no one gives a damn. In peace everything goes to pot." Those are the words of the sergeant who is defining the situation. The recruiting officer can only sigh in agreement: "How right you are!" Whereupon the sergeant continues his little lecture: "Like every good thing, war's also hard to get going in the beginning. But when it finally blooms, it's real tough. Then everyone becomes scared of peace. They're like crap-shooters, anxious near the end because they know they have to pay for their losses. But first they're scared back by war. It's something new for them."

One's ears prick up. What kind of a tone is that? It certainly is not the way a sergeant and recruiting officer talk (and talked in those times) with one another. Surely Swedish sergeants and recruiting officers in the year 1624 believed that peace was better than war when they talked about it. They were also very easily carried away by such great words as *heroism, holy war, mission,* and *salvation.* This was the way the commanding officers spoke, and their words were repeated by the men under them. Naturally they wanted the war to continue so that their business would continue to profit. But they spoke differently. It was all clandestine and hypocritical. They did not bend over and change their practice for the idealistically tainted theory. Even the sergeants and common soldiers had copied a great deal of the official tone. The topsy-turvy world and the plain martial ethics in the initial sentences of *Mother Courage* were consequently not what one would "naturally" expect: they were something completely different.

Here two men are saying what they actually think and want. This is the way you speak only if you do not want anything to count as your pure interest and if you know exactly what this interest is and can formulate it. The effect then is comical, for behavior which does not befit the situation or which breaks the social rules of the game generally provokes laughter. In laughter the shock comes afterward so that one actually cannot speak or act. One laughs over the lamentations of the sergeant and the recruiting officer because they talk openly about things that are generally taboo.

The sound is unmistakable. It was the chatter and the stubborn perseverance of the brave soldier Schweik. The beginning of this conversation in *Mother Courage* could also be inserted as the beginning of Hašek's *Schweyk,* and there is good reason for this. Not merely because Brecht later used the figure of the brave soldier to confront the Hitler regime and its activities, but mainly because Brecht was concerned with the same thing that concerned Hašek—pseudoheroics mirrored in the sober life and struggle of the common man.

In spite of this same concern, the function of the brave soldier was changed by Brecht. The tone was also altered. Here it is important to remember that the Schweik style which Brecht changed did not come directly from Hašek but from the German translation of Schweik by Lotte Eisner. This was much different from the Czech original by Hašek. Hašek wrote in a vulgar, often lewd Czech, but it was not a local Prague dialect. In contrast, the German that Schweik spoke in the translation was a so-called "Prague German" spoken by the German population in Moldaustadt, which differed greatly from the social habitat of the Schweik world. Since Brecht not only borrowed this particular tone for his *Schweyk im zweiten Weltkrieg* but separated this special way of speaking from its origins and gave it an individual identity so that it is heard again in the *Flüchtlingsgespräche* as well as in many scenes of *Furcht und Elend des Dritten Reiches,* he was able to change its function in two ways: the Prague German of the Eisner translation was claimed by Brecht as, so to speak, a model for slave language; in addition, the figure of Schweik himself had to be reutilized.

In order to accomplish this, Brecht the refugee who wanted to learn slave language, made use of a third functional change in order to be effective. He reintroduced a fundamental term of the Lehrstücke: the lesson of "consent" (*Einverständnis*). From then on, this became just as much a part of the satirical compositions in slave language as the Prague German of the Eisner translation. The reutilization was not so sweeping in effect to compel the playwright who had demanded genuine consent in the *Badener Lehrstück* to resort to advising hypocritical consent as the only means of fighting. The scenes of consent, compromise, and capitulation which run through such different works as *Mother Courage, Galileo, The Third Reich, Lucullus,* and *Schweyk,* not to mention the numerous battle poems against the Third Reich are much more inclined toward cunning pretense than anything else. Mother Courage's song about the Great Capitulation corresponds to Brecht's own experiences in life, and he never kept this a secret: one should not hold one's courage in reserve for great opportunities. Mother Courage advises against individual and emotional protests when one is alone and can actually achieve nothing by it. The commander-in-chief Lucullus never learned this. He wants to "complain" in the underworld and is gradually compelled to consent to the rules of the game established by an order completely different from the Roman hierarchy.

The first version of *Galileo* as it appeared on stage in the 1943 Zurich premiere also taught genuine consent: abjure in order to be able to continue working. There was no self-condemnation in this production of Galileo. The key sentence was delivered by the author of the *Discorsi* to his disciple Andrea: "Watch out when you pass through Germany. Keep the truth hidden." It is quite well known that Brecht was so impressed by the splitting of the atom and the atomic bomb that he revised his play and gave it a new meaning. The capitulation of Galileo became most important, and it was no longer to be understood as artifice in writing the truth but as betrayal, and what was even worse, as a failure of his analysis of society. Galileo had miscalculated the social forces. He was stronger than he supposed, and he overestimated the danger to his own life. Consequently, he failed as a man of science.

All of Brecht's texts in slave language deal with the *dialectics of heroism and agreement*. Where does cunning turn into betrayal in writing the truth? Galileo's famous words come to mind: "Woe to the country that needs heroes." Brecht did not always intend this statement to be understood as one of failure, of false agreement. In the *Flüchtlingsgespräche* Ziffel remarks: "It is unbearable to live in a country which needs humor." In an earlier dialogue Ziffel had explained almost in the same words of Mother Courage and the judge Azdak: "On the other hand, it is almost impossible to preserve humanity in our times without bribery, even a kind of disorder. You'll find humanity there where you find an official who accepts a bribe." With lines which reoccur in the poem "To Posterity," he confesses: "Just to get a sack of meal today you need the energy with which you could have made the land of an entire province arable. Just to determine whether you must flee today or perhaps it would be better to flee tomorrow, you need the intelligence with which you could have written an immortal work a few decades ago." In spite of this, the final result is not an affirmation of cunning and a cult of consent and a rejection of heroism. The *Flüchtlingsgespräche* ends on a genuine dialectical point. The "sympathizing" intellectual Ziffel is won over to Marxism by the worker Kalle. He had sought a country where the "virtues which demand a great deal," such as love of fatherland, thirst for freedom, and altruism, were just as necessary as their cynical opposites—hatred of the homeland, blissful servitude, and selfishness. "Socialism is this very condition," explains Kalle. However, in order to make this ideal condition more comfortable and not turn it into a situation that exhausts one's virtues, a great deal is necessary: "namely the utmost bravery, an unquenchable thirst for freedom, utmost generosity, and the greatest egoism possible."

It is for this reason that Brecht's Schweik figure should never be confused with Hašek's. Siegfried Melchinger has perceptively pointed this out: "Brecht's humor was never so grim, violent, and angry." In his review of the Milan production of *Schweyk im zweiten Weltkrieg,* he also gave the reason for this: "Brecht talks about refining the figure 'to suit the change in the balance of powers from the Hapsburgs to the Nazis.' If we follow this line of thinking to its end, then it means that the Schweik, who in Hašek's work yells, 'Soldiers, don't let me down. I want to continue serving his majesty the emperor,' is now no longer the outsider subject who experiences the demasking of militarism. He is purely and simply the object of power." Brecht's Schweik is no longer Hašek's Schweik. To be sure, he serves to demonstrate the thesis from the *Flüchtlingsgespräche* that one can always make fun of a good thing no matter what, but oneself is not at all funny. The reason *why not* is that in World War II just before Stalingrad Schweik cannot depend on the laughter and consent of the reader and spectator when he overcomes force by seemingly consenting to it. Schweik in World War II is *not* an affirmation of the teachings from the book *Tao te ching* (78):

> Nothing is weaker than water
> But when it attacks something hard
> Or resistant, then nothing withstands it,
> And nothing will alter its way.

In the emigration years this had to mean: making the contradictions and the points of disagreement sharp and visible through a language that seemingly meant consent. However, this way was possible only when one found readers, listeners, and spectators who showed understanding and were of the same frame of mind. All of Brecht's texts composed in slave language demand this dialectical cooperation and thinking of his audience. This is also true of the plays, of the *Kalendergeschichten,* not to mention the poems of this exile. There is one in particular that is most representative:

1940

My young son asks me: Should I learn math?
What for? I'd like to say.
That two pieces of bread are more than one.
That's something you'll realize in time.
My young son asks me: Should I learn French?
What for? I'd like to say. This empire has seen its day. And
If you rub your stomach with your hand and moan,
They'll have no trouble understanding you.
My young son asks me: Should I learn history?
What for? I'd like to say. Learn how to stick your head in the
    ground,
Then maybe you'll survive.

Yes, learn math, I say,
Learn French, learn history!

Mein junger Sohn fragt mich: Soll ich Mathematik lernen?
Wozu, möchte ich sagen. Dass zwei Stück Brot mehr ist als eines
Das wirst du auch so merken.
Mein junger Sohn fragt mich: Soll ich Französisch lernen?
Wozu, möchte ich sagen. Dieses Reich geht unter. Und
Reibe du nur mit der Hand den Bauch und stöhne
Und man wird dich schon verstehen.
Mein junger Sohn fragt mich: Soll ich Geschichte lernen?
Wozu, möchte ich sagen. Lerne du deinen Kopf in die Erde stecken
Da wirst du vielleicht übrigbleiben.

Ja, lerne Mathematik, sage ich
Lerne Französisch, lerne Geschichte!

The first three groups of four lines each have a similar structure. Each time the young son asks whether he should learn math, French, or history, and each time his father would like to advise him against this. The arguments follow without much difficulty. Finally, a short white space and two short lines combined in an entirely different rhythm. They advise the son to learn after the reasons against learning had been given three times. In spite of it all, the reasons for learning are not given. They are hidden in the white spaces. It is up to the reader to find them. He must ask himself how three arguments against learning can simply be outweighed by a short praise of learning. Three times the father contemplates "I'd like to say." However, it is never said. There is only the final "I say." Why? This must be determined by the reader. There is a clue given by the title of the poem, "1940." This was the year of the blitzkrieg and the defeat of the French. It would have seemed as though all arguments against learning were justified. But even this year has only twelve months. The "Song of the Moldau" in Brecht's play about Schweik expresses this:

Largeness does not remain large and smallness remains not small.
Night has twelve hours, then day arrives.

Times change. The great plans
Of the mighty always come to an end.
And even if they should run wild like bloody cocks,
Times change, and force won't be of any help.

Das Grosse bleibt gross nicht und klein nicht das Kleine.
Die Nacht hat zwölf Stunden, dann kommt schon der Tag.
Es wechseln die Zeiten. Die riesigen Pläne
Der Mächtigen kommen am Ende zum Halt.
Und gehn sie einher auch wie blutige Hähne
Es wechseln die Zeiten, da hilft kein'Gewalt.

In the poem "1940," the middle section with the counter-argument is lacking. It is a text in slave language, intended to be understood by fellow slaves, but slaves who are schooled in humor and dialectics.

Brecht the Roman

The language of slavery and plebeianism refers back to antiquity. Titus Lucretius Carus was expressly used as a model in the treatise concerning the difficulties in writing the truth. Brecht had a definite and strong attachment to Latinity. During World War I he had caused consternation in the Augsburg Gymnasium when he refused to write a school essay according to the dictates of the teacher and the institute. They had demanded unquestionable agreement with a sentence from Horace which said it was sweet and honorable to die for the fatherland. Brecht's essay disapproved of the sentence and its author and pointed to the fact that Quintus Horatius Flaccus himself did not live according to this principle. In the *Flüchtlingsgespräche* Ziffel reports about Brecht's cheating as a pupil in translating Latin when he refers to his "classmate B." On one occasion Brecht was jokingly criticized for using the present participle much too frequently in his poems and plays and thereby influencing other poets to follow bad usage. He replied in a mock tone: "One should only do that when one received an A in Latin, as I did." It is an open question as to whether he really had an A in Latin.

However, he did feel himself closely bound to the rules of Latin prose. He constantly made the attempt to achieve the conciseness and richness of Tacitus. He knew every detail about the Roman classical writers. When someone proved that he had taken entire sections with the dates from Sallust for his Caesar novel, he smiled with an air of satisfaction. The Roman references in his works, even in the minor ones, are too numerous to be counted. In the "Open Letter to the German Artists and Writers" ("Offener Brief an die deutschen Künstler and Schriftsteller," 1951) he employs the "great Carthage" along with the recollection of the three Punic Wars as his last and key argument.

This Roman tradition is largely noteworthy because it counters the German synthesis of Germanism and Hellenism with a certain polemical sharpness. Naturally this is also connected with Brecht's anti-Aristotelian position. In contrast to French classicism, which had sought Aristotle in the work of the Roman tragedians, in particular Seneca, Lessing's dramaturgy leaned on the alleged original texts of Aristotle and on Sophokles as models. German literature followed in Lessing's footsteps. Homer, Pindar, the Greek tragedians, Aristophanes. It was in this area that German literature perfected its knowledge of antiquity.

With Brecht there is no abrupt break with the Greeks, but rather a turn toward Romanism and Latin literature, which had to have an appreciable effect. It seems as though there is a development in process of completing itself by pushing Lessing and Winckelmann aside (and also French classicism along with it) in order to allow the Roman tradition to become productive again. This tradition, by the way, had not totally perished even in German classicism. One need only recall Schiller's poem "To Goethe" written when the Weimar theater director staged *Mahomet* by Voltaire. The turn from the Greeks cannot be explained solely by Brecht's opposition to the poetics of Aristotle. It seems that the playwright was not satisfied with a literature that was unthinkable without the system of the *polis*, of the Greek city-states. The Roman themes in the work of Brecht either treat the legendary beginnings of the *urbs* or they take place during Caesar's reign. If one studies the plays carefully, then it becomes apparent that Livy and Plutarch were his most important sources and provided him with themes. It was Livy for *Die Horatier und die Kuratier* (*The Horatii and the Curiatii*) and the adaptation of Shakespeare's *Coriolanus,* Plutarch for *Das Verhör des Lukullus* (*The Trial of Lucullus*). Naturally Brecht made use of all the pertinent literature on Caesar for his novel *Die Geschäfte des Herrn Julius Caesar.·*

Affinity for the Romans and their literature and a turning away from the Greek tradition in the German intellectual development. Aside from this, it should be made clear that Brecht attempted to treat all his most important Roman themes during the years of his exile, actually between 1934 and 1939.

The didactic play *Die Horatier und die Kuratier* (1934) completes the circle of Lehrstücke. The actors are supposed to learn from the play—as pupils. The lesson is taken from Livy (I, 26). Three Horatii and three Curiatii fight for victory in the battle between Rome and Alba Longa. Two Horatii are killed, two Curiatii are merely wounded. Livy describes what the third of the Horatii does: "Fortunately he had not been wounded, and though he could not match his three opponents at once, he could defeat them in single combat. In order to divide the battle evenly with them, he took to flight with the expectation that they would follow him at different speeds depending on the severity of their wounds. This way he separated his enemies from themselves, turned around and killed them one by one. First the strongest, and then the two who had been weakened by their wounds." Brecht creates this into a praise of thinking and learning. Thinking is more important than material superiority. Temporary victories should not lead to precipitous jubilation. Everything depends on the final victory. Even defeats can be changed into victories. This legendary event from the early days of Rome was to help place in proper perspective the forces and counterforces in the initial stage of the Third Reich. It cannot be denied that this Lehrstück of 1934 contained the right prognostication about the fate of the "Curiatii" of those times.

The unfinished novel about Caesar's business deals, the radio play about the trial and the condemnation of the general Lucullus, and the adaptation of *Coriolanus,* which was delivered, as it were, after his return from exile (1952–1953), have an inner connection: they are three works that deal with the plebeian tradition. Each one considers the hero and the rulers from the standpoint of their opponents, the subjects and the oppressed. It is like the poem "Questions of a Reading Worker" ("Fragen eines lesenden Arbeiters").

> Young Alexander conquered India.
> He alone?
> Caesar beat the Gauls.
> Didn't he even have a cook with him?
> Philip of Spain wept when his fleet
> Was destroyed. Did anyone else weep?
> Frederick the Great triumphed in the Seven Years War.
> Who triumphed besides him?
>
> Each page a victory.
> Who cooked for the victory banquet?
> Every ten years a great man.
> Who paid the costs?
>
> So many reports.
> So many questions.

> Der junge Alexander eroberte Indien.
> Er allein?
> Cäsar schlug die Gallier.
> Hatte er nicht wenigstens einen Koch bei sich?
> Philipp von Spanien weinte, als seine Flotte
> Untergangen war. Weinte sonst niemand?
> Friedrich der Zweite siegte im Siebenjährigen Krieg. Wer
> Siegte ausser ihm?
>
> Jede Seite ein Sieg.
> Wer kochte den Siegesschmaus?
> Alle zehn Jahre ein grosser Mann.
> Wer bezahlte die Spesen?
>
> So viele Berichte.
> So viele Fragen.

The dialectics of the Caesar novel come into play in the situation of a latter-day historian whose endeavors to clarify the past are impaired during his research by the unpleasant reports of Caesar's banker and by the notebooks of his administrator Rarus. The apologetics is contrasted with the economics. The Caesar adventure is mirrored in the manipulations of Caesar as the mighty banker as well as in the domestic miseries and transactions of Caesar as the general, politician, and writer. How can the conquest of Gaul be compared to the transactions of the Roman "city" in the final analysis? In Brecht's other novel, *The Threepenny Novel,* a similar question had been asked: What does the establishment of a bank mean when compared to a bank robbery? A stock compared to a picklock? The manner of portrayal in the Caesar novel, which consists merely of reflections, places Gaius Julius Caesar with all his business deals between the transactions of Mr. Mackie Messer and Mr. Arturo Ui.

Caesar or the hero and his business deals. Lukullus (this is the way Brecht writes his name, and he even has him called Lakalles "in the despised jargon of the suburbs," in other words, with the American pronunciation of the name) or the merits of a general in the eyes of his subordinates, the defeated, and the poor people. Coriolanus or the specialist who is ostensibly irreplaceable and who is forced to recognize only too late that the people are capable of doing without him and replacing him. This has no connection with heroism treated ironically as in Shaw. Brecht the playwright and novelist is not concerned with debasing the stature of heroes but in ordering the action of the hero in the total framework of social and, above all, of economic conditions. Caesar, Lucullus, and Coriolanus are to be seen at every moment from the viewpoint of the plebeians. The novel remained unfinished. It is impossible to tell how Brecht would have interpreted the figure in the end. Lucullus is thrown into nothingness by the plebeian judges of death. Plutarch reported the following about the funeral rites for Coriolanus: "When they learned of his death, the Romans showed neither a sign of respect nor disrespect toward the man himself. Yet, they allowed the women upon their request to mourn for him for ten months as was the custom when a father, son, or brother died. For this was the longest period of mourning that had been determined by Numa Pompilius."

Shakespeare, too, allowed his Coriolanus the deification: the senators of the Volscians as well as the enemy Aufidius grant a funeral march and festive burial. In the study *Coriolanus: Plutarch—Shakespeare—Brecht* Jürgen Kuczynski emphasizes that Brecht took Shakespeare's tragedy about Coriolanus and made it into a tragedy against Coriolanus. Yet, one must immediately ask whether any tragic elements have remained in Brecht's adaptation at all. In Brecht's play, the final scene is no longer played by the Volscians but is in Rome, in the senate. To be sure, it reads "Consuls, senators, tribunes," yet the action is like that in the Paris commune. Right in the middle of a useful deliberation about the distribution of land and aqueducts, the case of the murdered Coriolanus is briefly treated: they take cognizance of it and move on to the next point on the agenda. The general mourning period of the women reported by Plutarch is not granted. "Denied," decides the tribune of the people Brutus. The same word "denied" is spoken by the "faded voice" in *Das Verhör des Lukullus* when the advocate of the dead general raises objection. It belongs in Brecht's works to the vocabulary of plebeian justice used against class enemies.

The famous plea of the mother to the son, the leader of the enemy, also functions in a new way. Shakespeare's Volumnia (Livy calls the wife Volumnia, while the mother is named Veturia) makes use of classical rhetoric: the ideas were provided by Livy, the form was shaped in Athens, renewed in Rome, and finally taken over by Shakespeare. Homeland and honor, mother, wife, and children. Brecht surmised that Shakespeare purposely kept Volumnia's arguments weak. Yet, this is not the case. They are emotions and reflections from the domestic realm. In Brecht's play, she does not plead, she reports:

> Know
> That you march upon a different Rome
> Than the one you left. No longer
> Are you irreplaceable, only the deadly
> Danger for us all. Do not wait for the smoke
> Of submission. When you see smoke,
> Then it will be coming from the smiths, who are now
> Forging swords to be used against you.

> Wisse
> Dass du auf ein sehr andres Rom marschierst
> Als du verliessest. Unersetzlich
> Bist du nicht mehr, nur noch die tödliche
> Gefahr für alle. Wart nicht auf den Rauch
> Der Unterwerfung. Wenn du Rauch sehn wirst
> Dann aus den Schmieden steigend, die jetzt Schwerter
> Wider dich schmieden.

The lengthy discussion between Brecht and his associates Rülicke, Manfred Wekwerth, and Peter Palitzsch about Coriolanus, which took place in 1953 and was recorded in the essay *Dialectics in the Theater (Dialektik auf dem Theater)*, concerns Plutarch's statement that the common people volunteered freely for military service. Brecht explains: "Now we will then read this sentence with even greater interest since we want to find out everything about the plebeians." To which Palitzsch answers with a quotation from the poem "Literature Will Be Investigated":

> For it may be here that we're dealing
> With features of famous ancestors.
>
> Denn hier mag es sich um Züge
> Der berühmten Ahnen handeln.

It was exactly this point that concerned Brecht the Roman. During his years in exile the Roman motifs centered on the connections between victory and defeat, führer and people, heroics and economics. Brecht always meant the Roman world itself—because of the famous ancestors. Naturally Caesar and Lucullus were not placed on the agenda for the day merely because of themselves alone but *also* because of themselves. Brecht was not like Feuchtwanger, whose novel *The Wrong Nero* actually intended to portray Hitler and his satellites at that time. This is why the Roman themes remained productive for Brecht as novelist and playwright after World War II. The work on the Caesar novel continued; the adaptation of *Coriolanus* was completed. Even the reading of Livy and Plutarch produced useful insights in regard to new social problems. The general Coriolanus became the prototype of the *specialist* who puffs himself up in front of the people because he thinks himself irreplaceable. This is one of the many themes about the intellectual in the late Brecht period: Coriolanus as the counterpart to Galileo.

And then there was always Horace. Ever since Brecht's schooldays, beloved and mocked. One of the poems from 1953 deals with him.

ON READING HORACE

Even the deluge
Did not last forever.
Black waters
Once overran.
Of course, how few
Lasted longer!

BEIM LESEN DES HORAZ

Selbst die Sintflut
Dauerte nicht ewig.
Einmal verrannen
Die schwarzen Gewässer.
Freilich, wie Wenige
Dauerten länger!

It is remarkable how the impetus of the dactylic takes over from the third line and moves toward the classical hexameter, yet is throttled by the poet. The verse form as quotation. Antiquity in the present. Once again a poem about transformation, forgetting, and permanence. A modern variation of the sentence by the poet Horace: "Exegi monumentum aere perennius" ("I have created a monument for all times"). A poem by the older Brecht about the durability of poetry.

The Far East

Strange as it may seem, Brecht's involvement with Latinity and Roman themes makes it necessary to study the poetry and poetics of the Chinese. The original version of "Remarks on Chinese Acting" was written in 1938 during the exile in Denmark. Later on it was lengthened into the chapter "Alienation Effects in Chinese Acting," which appeared in the book *Dialectics in the Theater*. Brecht's visit to the Soviet Union in connection with his editorial work for the magazine *Das Wort* had introduced him to a great theater experience: the guest performance of China's most famous actor of that time, Mei Lan-fang. Brecht's reflections after this evening in the theater were in line with the entire direction of his theater work—the endeavor to formulate a non-Aristotelian dramatics. There was a continuity which went back to the 1920's. There also was an internal connection between the Roman themes and the study of the Chinese tradition. The common starting point can be found in what was later designated as the historicizing of the events to be portrayed in the theater. Brecht had repudiated the one-time cult of impermanence but had not, in contrast to Gottfried Benn, founded a cult of supposed permanence and transcendental timelessness. Just as always, dialectics was inimical to all social statics in Benn's case. Historicity and presentness had a mutual effect on one another. Caesar, Lucullus, and Coriolanus were both past and present as shaped by Brecht. The "Mother" Pelageya Vlasova was portrayed as a great *historical* figure of the plebeian tradition by the playwright as adapter, and not merely because her history took place in the year 1905. In both instances, in his study of the Romans as in his study of the Chinese, Brecht was determined to continue his reutilization of German classicism in a consequential manner.

He had worked with quotations for a long time. Famous poems by the German classical writers and familiar biblical sayings were never used for parody but to compel the spectator to reflect about the contrast between the origins of the quotation and its sudden use in an unusual connection. Brecht then moved from quotations of lines to whole scenes. In *Arturo Ui,* he quotes the courting scene in *Richard the Third* as well as the garden scene from *Faust.*

By studying Chinese acting Brecht learned that even the gesture, the entire scenic action of an actor, can assume the character of a quotation. In his late—quite cautious—attack on Konstantin

Stanislavski's dramatic art of empathy, Brecht had much to say against the tricks of such a mode of dramatic identification: "The Chinese artist does not encounter these difficulties. He rejects complete transformation. He limits himself from the very beginning to simply quoting the character to be portrayed. But look how artistically he does it! He needs only a minimum of illusion! What he shows is worth seeing even for someone not in his right mind. What western actor of the old tradition (with the exception of one or two comedians) could demonstrate the elements of his dramatic art like the Chinese actor Mei Lan-fang wearing a dinner jacket in a room without special lighting and surrounded by experts? Almost like King Lear's dividing his kingdom or the discovery of the handkerchief by Othello? It would be like the magician at a fair giving away his tricks so that nobody will ever want to see the act again. He would just be showing how to disguise oneself. The hypnotism would disappear, and all that would remain would be a few pounds of poorly mixed mimicry, a product quickly hashed together to sell to customers rushing in the dark."

The dialectical unity of the past and the present can be found in the quotation. The historical is actualized. The Chinese art of acting was fertile ground for Brecht's antibourgeois theatrics. The bourgeois theater, as stated later in the piece on the alienation effects of the Chinese theater, has worked out the timelessness of its objects. "The portrayal of a man is bound to the so-called eternally human." And Brecht opposes this: "The idea of man as a variable of the environment, the environment as a variable of man, i.e., the dissolution of the environment in the relations between men, stems from a new way of thinking, historical thinking." The experiences with the Chinese art of acting can lead to the elimination of the principles of a timeless bourgeois theater and the realization of a stage erected upon historical principles of knowledge.

The importance of the Chinese features in the work of Brecht is, however, not limited merely to experiences with the Chinese art of acting. In both Chinese art and philosophy Brecht found the unity of the pedagogic and the artistic that he himself had always sought to realize. The treatise concerning the difficulties in writing the truth had already praised the example of Lucretius, who combined embellishment with philosophical effectiveness. Yet Lucretius was a special case even in the Roman tradition. Brecht believed this synthesis in the Chinese tradition to be not an exception but the rule. His twenty-third Versuch bears the title *Chinese Poems* and most likely was written after his flight from Denmark while he was in Finland. Nine translations from two centuries. Four of the nine poems stemmed from Po Chü-i (A.D. 772–846). This poet was apparently a poet after Brecht's own heart. In the notes to this twenty-third Versuch, he remarks: "He came from a poor farming family, and he himself became an official. 'Like Confucius he regarded art as a means to communicate teaching' (A. D. Waley). He criticized the great poets Li Po and Tu Fu for their lack of *Feng* (criticism of the rulers) and *Ya* (moral guidance for the masses). He said this about himself: 'When the tyrants and their favorites heard my songs, they looked at one another and made faces.' His songs were 'on the lips of farmers and stable boys.' They were written 'on the walls of village schools, temples, and the cabins of ships.' Twice he was sent into exile." Furthermore, "his poems are in simple words, yet written with great care. There is one legend that Po Chü-i read many of his poems to an old peasant woman in order to determine whether they could be understood." There is no doubt about it: Brecht was intent that posterity should not be able to say that he did not criticize the rulers and provide moral guidance for the masses. He also wanted to follow the example set by the poet Po Chü-i by composing his poetic works in a manner that would make them comprehensible and even more artistic, as he had demanded in his poem "Literature Will Be Investigated," which was also written during the Danish emigration.

> But in these times they are to be praised
> Who sat on the bare ground to write
> Who sat among the common lot
> Who sat with the fighters
>
> Who told the suffering of the common lot
> Who told the deeds of the fighters,
> Artistically, in a language refined,

In former times reserved
For the glorification of kings.

Aber in jener Zeit werden gepriesen werden
Die auf dem nackten Boden sassen, zu schreiben
Die unter den Niedrigen sassen
Die bei den Kämpfern sassen

Die von den Leiden der Niedrigen berichteten
Die von den Taten der Kämpfer berichteten
Kunstvoll, in der edlen Sprache
Vordem reserviert
Der Verherrlichung der Könige.

The period of transition from Brecht's study of the Latin tradition to his particular involvement with the poetry and the wisdom of the Far East (the Chinese as well as the Japanese) can be determined exactly. The most important Chinese motifs and themes are to be found between 1938 and 1944. That first version of the essay on the Chinese art of acting and the translations belong here. Also the famous poem "The Legend about the Origin of the Book *Tao te ching* on the Path of Lao-tzu in the Emigration" ("Legende von der Entstehung des Buches *Taoteking* auf dem Weg des Laotse in die Emigration") must be taken into consideration here. In September 1944, the work manual of the poet talks about a plan to compose a play about the life of Confucius, another doctrine play for children. It would mean treating an old dramatic project. Confucius had been evoked quite earnestly in the treatise about writing the truth in 1934. Thus far, only one scene of this dramatic project has become known. The note by the playwright endeavors to explain why such a great figure as Confucius should be entrusted to a theater for children: "Children are not capable of providing the fine psychological *interieurs* —a strong reason to entrust them with the portrayal of a great public figure who himself formulated everything that would be useful information for them." All motifs converge here: the figure of Confucius; the treatment of the historical figure as one of the actual ones; the communication of useful information instead of the release of useless emotions; the rejection of psychological empathy in favor of demonstrations according to history and quotations. Brecht moved toward the Far East to look for witnesses and compatriots to help him in his fight against the bourgeois aesthetics of timelessness, against the culinary theater,* against Aristotle.

Anti-Aristotle

When one examines Brecht's Roman and Chinese themes more closely, two things become obvious. To begin with, the Roman motifs are much more concerned with myths and legends than with actual Roman history. Livy's writings about the battle of the Horatii and the Curiatii or the general Coriolanus belonged to the tradition of Roman sagas about the cities. It was more "golden legend" than pragmatic historical writing. On the other hand, the general Lucius Licinius Lucullus was a historical figure who remained alive in the general historical consciousness merely because of the reports gathered from banquets and table talk and because he introduced the cherry tree into Europe. He came so close to being a mythical figure that the dramatist could manipulate him for special dramaturgical and political reasons any way he saw fit. In the case of Caesar, this was impossible: the historian of the Gallic Wars and the civil war was too well known in the Latin classes of the school system. In the Caesar novel, Brecht did not allow Caesar to appear himself but resorted to dialectical reflections in which Caesar was discussed by others—sometimes by intimates, other times by mere acquaintances, sometimes by contemporaries, other times by people from a later generation. Contradictory testimonies produced the desired distance and prevented

---

* *Translator's note:* During the 1920's Brecht argued that the bourgeois theater of illusion provided nothing but mental refreshment for the audience. He coined the term *culinary theater* for that theater which produced plays as though they were goods to be consumed by the audience, digested, deposited, and forgotten. *Culinary theater* might also be termed *commercial theater*. Brecht opposed this type of theater with his own *epic theater*, which was conceived in order to smash the illusion of reality on the stage and raise the political consciousness of the spectator.

empathy even though the biographical details were not manipulated this time but were reported exactly as they were. Nevertheless, there must have been a certain amount of discontent in writing the novel. It was never finished. If asked when the novel would be completed after he had already published some fragments upon returning from exile, Brecht would avoid an answer by intimating that his theater work exhausted his time and energy. The connection of the writer Brecht with the actual Roman and historical material remained suspect. In the final analysis Rome was more of a parable for him than history.

Even in his study of the Chinese tradition the limits he set for himself soon became visible. Brecht was plainly intent on borrowing the forms and not the substance of the Chinese theater for his own work. This could not be avoided since the historicizing gesture of the Chinese actor corresponded to a common historical consciousness of the artists and their audience. Moreover, it signified, according to its function, almost the opposite of what Brecht was seeking with his attempt at historicizing. The seemingly extraordinary succession of events demonstrated to the audience by the Chinese actor, rather in the manner of a trip on a barge, was portrayed as a historical process. To use an example from Brecht: "Many songs sing about an unusual trip known to everyone." These words conveyed a sense of agreement between the actors on stage and the spectators in the audience. Agreement immediately becoming confirmation. A common and binding tradition. The present was demonstrated as part of a continuous tradition. The heritage itself was acknowledged, never doubted. Brecht could only adopt forms here, and he had to forgo making use of the substance and function of this socially conservative dramatics. On the other hand, Brecht's aim to historicize portrayable events from daily life was designed to make the *changeable* and the *changeableness* of the demonstrated events visible for the new audience with the help of a new *art of audience participation*. When Brecht thought one time of turning to a specific Chinese theme as an experiment, as in the case of *Leben des Konfutse* (*Life of Confucius*), he was once again not able to finish it. In addition, it is important to note in his chronicle about the origin of the book *Tao te ching* what Brecht does and does not take from the teachings of Lao-tzu and use for his purposes in the report.

He must have felt closer to the Chinese poetry than to the special forms of the dramatic art in the Far East. It is impossible to consider his late poems without the original Chinese models. As the affinity for Po Chü-i demonstrated, there was also an idea about the purpose of poetry that he held in common with the Chinese poet. With regard to the Chinese theater, however, Brecht felt it to be exemplary mainly in that it was not Aristotelian.

It is well known that Brecht conceived his dramas and dramaturgy in direct opposition to the principles of Aristotelian poetics. He himself never tired of emphasizing this. As late as 1954 he made this doctrinaire statement: "Non-Aristotelian dramatics is a dramatics which portrays contradictions and takes pleasure in the contradictions. Aristotle is not entirely an undialectical thinker but his dialectics is one-tracked. For instance, he gives us the example with the starlings that swoop down to painted grapes because they are painted to look so real. Essential here is naturally the similarity—but the dissimilarity is also essential." This late formulation is, relatively speaking, conciliatory. Earlier statements about Aristotle the Stagirite are more brutal. Especially in *Galileo,* Aristotle—this time with his physics—is not given a very admirable role to play.

Brecht's argument with Aristotle did not remain confined to their opposing views about the function of drama. There was much more behind all this. Hence, it was rather strange praise when Georg Lukács on the day after Brecht's burial announced to a gathering of mourners in the Theater am Schiffbauerdamm that Brecht's death signified the departure of the legitimate heir of Lessing and Aristotle. This was not an interpretation of Brecht; rather the theoretical contrast between Bertolt Brecht and Georg Lukács was underscored once again. Lukács himself had always taken an Aristotelian position. Brecht's complaint about Aristotle also applied to the Hungarian aesthetician: like the Greek, he was, indeed, a dialectician but a one-tracked dialectician. There was still the question whether that was not a contradiction in itself: a one-tracked dialectician.

In 1938 Georg Lukács had written an essay in exile with the

title *The Question Concerns Realism* (*Es geht um den Realismus*). He referred to a debate within the German literary emigration concerning the productive potential and the sterility of expressionism with regard to future generations. The dispute, which had also involved Ernst Bloch, was printed in the magazine *Das Wort,* coedited by Brecht. Lukács pointed particularly to the series of discussions on this subject and set the task of "determining the internal versatile connection which linked in various ways the people's front, the *Volkstümlichkeit** of literature, and the real realism." His arguments were directed toward Bertolt Brecht as well as Ernst Bloch. The author of *Geist der Utopie* (*Spirit of Utopia*) did not want to admit that there was a contrast between expressionism and Volkstümlichkeit. Bloch meant exactly the opposite: "Expressionism did not have an arrogance that was alien to the people. On the contrary, the 'Blue Rider' imitated the Murnau glass pictures. It began to open our eyes to this moving and fascinating peasant art, to the sketches of children and prisoners, to the shattering documents of the insane, to primitive art." Lukács retorted sharply: "This idea of Volkstümlichkeit confuses everything. Volkstümlichkeit does not mean the ideologically eclectic, artistic, refined acceptance of 'primitive' products. The real Volkstümlichkeit has nothing to do with all this. Otherwise, any pretentious person who collects glass painting or Negro sculpture, any snob who celebrates in his insanity the liberation of man from the shackles of his mechanical reason, would be a champion of Volkstümlichkeit." The conclusion expressly took Thomas Mann as an example to substantiate the argument: "And since the checks to progress and democracy (in the field of politics as well as culture) brought about an imperialistic period, then it is necessary to criticize the political, cultural, and artistic signs of decadence in this period rather sharply if we are to have a breakthrough to a real Volkstümlichkeit."

Tactics for the people's front, the struggle for realism in art and literature, Volkstümlichkeit, the legacy of German classical

---

* *Translator's note: Volkstümlichkeit* is a difficult word to translate into English, especially since the Nazis used it to extol the "great" traits of the Aryan race. It usually carries the meaning of "ethnic character," "national trait," or "popular aspect."

aesthetics, Thomas Mann as literary representative, the poetics of Aristotle. Indeed, the question concerns realism! Brecht had not been an expressionist. Hence, he thought much differently from Ernst Bloch about these questions. Still he was much closer to Bloch's position than to Lukács' at the time of the debate in 1938. Lukács' reference to Thomas Mann signified a negation of Bertolt Brecht's aims. Opposites in the realm of politics: the people's front and the conditions of ownership. Different literary models: for or against the author of *The Magic Mountain*. Opposite ideas about the actual possibilities of German classicism. Contrasting views about Aristotle. The philosophy of the founder of peripateticism meant for Lukács an avowal of Lessing and the unchanged validity of German classicism and the endeavor of literature to mirror reality. Starlings that fly to the grapes because they are painted like real ones. Comprehensibility and Volkstümlichkeit as the artistic criteria. The endeavor of art to have a direct effect on the masses. The endeavor of anti-Fascist politics to take on a wide unified front.

Brecht differed here everywhere. Emphasis on the opposites between Marxists and non-Marxists despite their mutual anti-Fascist views. Transformation of the consciousness of the masses through dialectical thinking instead of the stipulation of Volkstümlichkeit, which does not recognize the situation of the real people. One should take the folk scenes in *St. Joan of the Stockyards* or in *The Good Woman of Setzuan* along with the corresponding explanations of the *Flüchtlingsgespräche* and confront them with the demand for Volkstümlichkeit. Realism does not have to preclude dialectics. Mere imitation of reality without contradictions will not do the job. German classicism must take on a new function. Aristotelian dramatics should give way to a non-Aristotelian dramatics. Brecht's essay *Volkstümlichkeit und Realismus* was first published from his posthumous papers in 1958. However, it had been finished during his exile in 1938, that is, in the same year that Lukács wrote his polemical *The Question Concerns Realism*. This is Brecht's answer to a charge that he had thoroughly understood. The man who made this charge is only mentioned in a footnote when the word *realistic* is clarified: "In particular, *Das Wort* owes a great deal to Georg Lukács for some notable essays that shed light on the term realism even though they, in my opinion, define it somewhat too narrowly." In actuality, Brecht's entire essay, which contained the Hungarian critic's central formula right in the title, is directed against Lukács. The antithesis is as follows: "The criteria for Volkstümlichkeit and realism must be selected not only with great care but with an open mind. They should not be taken just from the existing realist works and the existing folk works, as is frequently the case. Such an approach would lead mainly to formal criteria, and the definition of the folk and real world would be established according to form." This is also the position of Brecht's complementary essay, *Breadth and Diversity of the Realistic Mode of Writing* (*Weite und Vielfalt der realistischen Schreibweise*), which was included in volume thirteen of his Versuche (1954). Brecht indicated at the beginning of the article that "it was written in 1938 and was directed against the tendency to set limits on the realistic mode of writing in any formal way." Lukács had supported his case by calling upon Balzac, and now Brecht answered with the name of Shelley: "There is a great deal to learn from reading Balzac—provided that one has already learned a great deal. But poets like Shelley must be given more of a definite place in the great school of realists than Balzac since Shelley renders the abstractions more feasible than Balzac and is not an enemy of the lower classes but their friend. One can see that Shelley's realistic manner of writing does not mean renouncing imagination or genuine artistry." Lukács prefers Goethe, Balzac, Tolstoi. Imitation of reality. Renunciation of moralizing. Empathy made easy. Brecht favors Grimmelshausen, Voltaire, Shelley, Hašek. The portrayal of reality in contradictions. Prevention of vicarious identification. Didacticism with the aim of demonstrating that conditions can be changed and are worth changing. Literature of empathy versus literature of alienation. Aristotle versus anti-Aristotle.

From the beginning, Brecht meant the historical figure of Aristotle. He rejected not only the poetics of Aristotle and his physics, but most of all his politics. The conservative system, which was based on degree, medium, and compromise, by the philosophy teacher of Alexander the Great was most suspect for him. The dramatist Peter Hacks, strongly influenced by Brecht, has likewise cast Aristotle as the symbol of socially conservative ideology. According to Hacks, the question concerning Aristotle is about "a man whose claim to fame is that he weakened and made the drama harmless for the societies that exploit." Therefore, it is "not superfluous to warn people about this old apologist." With the fundamental ideas of his dramaturgy rooted in bourgeois compromise, Lessing definitely stands closer to the basic Aristotelian outlook than Brecht's dramaturgy, which seeks revolution. Aristotle and Lessing endeavor to gain the recognition of moral values and actions through the spectator. Catharsis of emotions. The provocation of sympathy and fear requires the acknowledgment of constant values *a priori*. In contrast, Brecht continually asks about the concrete connections, and he questions the seemingly authentic values set for everyone. Where Lessing understands catharsis as a stage in humanization, Brecht sees only barbarity. In *Conversation about Being Forced into Empathy* (*Gespräch über die Nötigung zur Einfühlung*, 1953) the playwright begins a talk to his colleagues with the following introduction: "I have here Horace's *Ars Poetica* in Gottsched's translation. He takes a theory from Aristotle that has often concerned us and formulates it rather nicely:

> You must captivate and win the reader's heart.
> One laughs with those who laugh and also lets tears roll
> When others are sad. So, if I am to cry,
> First show me your eyes filled with tears.

"Gottsched immediately alludes to the famous passage from Cicero dealing with the art of recitation. Cicero tells about the Roman actor Polus, who was supposed to play Electra mourning her brother. Since his only son had just died, he brought the urn with his ashes onstage and spoke the appropriate verses 'with such strong personal devotion that his own loss made him weep real tears. And there was no one present who could have refrained from crying with him.' Truly, there is no other word that can be used to describe this event other than *barbaric*."

The dispute with Aristotle presents one of the most important processes of convergence in Brecht's work. "The question concerns" the historical Aristotle and the historical mission of his philosophy, in particular, his poetics. The question concerns the contradiction between formal and real dialectics, an aesthetic of tenacity and corroboration as opposed to a theory of art that strives for real change. When writing about Aristotle, Brecht is at the same time implicating all those supposed or real heirs of German classicism. When Brecht speaks about "German misery," he means the classical Aristotelian art and idea of art as the expression of this misery, the crippling and inadequate German conditions. This also pertains to the historical function of Aristotle the Stagirite and the polemics of the people's front in 1935, the much too restricted concept of realism as well as the unrealistic concept of folk and the supposed Volkstümlichkeit. The disagreement with Lukács and his followers in 1938 had lasting effects for Brecht, especially since it became relevant again for him and his Berliner Ensemble ten years later when he made that snide remark: "The people are everything but 'popular.' " ("Alles is das Volk, bloss nicht tümlich.")*

Nevertheless, the playwright worked on two dramatic projects in those years filled with political and philosophical disputes, and both must be counted as belonging rather unabashedly to the traditional Aristotelian dramatics on the basis of their form and also their function: *Die Gewehren der Frau Carrar* (1937) and *Galileo* (*Leben des Galilei,* written in 1938/39).

Brecht conspicuously included *Die Gewehren der Frau Carrar* in the series of his Versuche in 1953 without giving it a volume number and designating it as a special issue that did not have a place in the numerical order of the other volumes. That points to a secret illegitimacy, to the shamefaced special existence of the play, which has as its theme the Spanish Civil War.

Teresa Carrar belongs to the series of mother figures in Brecht's works, and she is the new type that had already replaced Widow Begbick and Mrs. Peachum before his emigration. The camp-follower Anna Fierling, called Mother Courage, was an amalga-

---

* *Translator's note:* Brecht attacks the racial and chauvinistic implications attached to the word *Volkstümlich* by the Nazis. Brecht was very much the champion of the people but not any one people or nation in particular.

mation of both female types as it were. On the other hand, Señora Carrar (as well as the fisherwoman from *Verhör des Lukullus*) approximates the figure of the "Mother" Pelageya Vlasova rather strongly in her disposition and manner of speech. (It is common knowledge that the author had the actress Helene Weigel in mind in each case. She played the first Señora Carrar in 1937 in a German emigrant theater located in Paris.) The decisive and conclusive argument of the Andalusian fisherwoman that explains her son's death—"The cap was responsible for it all . . . . It's so shabby. A gentleman would never wear something like this"— could have been spoken by Pelageya Vlasova to explain the death of her son, the revolutionary Pavel Vlasov. Despite this similarity, the "Mother" is a figure from the epic theater, while Señora Carrar is not. According to its dramaturgy, *Die Gewehren der Frau Carrar* is a work structured on Aristotelian principles.

Brecht's advice on how to receive a non-Aristotelian play had already been conveyed in the closing lines of the didactic play (*Schulstück*) *Die Ausnahme und die Regel* (*The Exception and the Rule*, 1930):

> You saw the usual, what always happens.
> Now we request:
> Whatever's familiar to you, find it strange!
> Whatever's usual for you, find it puzzling!
> Whatever's normal should astound you.
> Whatever's the rule see it as an abuse,
> And wherever you have recognized abuse,
> Then remedy the situation!

> Ihr saht das Übliche, das immerfort Vorkommende.
> Wir bitten euch aber:
> Was nicht fremd ist, findet befremdlich!
> Was gewöhnlich ist, findet unerklärlich!
> Was da üblich ist, das soll euch erstaunen.
> Was die Regel ist, das erkennt als Missbrauch
> Und wo ihr den Missbrauch erkannt habt
> Da schafft Abhilfe!

The transformation of Pelageya Vlasova was demonstrated and didactically explained by an epic report that closed like an oration. In the Berlin performance film montages were added. The transformation of Señora Carrar reaches completion within the confines of a traditional theater. Only the figures themselves are in the play. The most important elements of the action are portrayed, not reported. There are no songs, no montages. The spectator is able to receive an "accompanying interpretation" of Señora Carrar and her decisions: the spectator never becomes alienated from her. The traditional method of presentation is possible because the complex process of revolutionary insight is not to be shown but, according to the intention of the author, simple transition from neutrality to action in a political-military conflict which has its fronts clearly designated. In particular, the play is to provide information. Brecht would like to portray who is fighting in the Spanish Civil War and what the battle is about. Here is a play written after Lukács' own heart: realism and Volkstümlichkeit, the heroine's transformation. Perhaps there is no sympathy and fear, but there is possibly "defiance and hope," to borrow an expression from Ernst Bloch. And there is also a greater unity, a people's front in the Civil War, as the conversation between the worker Pedro and the padre indicates.

It is more difficult to explain the return to Aristotelian principles in *Galileo*. In the study *Brecht's 'Galilei': Form und Einführung*, Ernst Schumacher examines the work procedure and how it was reflected in the work journal of the author. He demonstrates why Brecht could note the following on July 30, 1945: "I cannot defend the formal aspects of this play strongly." Schumacher also shows why Brecht essentially valued the play as an interesting contrast to the parable plays from the standpoint of dialectics in the theater, and he believes that he can explain the return to a modified Aristotelian form by studying the requisites of the real Galileo material. The "historicizing" of real history cannot be achieved through manipulation and montage. This can be seen in the contrast between Galileo and the Chicago play. "In the case of Galileo he, therefore, had to follow history. In the case of St. Joan he did not have to worry about it." From this Schumacher concludes "that the demonstrative method of acting could consequently be accomplished only with the imitation of conceived events not with events that have been passed down

through history." There is a great deal to support this point of
view: the repetition of the formal difficulties with the Galileo
material while working with the historical material of *Die Tage
der Commune* (*The Days of the Commune*, 1948/49); the unfinished Caesar novel; the failure with *Leben des Konfutse*. Admittedly, *Arturo Ui* also deals with historical subject matter and,
to be sure, with double alienation: Hitler history as gangster history. To top it all off, in Elizabethan style. Only here, the present
was unfinished—there was an open history which allowed itself
to become alienated from itself.

However, the fact is that *Galileo* did not in the least mean that
Brecht had turned from non-Aristotelian dramatics. It mainly
showed remarkable signs of resisting much of the historical subject matter in the transposition to non-Aristotelian theater. This
cannot be considered a subsequent triumph of the Aristotelian
over the non-Aristotelian, for, in spite of it all, Galileo Galilei did
not allow for the catharsis of the spectator: the clever device of
the famous physicist with the revealing self-analysis took care of
this. Yet, a specific difficulty of dialectical theater work had become apparent. Brecht's demand that the realistic manner of writing have breadth and diversity corresponded to the necessity for
dialectics in the stage practice with a wide range of diverse forms
that have depth.

Theater Work

In Diderot's *Paradoxe sur le comédien,* two writers who admire
the theater discuss the themes of drama and the art of acting. One
of the speakers defends the traditional idea that the actor's sensitivity and rapport with certain characters of tragedy and comedy
will determine whether he will be a great actor. Consequently,
only the actor who is truly in love can amount to anything as an
accomplished lover on stage; only a passionate, jealous soul can
play Othello. The other speaker, who clearly represents Diderot's
position, and yet should not be completely identified with Diderot, is of another opinion. He argues that the feelings of a private
individual can never fully coincide with the chart of life and feel-

ings on which a dramatic figure must plot his course. If there should be a coincidence between real life and art in some unusual cases, then it might lend the evening in the theater a certain additional attraction. However, on the whole such a rapport between the actor and the figure to be portrayed is damaging. An actor's greatness depends on his ability to appear real, to imitate, and to exhibit reality—to transform himself, as it were, with great craftsmanship and confidence. This is why superb stage presence is necessary in every moment of the play even when extreme passion is to be expressed.

Diderot shows that this was always the case with the great actors by recalling numerous anecdotes from the theater history of the eighteenth century that supported his argument. The most famous one, which is often quoted, concerns the actress who is dying in the arms of her lover during one scene and complains to him softly about his bad odor. But there is also another highly ingenious example, which Diderot uses for the same purpose, in Molière's *Le Dépit Amoureux,* in which an actor and his wife play a pair of quarrelsome lovers. In reality the actor and his wife detest each other. They succeed in inserting unfriendly prosaic remarks between the lines of the verse dialogue that have meaning in regard to both the play and their own marriage. Is this a sign of "coldness"? For Diderot, it is a factor in dramatic skill. The verity of the stage is not the verity of life but its illusion. "The actor is at his best," remarks Diderot's second speaker, "when he best knows the outward signs of the conceived ideal type and is best able to render it." Whereupon the first speaker responds: "However, he who leaves the least room for the imagination of the great actor is the greatest poet."

As one reads Diderot's dialogue, one finds oneself immersed in a debate about the theater work of Bertolt Brecht. It is not necessary to determine whether Brecht was familiar with Diderot's statements about actors.* The important fact here is the objective historical relationship between Diderot's fight against the theater and drama of his epoch and Brecht's concept of theater work

* He was, of course. In his Danish exile Brecht planned to form an organization of anti-Fascist writers under the name of the "Diderot Society."

(*Theaterarbeit*). The objective historical connection between the dialectical basic ideas of Diderot and Brecht may at the same time even explain the special function of this theater work. The question does not concern analogues or literary parallels but the similarities of the social situation which in both cases must lead to the same theses and paradoxes.

Diderot fights for a bourgeois literature and a bourgeois drama. His enemies are the followers òf the courtly dramatists, Corneille and Racine. Brecht fights against the bourgeois theater. His opponents are the followers of bourgeois dramatic practice, particularly in Germany, the followers who accept the traditional manner of producing plays. Hence, he knows what he is doing when he opposes the followers of the late bourgeois theater, turns from the naturalists, neoromantics, expressionists, and existentialists, rejects the bombastic theater of Max Reinhardt as well as the artificial and dry approach of Leopold Jessner—all this was to question the underlying principles of the bourgeois theater and its audience. The dramaturges of bourgeois dramatic literature who, like Diderot and Lessing, aspired to a higher place, wanted nevertheless to remain on Aristotle's side. Brecht entitled the ninth volume of his Versuche *On a Non-Aristotelian Dramatic Theory* (*Über eine nicht-aristotelische Dramatik*).

The similarities as well as the decisive differences between Diderot and Brecht in regard to their concept of theater are determined by social factors. Both are opponents of that widespread view that the actor is to portray characters in the theater that correspond most to his own natural disposition. In paragraph 50 of *A Short Organum for the Theater,* there is the following sentence: "Just as the actor's task is not to pretend to the audience that it is he himself who is standing on the stage but that it is a fictitious character, it is also his task not to pretend that the events taking place on the stage are not rehearsed and are now happening for the first and only time." In paragraph 48 Brecht had said the following about the *acting* of an actor: "At no moment should he allow himself to be wholly transformed into the figure he is playing. The review which states that 'he didn't play Lear but was Lear' would be a devastating critique." The incriminating sentence was taken from a review by Alfred Kerr and was directed against Kerr, the champion of a bombastic, self-indulgent, "culinary" concept of the theater. After a production of Goethe's *Iphigenie auf Tauris* Kerr had written: "Destiny gave birth to the actor Friedrich Kayssler just so he could play the role of Thoas." Brecht would have considered this an obituary notice for the actor Kayssler. Diderot would have agreed.

The common demand that the actor possess great craftsmanship and conscious artistic skill, along with keen powers of observation and worldly experience, corresponds to the moral and political demand placed on the dramatist in the eyes of both Brecht and Diderot. Diderot, from his bourgeois standpoint, considers the poetic rhetoric of the classical drama in France "false": he compares the historical Henri IV and his real premonitions of death with the Alexandrian couplets depicting Agamemnon's premonitions of death and asserts that it is absurd to assume that Henri IV would have conducted himself and talked in the same manner as Agamemnon does in Racine's play. Diderot brings a real aesthetic problem to a head in a sharp and satirical way. He attempted to introduce bourgeois problems of everyday life on the stage and to ban the kings, martyrs, and heroes of courtly classicism. But he overlooked the other side of the problem: in regard to social conditions of French absolutism, the dramas of Racine and Corneille were able to be "true to life" in spite of the Alexandrian couplets. Diderot was aware of the fact that he was being unjust. However, his criticism still centered decisively on the weak spot of the successors of French classicism: their works and characters had nothing new to convey in the way of consciousness to the new bourgeois theater. This is why he played Shakespeare against the courtly successors. This is why he referred to the example of the Greek tragedians and explained: "They did not merely want to entertain their people but wanted to improve them." Here we have the bourgeois man of the Enlightenment speaking, the moralist who represented the position of social reform in the theater.

Even here the similarity with Brecht is surprising. Brecht expressed his main objection to the culinary theater, which allowed bourgeois entrepreneurs to have the best seats in the house due to high prices, by attacking the moral and social irresponsibility of the late bourgeois theater. There one might enjoy beauty and ugliness, the fate of kings and impoverished figures from Gorki's *Lower Depths,* the frivolity of harmless love quarrels, and a view of the hell in the everyday routine of the bourgeoisie. Max Reinhardt's theater knew how to make everything enjoyable and palliative: miracle plays and bourgeois classics, *Oedipus* and *Lysistrata,* the trial of Joan of Arc, or a marriage tragedy by Strindberg. Yet, even with all its artistic perfection, this theater had no real function at all—aside from its culinary job. To use Diderot's words: it merely wanted "to entertain" the spectator. To entertain by means of humor or horror, beauty or ugliness. However, it did not want "to improve," as Diderot insisted it should, that is, it did not intend to change the spectator.

Brecht made new demands, but from a position that was no longer like that of the bourgeois society. He believed that drama was to fulfill a responsible, didactic task of social transformation. It was not to involve people in an audience merely for the duration of an evening but was to lead to significant social action by providing insights by means of acting and enactment. Consequently, the problem of consciousness in Diderot's "paradox of acting" was given an entirely new meaning. The question no longer concerned the consciousness of an able craftsman who was constantly to remain master of his manner and technique in scenes requiring utmost passion. Now the question dealt with the theater and how it should make the social connections clear and affect the consciousness of the spectator through the acting. Here Brecht is demanding a new type of spectator as well as one with a new social function.

However, this theory of drama required a new, adequate theatrical and stage style. It was not sufficient to turn away from the culinary theater: new dramaturgical and staging methods had to be uncovered for this dramatics. Diderot could no longer be of help here. Much more was demanded from the actor than adaptability, technique, and conscious characterization. It was impossible to think about creating from nothing. Brecht searched for theatrical and dramaturgical traditions with which he might establish a connection. In a conversation with the director Erich Alexander Winds, he explained: "One has to free oneself of the usual prejudice against copying. It is not 'the easier thing' to do. It is not a disgrace but art. That is, it has to be developed into an art. Above all, there can be no rigid patterns that lead to torpidity. Speaking from my own experience with copying, I have borrowed from Japanese, Greek, and Elizabethan plays as a dramatist, have copied the arrangements of the folk comedian Karl Valentin and the skits of Caspar Neher as a director, and I have never felt tied down." Furthermore, "Reality is to be copied in order to influence reality."

Even though it was most important that a dramatist and director be schooled, this did not mean that the actor did not have to study. In an essay entitled *Short Description of a New Technique of Acting (Kurze Beschreibung einer neuen Technik der Schauspielkunst)*, which belongs to Brecht's studies on a non-Aristotelian dramatics, he demands this new manner of acting from the actor: "The position he takes is a position of social criticism." In one poem, Brecht appoints the figures of a drama (meaning also the actors who play these roles) as "accomplices of the playwright" at certain high points. The actor is to have just as much a "critical attitude" as the dramatist.

This is also true of the spectator. If he is to learn something from the events portrayed, then he must remain awake, compare his own experiences with those on the stage cautiously and hesitatingly, and follow the lessons as enacted. This is the reason why Brecht dreamed of smoking spectators who were to sit in rocking chairs. This was to prevent delirious and helpless "empathy." Since Brecht's theater work did not make use of revelry, it was not to produce revelry. The dramatist, director, and actor will do everything to help the spectator in his new attitude in the theater. But the spectator must be ready to allow himself to be helped. Brecht asserts that the art of audience participation must be developed and changed according to new basic principles just like the art of acting and staging. This is the reason why the characters themselves do not succeed in gaining full insight in most of Brecht's plays, whereas the spectator is supposed to achieve this. Joan Dark may remain at the beginning of a discovery; yet the spectator must go further and discover. The good woman of Setzuan may throw up her hands to the gods; yet the spectator is not to imitate her. Mother Courage need not "become fully aware" of the real meaning of the affairs of war and the business of war; yet the spectator should learn what she herself does not learn.

From Brecht's point of view, the theater audiences of the late bourgeois era were not able to fulfill these tasks. He did not have these audiences in mind. He did not want to change an audience filled with Puntilas into revolutionaries while they watched the play about Puntila. He knew what to make out of a character like Puntila both on the stage or in the audience, a type who would announce that he was actually "something of a Communist."

Now, however, with a new audience and with new tasks, a new element of his theater work entered into his productivity on the Schiffbauerdamm in East Berlin: *the endeavor to create artistic beauty in demonstrating social reality*. It has often been asserted that this emphatic allusion to the artistic tasks of his dramatic productions and his dramatic practices in general was a new feature in Brecht's development. This is obviously incorrect: Bertolt Brecht had always conceived his Lehrstücke as poetic works. His dramatic productions were always designed as works of art, even for audiences of exiles and while he was working in misery. The question had already been raised in the essay *New Technique of Acting* whether "a critical attitude is inartistic." Brecht answered with a no. Another essay written in 1940 dealt expressly with the "artistic value of the epic theater." Then there was the essay written on the Zurich production of *Puntila*. The title was *On the Folk Play* (*Über das Volksstück*), and it stressed this point: "The theater which is really cultivated will not have to sell itself by giving up its artistic beauty." The new feature in Brecht's work can be found then not so much in his "rediscovery of the artistic" but in his endeavor to unfold those artistic potentialities of his work and theater to a greater degree in a new society. An inordinate degree of the "artistic" during the time of the struggle against the Nazi state and society would have distracted the people from the more pressing social tasks. On the other hand, the spectators in a new society had, in Brecht's opinion, a right to those beautiful things and blessings that great theater might be able to offer.

This did not mean, however, a return to revelry and culinary theater. The new art of audience participation adhered strongly to the dialectical synthesis of the spectator's consciousness and feeling for the beautiful. It demanded that the new actor be able to present the synthesis of social insight and dramatic and artistic craftsmanship that could be constantly rendered anew. This was Diderot's demand—and yet it is also something completely new. Grace and ability, but at the same time a genuine and extensive knowledge of reality, of human nature and human conditions. The productions of the Berliner Ensemble under Brecht's artistic direction often made this aim beautifully visible.

There is a poem by Brecht written in 1951 which sums this up as a poetic confession. What the poet says here about his own poetry was also true for the entire range of his theater work:

To a Chinese Tea-Root-Lion

The bad ones fear your claws.
The good ones rejoice in your grace.
This
Is what I'd like to hear
Said
About my verse.

Auf einen chinesischen Teewurzellöwen

Die Schlechten fürchten deine Klaue.
Die Guten freuen sich deiner Grazie.
Derlei
Hörte ich gern
Von meinem Vers.

Brecht and the Consequences

Shortly before Brecht's death, one of his assistants, Manfred Wekwerth, recorded a conversation that Brecht had with members of the Berliner Ensemble at the beginning of August 1956. Wekwerth called the recording "The Discovery of an Aesthetic Category" ("Auffindung einer ästhetischen Kategorie"). The discussion centered on *Die Tage der Commune,* which was yet to be performed. During the session Wekwerth made some notes: "Our method of acting cannot be approached in any purely theoretical way. It would be a good idea just to publish living examples of the dialectical method of acting. I mean those unusually beautiful photographs of *The Caucasian Chalk Circle.*" He continues: "Just in general we have to consider dialectics for the theater in a new way. More practical. He thinks it's possible to present an event as actuality." In addition, "all philosophy is interesting for his theater work only insofar as it can help bring about the presentation of social events in an actual manner, nothing more than that." Naturally, as Wekwerth fully realized, these statements do not signify a sudden emergence of dialectical thinking but a culmination. The unity of theory and practice, the basic element of the dialectical process, was carried to perfection by Brecht in his theater work. Yet, in the years before his death, he had to experience—as a playwright who was winning international laurels—more and more frequently that his theoretical writings were being mistaken for pure "philosophy" without reference to the poems, plays, and prose narratives. They were also completely abstracted from his theater work, or some culinary aspects of the traditional theater were found in them so that they allowed the preparation of his plays for the usual theater audiences according to the old recipe and familiar sauce. No consideration was to be given to the non-Aristotelian dramatics and the new art of acting and audience participation in the theoretical writings.

Brecht, who had become a success by 1956, saw himself threatened by the fanatical commentators of *A Short Organum for the Theater,* who were secretly alien to art, or at least alien to the theater. He was also damaged by the productions of *Mother Courage* in the average German municipal theater, which proudly proclaimed its "premiere" after a short period of rehearsals. It would seem from this development that Brecht would have become more rigid in his theater work, emphatically more didactic. Instead he moved toward a discovery of the naïve as an aesthetic category, and this is recorded in his discussion with the members of the Berliner Ensemble. Brecht believed that the naïve was a most natural part of the theater. He did not include it in his writings simply because he assumed that naïveté was there as a matter of course. "Yet, they seriously believe that there would be great beauty in art without naïveté. The naïve is an aesthetic category, the most concrete." Naturalism is not to be confused with naïveté; it is just the opposite.

Once again, Brecht has examples from tradition ready to support his case and not merely from the realm of dramatic literature. Brueghel is naïve in the manner in which he paints "The Fall of Icarus." The aesthetician Hegel is "naïve" in his analysis of literary works, though, to be sure, not in his conclusions. The recorded conversation of August 1956 shows Brecht's relationship to tradition as that of a *negated* relationship in the Hegelian sense of the word. Critical selection, adoption, and establishment. It would seem here that Brecht was following Schiller as dramatist and director with his references to the naïve. Once again, observations on the naïve and sentimental poetry. Yet even here German classicism is *reutilized*. The new naïveté of dramatic acting resulted from the most exact and concrete knowledge of human relations. Brecht's naïveté is not, as it is with Schiller, presentimental. Schiller as a sentimental poet had questioned the possibility of recapturing the ancient naïveté to make it yield productive results for modern art. He considered poetry in a strife-ridden society possible only in the typical forms of the sentimental: the artificial idyll as a Rousseau fantasy and as the dairy farm of Marie Antoinette; the elegy as bereavement over the annihilation of greatness by the vulgar; the satire. Schiller equated the modern poetry of his times with sentimental poetry.

Brecht does not mean Schiller's naïveté when he uses the term *naïve*. According to Wekwerth, Brecht made this remark: "When undifferentiated, the naïve is primitive." Hence we have a new naïveté which can unfold itself on a higher plane when linked to the dialectical process of cognition. Naïveté as synthesis, as negation of negation. For the theater, this must mean understanding the events on stage in their contradictions so exactly that they can be demonstrated just as clearly through the directing and acting of the play. The result is an intelligible, bright, and cheerful theater, not a theater determined by grim, heavy doctrine.

Still, the crucial question always led back to the effect, the effect on the spectator. Brecht's concept of the naïve was not a return to Schiller, nor did *Dialectics in the Theater* signify a return to Hegel, who had said the following about comedy in his *Lectures on Aesthetics*: one has "to distinguish whether the characters are comical for themselves or only for the spectators. We can classify the first case as true comedy which has as its master Aristophanes." A character who is comical to himself and in himself and who simply feels "damned satisfied" in his own skin, as Hegel occasionally phrased it, could not win Brecht's interest in the least. He was concerned most with the comical effect on the spectator. Joviality and jovial recognition. Recognition of contradictions. Naturally, they are all of a different kind whether they be antagonistic or not. In each case it depends on whether the contradictions deal with those within the bourgeois society or in the social development. Brecht had learned this lesson about contradictions by studying Mao Tse-tung toward the end of his life, and had then endeavored to work out the individual kinds of jovial recognition according to whether the true history that was to be portrayed took place in an old or a new social order. This is why the question about the new naïveté had to be discussed right before the play *Die Tage der Commune* was to be produced. It was to present the differences between the bearers of conflicting social concepts as they stood in contrast to one another *and* as they contained contradictions within themselves.

Brecht died while working on this problem. After his death the Berliner Ensemble showed how this new, cultivated naïveté that was rich in knowledge was to be realized in the portrayal of the actual, particularly in the performance of *The Resistible Rise of Arturo Ui*. The volume *Theaterarbeit,* which was edited by Brecht himself, should substantiate this point. To believe that "provocation" lost its object for Brecht with the end of the bourgeois society would mean that a society which was no longer bourgeois did not have any contradictions and therefore did not need to be provoked to recognize contradictions through theater work. Yet, Brecht remained concrete here, without illusions, provocative. He continually endeavored to study the old as well as the new contradictions in order to provoke recognition. A provocative life equals provocative recognition. And once more, at

the very end of his life just as in 1920, there was the contrast
between Brecht and Gottfried Benn. Both died in the summer of
1956.

If one of the elements in his practice of concrete social recognition is overlooked, then it does, in fact, seem as though the
entire work of Brecht reverts to "eschatology." If Brecht is absorbed into the normal repertoire as a classical supporter of
traditional values, and if the director has brainstorms instead of
understanding, then Puntila becomes a "remarkable fellow,"
Mother Courage a "moving heroine," Galileo a "noble man of
patience," and the situation of the stockyards in Chicago appears
as an anachronism in the period of the "second industrial revolution." This can be seen in each instance when the attempt is
made to play "poetry" against consciousness. It might be accepta-
ble for a theater director, but in most recent times it has not
worked for a dramatist who has come after Brecht and has had
to fight it out with Brecht's work and teachings.

This reveals the great difference between Brecht and Friedrich
Dürrenmatt. Dürrenmatt's Schiller speech of 1959 underscored
the fact that one could not separate Brecht's Marxism from his
artistic works, that one could understand the peculiar nature of
his literature only by analyzing its dialectical structure. The
Swiss dramatist characterizes Brecht as an eminently sentimental
poet in Schiller's sense of the word. This is correct if it is set
against Schiller's concept of the naïve (understood in Brecht's
sense of "primitive"). Yet, it still fails to recognize the endeavor
of the sentimental dialectician Brecht to reach a new and higher
naïveté. Four years before the Schiller speech, which was held
in Mannheim, Dürrenmatt had attempted to come to terms with
Brecht in his essay *Problems of the Theater (Theaterprobleme,*
1955): "The world is greater than man. It necessarily has to take
on threatening features that would not be so threatening when
viewed from a point on the outside. Yet, I have no right, nor do
I have the ability to set myself on the outside. Consolation in
poetry is often rather a cheap way out. It is more honest to maintain the human point of view. Brecht's thesis developed in his
'Street Scene'—to take the world as an accident and show how
this accident came about—may make for great theater, and

Brecht has certainly proved this. However, he has had to conceal much of the evidence in his demonstration: Brecht's thinking is inexorable because he will not think about many things inexorably." This is basically an unfair interpretation of Brecht's theater, but it does reveal a great deal about Friedrich Dürrenmatt. Even here we have a dramatic "world without transcendence"—something that many people in turn will take amiss. The observation of mankind and the world "from a point outside" may be consoling and less threatening, but one loses, according to Dürrenmatt, insight in the process. This is the human point of view but not Brecht's dialectical manner of observation.

Toward the end of his life, Brecht lived in an old house on the Chauseestrasse in the northern section of Berlin, and from a window in his study he could look down upon the Dorotheenstädtische cemetery. This is where he lies buried. He had even selected the site of his grave. Only a few feet away from his grave, somewhat diagonally, lies Hegel's grave.

"It was toward noon," Wekwerth states in his report about the conversation on that August day in 1956, "when Brecht took three pages clipped together from a tottering mountain of paper and books. On his advice, his son had written down fifty popular sentences about dialectics, and we were to look through them to see if we could use them for the theater. In his last days, Brecht talked a great deal about dialectics in the theater." Even in one of his last poems, the lesson regarding the unity of contradictions was counted among those things which meant happiness.

PLEASURES

The first view from the window in the morning
The old book found again
Enthusiastic faces
Snow, the turning of the seasons
The newspaper
The dog
The dialectics
To shower, to swim
Old music
Comfortable shoes

To grasp
New music
To write, to plant
To travel
To sing
To be friendly.

VERGNÜGUNGEN

Der erste Blick aus dem Fenster am Morgen
Das wiedergefundene alte Buch
Begeisterte Gesichter
Schnee, der Wechsel der Jahreszeiten
Die Zeitung
Der Hund
Die Dialektik
Duschen, Schwimmen
Alte Musik
Bequeme Schuhe
Begreifen
Neue Musik
Schreiben, Pflanzen
Reisen
Singen
Freundlich sein.

It seems as though this were all merely a compilation of factors that contribute to personal happiness. However, when the words "the dialectics" appear, we have a transition from a happy condition to producing happiness, a transition to an activity which *makes* for happiness. "To be friendly"—that is both infinitive and imperative: a joyful condition and a self-imposed task. On August 14, 1956, Brecht died in Berlin.

Friedrich Dürrenmatt:
The Worst Possible Turn
of Events

The fact that many of our present-day spectators see nothing but nihilism in my plays is merely a reflection of their own nihilism.

Dürrenmatt in a note to *Die Wiedertäufer* (1967)

After the premiere of a new play by Dürrenmatt the reviews almost always contend that the work lacks formal and internal unity. Even when Dürrenmatt constantly uses the general term *comedy* as a designation for works of a highly different nature, he cannot conceal the fact that it applies only to one basic element in his plays, often just a surprise effect. The critics argue that Dürrenmatt's productions are in need of central themes and ideas to hold them together. Thus far, his works have shown themselves to be rather spotty attempts to dramatize a comical idea. Sometimes they stretch a mere paradoxical statement into a play and sometimes into a prose narrative, as in the novel *Grieche sucht Griechin* (*Once a Greek*) and in *Die Panne,* the short-story version of the radio play *Traps.*

In actuality all Dürrenmatt's works can be clearly arranged and classified. The transition from one literary genre to another does not have to be forced but develops from a new intellectual situation and from structural necessity. Even the detective novels of his earlier period are anything but the embarrassing products of a writer who had to scrape money together to support his family, and hence, it would be best not to talk about them. In fact, they are authentic Dürrenmatt and belong to the volume of his early prose works which he himself edited under the title *Die Stadt* (*The City*). Here the connection between the novel *Der Richter und sein Henker* (*The Judge and His Hangman*), which has been called trivial literature; the early story *Pilatus,* written in 1946; and his first great drama *Es steht geschrieben* (*Thus It Is Written*) is evident.

It is also easy to distinguish the phases of Dürrenmatt's gradual break from his literary mentors. At the beginning Dürrenmatt's dramas were influenced by the German playwright Frank Wedekind, who had schooled Brecht. The composition of various scenes that revealed a dependence on Wedekind brought forth the usual accusation of plagiarism from Wedekind's widow. Dürrenmatt, who was thirty-one at the time and already well-known as the author of *Romulus the Great* (*Romulus der Grosse*) and *The Marriage of Mr. Mississippi* (*Die Ehe des Herrn Mississippi*), wrote his reply in the Zurich *Tageszeitung* on August 9, 1952, giving it the title "Confessions of a Plagiarizer." Basically the early work of Dürrenmatt was a highly productive falling-out with Wedekind. It ended temporarily with *Mississippi.*

After this, there was a new rift which proved to be productive— this time with Brecht. It began with the first version of *Ein Engel kommt nach Babylon* (*An Angel Comes to Babylon*) and ended with *The Physicists* (*Die Physiker*), which had its premiere on February 20, 1962. This comedy, which was intended to counter Brecht's *Galileo,* can be considered another caesura in his development. The dramas that have followed from this point, *Der Meteor* (*The Meteor*) and the new version of his first work *Es steht geschrieben* with a different title, *Die Wiedertäufer* (*The Anabaptists*), seem to represent a return to the philosophical and literary position of the early Dürrenmatt.

Behind all these breaks with his literary mentors, there is a basic theme that persists in all his works. Dürrenmatt is far from sacrificing the actual structure of his work to ingenious ideas. It is the other way around: Dürrenmatt is a master at transforming all structure into a new formation of themes and investigations. This is a skill that he has had ever since his debut in the literary limelight, and he has stubbornly held onto this skill and has constantly modified it.

In his superb essay *Problems of the Theater* (*Theaterprobleme*, 1955), Dürrenmatt has written that "the world is greater than man and perforce takes on threatening features that would not be so threatening if one could view them from outside. However, I do not have the right nor the ability to place myself outside. It is rather a cheap way to find solace in poetry. It is much more honest to retain the human point of view."

This has always been Dürrenmatt's starting point. Basically, Dürrenmatt works with a theology without God in his plays. The original situation of man is paradoxical; yet God does not take on a meaning or explain things—even if he may have meant something in the past. In an early short story, *Der Tunnel*, a "chubby" young man, about twenty-four, undoubtedly a self-portrayal, travels on the lackadaisical commuter train from Zurich in the direction of Olten. On the dull, routine trip the train passes through an interminably long tunnel which leads into the middle of the earth. "What should we do?" the conductor yelled into the ear of the young man as the train roared through the walls that raced toward them. The chubby man's body was useless now and could not protect him. It was planted against the windowpane that separated him from the abyss. With his eyes wide open he was soaking everything in for the first time. " 'What should we do?' 'Nothing,' he answered mercilessly without turning his face from the scene that meant death. He did show, however, a ghostlike serenity while glass splinters were strewn about. They came from the broken dashboard, while two balls of cotton shot above them as swift as arrows into the ʾnnel. They had been caught up in a draft which had suddenly broken through, and the first crack became visible in the windowpane. 'Nothing. God let us fall, and so we're plunging right at him.' " This is the way it is. God let us fall. And yet, this means that there must have been a God at one time. This is also what the governor Pilate realizes in the story, written in 1946, that bears his name. As the Son of Man entered the courtroom, the Roman governor still thought of him as "a god." After the flagellation he knew without question that he was God himself. "It's clear that all those things—the legions and the burning torches, the stake which extended into heaven, the rough square stones of the walls, the hard surface of the ground, the soft breathing of the slaves, and the massive fires of the stars—all were there because God was there, and it was him and nobody else. They were all there because there is no other means of understanding between man and God except death, and no other grace except the curse, and no other love except hate."

The strands in the dramatic works of Friedrich Dürrenmatt are held together by this outlook. God is there, but he is useless in human relations. Man must learn to master these relations himself, even the dramatist, who works with fictional figures created in man's image. For Dürrenmatt, the son of a pastor, transcendence is always present but mainly as the opposite position and a threat. When Dürrenmatt calls for the preservation of the "human point of view," he does not do so because he is considering a move toward "existentialism" and the "integral atheism" of Sartre. On the contrary, the critic Dürrenmatt denounced Sartre's most important play on this subject, *Lucifer and the Lord,* as a "most devious type of weapon," something like "philosophical brass knuckles."

Dürrenmatt himself has no desire to be a star slugger along Sartre's lines. In his work, death dies. Meaningless death. Corpses pile up on the stage. Farcical death is experienced, and one is disconcerted about not being able to understand and explain the deaths. In the strange case of the "meteor" Schwitter, one even reaches the point of becoming upset by the fact that he does not die. Religion is inhumane. It is only capable of disturbing because it makes a farce out of serious humane things. The prime minister in the religious play about the angel in Babylon has the following to teach: "If heaven becomes real due to the appearance of the angel, human order collapses, since the state is perforce reduced to a farce when confronted by a visible heaven, and the result of this comical mess is this: a people has risen up against us. Why? Because we did not solemnize the marriage fast enough. An angel just has to flutter about, and already the people begin to lose their respect for us."

When the other world, the world above, makes itself visible on earth, it causes nothing but trouble. The writer and Nobel prize-winner Schwitter, likened to a "meteor," has been falsely pronounced dead by highly competent doctors. So we are not involved in a trite farce. Not at all. Dürrenmatt's comedy depends on the double death of this famous man. Lazarus rising from the dead with worldwide coverage by press, radio, and television. This is the reason for the exact diagnosis: the show is stolen, to sum up the situation correctly, by some "metaphysical" proceedings.

This is Dürrenmatt's basic theme. His main concern is to portray the condition of a world that must manage itself without God. This is why it is anything but a joyous exultation when Dürrenmatt replies to his critics in the note to one of his recent plays, *Die Wiedertäufer,* that he who sees only nihilism in the comedy merely reflects his own.

It is from this theme that Dürrenmatt has derived all his dramaturgical theory and practice. In a remarkable analysis of *Es steht geschrieben,* Beda Allemann makes the observation about Dürrenmatt's works that "tragedy itself as the way of life of the western world is threatened by parody." The death of the hero is no longer possible "because the pathos with which this death would have to be expressed would sound incredible." Allemann has demonstrated that Dürrenmatt has found an answer to this dilemma by replacing "the tragic death with death by the hangman." It is quite well known that the theme of death by the hangman and judge plays an essential role in the early works of Dürrenmatt. Later on he concentrates on this question in the famous *Nächtliches Gespräch mit einem verachteten Menschen (A Noctural Talk with a Despised Person)*, published in 1957 but written, as Dürrenmatt has informed us, in 1951. A talk between the hangman and his victim. The tragic death of a revolutionary who gives a farewell speech is no longer possible. In this nocturnal talk, the victim comes to realize: "What a comedy! I fight for freedom and yet don't even have a weapon in my hand to shoot the hangman in my own house." Here the nexus of guilt and atonement takes on the features of a parody.

Even though Dürrenmatt has sought to replace death by the hangman with murder and other devices of the mystery novel in his later works, he has remained basically true to his principle. In the gangster opera *Frank the Fifth* murder is piled upon murder and can be matched only by those that occur in comic books. The effect is the same: the audience is not shaken in any tragic sense when someone is killed but tends to be more relieved when someone is killed off once again. The three murdered nurses in *The Physicists*, especially the third one, who is strangled following and during a love scene, are intended only to cause mirth, not the Aristotelian catharsis of emotions. It is just as in a mystery novel or film where no one thinks of feeling for one of the people who must be murdered. What matters most is finding the murderer and bringing him to justice. Because of this the numerous murders that occur in Dürrenmatt's dramas stem from the same considerations that obliged Brecht to give up the requirement of the theatrical death. To repeat Dürrenmatt's words: "For us, only comedy is possible." Naturally it must be a comedy that knows how to get along with corpses.

Dürrenmatt also reconsidered and modified the theme of alienation in his early theoretical writings. On February 22, 1952, the Zurich magazine *Die Weltwoche* printed an essay *A Note on Comedy (Anmerkung zur Kömodie)* by its drama critic, who at that time was Friedrich Dürrenmatt. Here Dürrenmatt already showed signs of taking a stand against the genre of tragedy, as he did three years later in his more detailed study *Problems of the Theater*. Dürrenmatt argued that a writer of tragedies can fall back on the myths at hand and modify each one according to the times. On the other hand it is impossible to think of the writer of comedies, as far back as Aristophanes, who did not have his own original ideas. "Nevertheless, Aristophanes becomes relevant only when he takes up the question of distance. The tragedies portray the past as present in order to make us tremble . . . . Aristophanes does it the other way around. It is because his comedies take place in the present that he is able to create distance, and I believe that this is essential for a comedy." Here

Dürrenmatt takes a position as dramaturge that is actually close to Brecht's idea of epic theater. It is interesting that Dürrenmatt defined the limitations of Brecht's essay *Street Scene (Die Strassenszene)* three years later but also used the same ideas as his starting point: to give the spectator an actual event in a form that provides distance.

Even in *Problems of the Theater* Dürrenmatt is not completely successful in providing the necessary distance between his basic tenets that concern distancing and the actuality of comedy and those of Brecht. "Brecht's thesis developed in his *Street Scene*— to take the world as an accident and show how this accident came about—may make for great theater, and Brecht has certainly proved this. However, he has had to conceal most of the evidence in his demonstration. Brecht's thinking is inexorable because he will not think about many things inexorably." These are witty words, nothing more. At present Dürrenmatt stands right between the tradition of Aristotelian drama and the Brechtian school of drama, which takes an anti-Aristotelian course. It is also incorrect to say that Dürrenmatt has opposed Brecht from the beginning on the issue of the function of the dramatic event. In his *Note on Comedy* of 1952 Dürrenmatt is far from demanding a theater without purpose or even a theater of the absurd such as Ionesco was promoting at the time. Comedy is a theater of its times and depends on flashes of inspiration. "It is discomforting but necessary. The tyrants of our planet are not moved by the works of poets. They yawn at their lamentations. They consider their heroic epics silly fairy tales. They fall asleep upon reading their religious poetry. There is only one thing they fear from their poets—their mockery." This sentence alone could have also been written by Brecht.

As in the case of Brecht, and yet completely independent of Brecht, Dürrenmatt was fascinated by trivial literature, and an intensive study of his plays and theoretical works will show that this began during the early 1950's. Light comedies, mystery novels, cabaret skits. All these along with a rejection of so-called "serious art." This was also true of Brecht during the 1920's.

The combination Dürrenmatt-Brecht has some definite objective and historical features. Dürrenmatt's initial phase seems to be a repetition twenty-five years later of Brecht's. This has nothing to do with literary metaphysics but with the given realities of literature and theater at the end of the bourgeois period. Dürrenmatt and Brecht share the same starting point. The abstract nature of this combination has taken on an added dimension for Dürrenmatt and has become second nature in that he has become conscious of the dialectical correspondences through a study of Brecht's works and theories. This is why the essay *Problems of the Theater* cannot be taken as a real resolution yet, and it is also the reason why Dürrenmatt returns to this theme once again in his Schiller speech of 1959.

In the meantime the dramatist Dürrenmatt has moved closer and closer to the playwright Brecht. After *The Marriage of Mr. Mississippi,* which had been a great success and simultaneously had led up a dead end, it was apparent that Dürrenmatt began more and more to employ Brechtian motifs. It was unmistakable especially in the second version of the comedy *An Angel Comes to Babylon,* as it was also in *The Visit* and most of all in *Frank the Fifth,* "the opera about a private bank," which was not a plagiarism of *The Threepenny Opera,* as was so readily assumed, but an attempt to give a new purpose to Brecht's idea. For Brecht, even gangsters are good citizens. For Dürrenmatt, the good citizens are actually gangsters.

The Schiller speech given in Mannheim during 1959 was to have established the dialectical interchanges between Dürrenmatt and Brecht, and it was also supposed to have determined the differences as well as the similarities between the two writers more closely than ever before. Brecht is dead, but for Dürrenmatt he is more alive than ever before. According to Dürrenmatt, Brecht is in our times the epitome of the "sentimental poet" in Schiller's meaning of the term. Marxism is an integral part of Brecht's artistry, and Dürrenmatt's speech makes this clear to all critics who want to separate the pure poet Brecht from mere communism no matter whether their approach be positive or negative. "It has been upsetting to see that the greatest German dramatist in our times who believed in acting humanely and took the side of revolution asks us to answer the question about our present state. Do we actually have an answer, or do we pretend that we have one?"

Now that we are familiar with Dürrenmatt's play *The Physicists,* we can look back at the Schiller speech of 1959 and see both his involvement with Brecht and the beginnings of his opposition and rejection of Brecht, which three years later was to lead to the rejection of *Galileo* and Brecht's dramatic theory of purpose. Toward the end of the Schiller speech, where the middle section about Brecht as a sentimental poet came to a close and Dürrenmatt began talking about a new confrontation of our times with Schiller's period, there is a remark that is directed simultaneously against Schiller and Brecht: "It is our task to determine anew what belongs to the state, what belongs to the individual, where we are to adapt, where we are to resist, and where we are free. The world has changed itself not so much through political revolutions, as everyone assumes, as through the population explosion, through the necessary development of an automated world, through the compulsory transformation of homelands into states, people into masses, love of the homeland into loyalty to the firm." A sentence following this passage can now be considered the intellectual seed of the play about the three physicists, for Dürrenmatt believes that it is incumbent upon him to probe the following issue: "The old revolutionary dogma that man can and must change the world has become impractical for the individual and has been taken back. This principle is still useful for the masses but only as a slogan, as political dynamite, as inducement for the people, as hope for the gray armies of the starving."

This is Dürrenmatt's first real answer to Brecht. Though the 1959 Schiller speech unmistakably questioned whether the contemporary world could be reproduced on the stage and whether theater could change the world, it did so in an unobtrusive way In 1955, when Brecht was critically ill, he sent a letter to the Darmstadt Conference of Dramaturges asserting that it was possible to make the contemporary world visible on stage and also to bring the spectator to recognize and change the world with the help of the play that shows it correctly. "In an age where science knows how to change nature to such an extent that the world almost seems livable, man cannot continue for long to describe man as a victim, an object in an unknown world with fixed conditions. From the standpoint of a billiard ball, it is difficult to conceive of the laws of motion." In 1955 this was Brecht's answer to Dürrenmatt, who had praised the victim in *The Marriage of Mr. Mississippi* and had raised the question whether it was at all possible to reproduce the contemporary world in the theater. Therefore, Brecht's answer implies the name Friedrich Dürrenmatt in its very first lines. It is not the perspective of the victim, nor the standpoint of the billiard ball. The development of science has created the possibility for "humane and decent" social conditions. Hence, the world can be reproduced in the theater but only when it is considered changeable. And who should do the changing? Brecht's response: "I have maintained for many years that this is possible and am now living in a state where an enormous effort is being made to change society."

Only when Brecht's tenets have been included in the Brecht-Dürrenmatt dialogue can one understand some of the sentences in Dürrenmatt's Schiller speech that stipulate the opposite: the development of modern science has not only continued to make the earth unlivable but has also made it possible to divide natural and social science so that both can be annihilated. Here Brecht's thesis that a changeable world cries out for change is answered by Dürrenmatt from a sociological point of view: the changing of the world by the individual "has become impractical . . . has been taken back."

From here Dürrenmatt moved to the play *The Physicists,* which once again picked up all his early themes: the value or senselessness of sacrifice, the impossibility that the individual can influence the course of the world, comedy with dead people, the playwright's effectiveness or ineffectiveness in regard to changing the world. In spite of all this, Dürrenmatt did not simply dramatize the ideas in his Schiller speech of 1959. The play itself meant taking a new position—a new one also vis à vis Brecht. The twenty-one points in the afterword of the play about the physicists make that clear.

Here it is worthwhile to consider the poet Gottfried Benn's

objection to Dürrenmatt's *The Marriage of Mr. Mississippi.* Even
though it was made ten years earlier, it still applies to *The Physicists.* Benn seldom took an interest in contemporary literature,
but this one time he remarked that the author of the remarkable
play *Mississippi* had not shown enough respect for the strict division between the two worlds of art and life. As the critic of
Friedrich Dürrenmatt, Benn postulated that "art is something
concrete if it is real art. It brings about and demands decision.
Now what about the decision of our author? Is it possible to give
expression to the inner condition of modern man on stage, to
both his basic features, the individualistic side and the side conditioned by his birth, when time and space have been atomized,
and when it is no longer possible geographically to choose either
the south with its cypress trees or the north with its apple trees?"
The inference here about a play that deals with absolute justice
and sacrifice is that "one is forced to say that the author who tries
to make things relative and discuss them is often not at all successful in separating himself from his characters."

With this remark, Gottfried Benn hit upon the prime difficulty
in Dürrenmatt's dramaturgy. However, the playwright's response
(or nonresponse) concerning the purpose or purposelessness of
his plays has basically little to do with Benn or Brecht. That is,
little to do with the apodictic division between life and art set
by the poet of soliloquies, or with the "sentimental" works of a
Marxist, who would like to change the world with the help of
the stage. Still, Dürrenmatt's negative attitude cannot avoid the
contradictions it generates. For some time it had seemed as
though Dürrenmatt's dramatic works presented only various versions of the necessity and greatness of human sacrifice. However,
it was already apparent from Ill's sacrifice in *The Visit* that tragic
greatness was lacking. The relationship between the old lady and
the town of Güllen no longer allowed for the traditional play of
guilt and atonement. In *The Physicists,* the total "sacrifice,"
which the physicist Möbius wanted to take upon himself—"that
it is the duty of a genius to be misunderstood today"—is neither
tragic nor successful. At least Ill's sacrifice had guaranteed the
little town of Güllen some prosperity for a while, as is borne out
by the frightening final chorus. However, Möbius' decision to

give up his research remained of no consequence, for the "old lady" in this new play could still consolidate her monopoly of world domination or world annihilation with the help of the research he recanted. If it had originally seemed that Dürrenmatt leaned toward those ideas that Benn had put forth in his radio play *The Voice Behind the Curtain* (*Die Stimme hinter dem Vorhang*), written exactly ten years before *The Physicists*—"Living in darkness we do what we can"—then Möbius' case shows that even this is no longer possible with the situation in society the way it is. The physicist Johann Wilhelm Möbius would like to live in darkness and abandon his research and active life. Yet here the eighteenth point in Dürrenmatt's thesis at the end of *The Physicists* proves to be true: "Each attempt made by an individual to solve a problem that concerns everyone must fail." Brecht's philosophy seems preferable here to Benn's? Or is it?

The reason for this question can be found in Dürrenmatt's *Writings on the Theater* (*Theaterschriften*): "The course I have taken with my dramas cannot be comprehended at first glance. It has made the transition from 'thinking about the world' to 'thinking of worlds,' without dropping the comic and playfulness as its means. All this was done not to criticize philosophical, scientific, or theological thinking but to become concerned with something else. *Frank the Fifth* takes this direction, not as an economic play —it would be too naïve and superficial for this—but as a work about a fictitious model. What kind of a model? Of possible human relations." As a dramatist, Dürrenmatt does not interpret the world because this is not his task. Nevertheless, the events in the contemporary world can definitely be grasped as part of the plots and situations of his plays—either by the critic or by the spectator—and interpreted. Dürrenmatt has admitted this. He finds it quite understandable that a spectator (even though he is not always a critic) should relate the actions of the characters on stage to his own reality. It is difficult to predict and certainly cannot be predicted dramaturgically what will come of this. Dürrenmatt does not seem to acknowledge the dialectical relationship between theory and practice in the Brechtian sense. Evidently he would never think of founding a new art of writing plays in the manner of Brecht, nor of initiating a new "art of participation" for the audience. Once again we have different ideas about the possibility for change in the world.

The final point of Dürrenmatt's thesis at the end of *The Physicists* summarizes his view about the connection between the substance and purpose of a viable theater for the present, and it departs from the thinking of both Brecht and Benn: "Drama can trick the spectator into contending with reality, but it cannot force him to resist it or even master it." The point here is that individual sacrifices have no meaning today. The individual cannot save the world by making a sacrifice, nor can he basically change it by his thinking and actions even if he be the greatest physicist in the history of mankind. The period in which great individuals such as heroes and saints changed the world appears to have come to an end for Dürrenmatt. Hence, we are led to the conclusion emphasized in point seventeen: "The problem that concerns everyone can only be resolved by everyone." Physicists are to deal with physics, that is, with research in physical science. The results of their work, however, concern everyone. Therefore, only all of mankind together, according to Dürrenmatt, can avoid the worst possible turn of events.

The third point of Dürrenmatt's thesis reads: "A story has only been thought to its finish when it has taken its worst possible turn." One must be familiar with this sentence if one is to grasp the meaning of that other sentence which appears in the afterword of his comedy *Die Wiedertäufer* (1967). Once again Dürrenmatt adds a dramaturgical self-interpretation to one of his plays. After making some reflections, he ends his chain of thought with the following formulation: "The worst possible turn a story can take is the turn to comedy."

If one were to attempt to draw a logical conclusion from these two sentences, which were conceived five years apart (1962 and 1967), then the synthesis would have to read: *"A story is thought to its finish when it has taken a turn to comedy."* We have here, possibly, a guideline that can help us grasp the operations and intentions of the playwright Friedrich Dürrenmatt. The formula is certainly applicable for the author's new adaptation of some of his earlier material. The course taken by Dürrenmatt's first play, *Es steht geschrieben,* up to the reshaping of the material into the comedy about the Anabaptists shows the turning point of the story into the comical. In his collected works *Es steht geschrieben* has the subtitle "A Drama." The new version with the Anabaptist title is presented as "A Comedy in Two Parts." These are admittedly superficial indexes, but they are nevertheless connected with a fundamental change. The biblical title was replaced by one that is objective and historical. With this, *Die Wiedertäufer* took a place next to *The Physicists*. When Dürrenmatt began to make a drama out of this material, he was a twenty-five-year-old student of German and philosophy who basically knew that he would not receive his "passport diploma" in either field. On the other hand, the comedy dealing with the Anabaptists (1967) was written by a famous playwright who in the meantime had been putting his own dramatic theories into practice. They all had the same starting point: tragedy is no longer possible in our time. "Only comedy is possible for us." Hence, we have the origin of comedies in which a story leads to the worst conceivable ending: the perversion of human misfortune through laughter. Of course, this laughter is legitimate, not simply cold-hearted.

Es steht geschrieben was typical of his entire early work, which constantly propounded the primacy of sacrifice over any type of action. The sufferer stood morally and metaphysically higher than the man of action. Here the young Dürrenmatt proved himself to be a conscious disciple of Frank Wedekind and the expressionist dramatists. The ideal situation for all of Dürrenmatt's early plays was set by Wedekind's comedy *Der Marquis von Keith*. Wedekind's two tragicomical Don Quixotes, Keith and Scholz, symbolized a twofold failure that had a comic effect. On the one hand there is the adventurer whose energy is sapped by the yearning for the respectability of the bourgeois life, and on the other there is the confirmed moralist, who would like to play the enterprising *bon vivant* but is prevented from doing this by his own moral scruples. In both cases, their consciences make them into pitiful and comical fools. The defeated moralist Scholz retires in the end to an insane asylum of his own will. This was Dürrenmatt's ideal dramatic situation. One can see traces of it not only in *The Marriage of Mr. Mississippi* but also in *The Physicists*. Even the "meteor" Schwitter has something left over from the Marquis of Keith, and Dürrenmatt has revealed that he had thought of giving the immortal Nobel prize-winner, who destroys everything around him, a counterpart. Then we would have had another Dürrenmatt version of Ernst Scholz.

In the play *Es steht geschrieben*, the roles of Keith and Scholz are unmistakenly taken by the Anabaptists Knipperdollinck and Bockelson. The rich burgher Knipperdollinck is the descendant of the rich moralist Ernst Scholz, who is a fool according to the laws of his surroundings. With Dürrenmatt, this character is truly serious about the evangelical promise, in other words, about the "spirit of utopia." So he falls into the hands of Jan Bockelson from Leiden, who desires only to have great adventures and to enjoy himself, and knows that he will be beaten to pulp if he fails.

Dürrenmatt built his parable play in the first version around the common features of these two men. They danced together in a neoexpressionist scene entitled "The Dance on the Roof," a lyrical, wildly romantic pas de deux, which let loose a theater scandal at the 1948 premiere in Zurich. And they were together in the final scene of the drama moaning and dying on the wheel. Bockelson remains silent in the end, but Knipperdollinck, who represents the primacy of human sacrifice, is given the last word by Dürrenmatt. The victorious Count von Hessen watches the dying man and remarks that Knipperdollinck has led a meaningless life. "Despised by everyone." However, the aged Bishop of Münster, Dürrenmatt's mouthpiece in this play, who was wisely left unchanged in the new version, replies: "The meaning is in their pain." The count accuses the defeated men of having lost God. Once again the bishop answers: "Blessed are those who find him again on the wheel."

Knipperdollinck praises God while dying on the wheel: "The depth of my despair can only be equated with your justice, and my body lies on this wheel as in a cup which you in all your mercy are now filling to the brim."

Dürrenmatt's alternative verion of 1967, *Die Wiedertäufer*, has essentially retained the plot action of *Es steht geschrieben*. He never contemplated writing a historical drama. As a child,

Dürrenmatt had a popular book on world history in his father's parsonage, and he read about the Peasants' War, the emperor Charles the Fifth, the three cages with the executed ringleaders on top of the tower of the Lamberti Church of Münster. "And so, Münster became for me during the next thirty-seven years the epitome of a very particular city, a city of rebellion, of hope and defeat, a city that was naturally more imaginary than real."

In both versions, the events are more imaginary than real. But in *Die Wiedertäufer* the story took its worst possible turn for Dürrenmatt: the turn to the comic. This serves to enhance the play's fundamentally new dramaturgical idea. The original equation of Knipperdollinck with Bockelson is dropped, and Bockelson alone becomes the center of the new comedy. Dürrenmatt was quick to make use of the fact he picked up from historical sources that this man Bockelson, who became king of the New Jerusalem in Westphalia, had been a tailor's apprentice, a bartender, a manager of a brothel in his homeland Holland, and had sometimes tried his hand at acting. These part-time occupations of the historical John of Leiden become his main occupations in the play.

The utopia that is realized in Münster is ruled by an actor. Even worse, it is an actor who was previously a flop. The Bishop of Münster, Minden, and Osnabrück, a patron of the theater, did not think him worthy enough to act in the elite ensemble of the espiscopal court theater. The neglected actor revenged himself by driving the bishop out of the city and demonstrating great talent as a thespian. Unfortunately, not on the stage but on the contemporary world scene. The result of his personal failure in the theater is terrible misfortune for everyone. However, the causes and consequences in this story about an actor turn into a joking matter. The sacrificial death of the Anabaptist Matthison is also a joking matter. Here we have a man who remains credible and sacrifices himself while others are making a business out of the faith. His head is brought to the bishop.

The pronouncement made by the ancient bishop over the head of his enemy was also in the first version. There it was an incidental scene. Now it is the core of the new comedy. Since the actor from Leiden, Bockelson, has succeeded the true believer,

Matthison, the bishop is now able to recognize the true pattern: "As a friend of actors I am now faced with a fanatic actor desirous of playing all the great roles, driven by a vulgar imagination, experienced on the stage, stuffed with all sorts of literature and hackneyed phrases. He is more dangerous than you. Be satisfied, you baker from Haarlem, your death was ludicrous. Don't be bothered about it. The only thing that will continue to exist, prophet, is that which annoys us and makes us laugh."

The end of the play is both excruciating and comical because it is so thoroughly vile. King Bockelson betrays his people, who are starving in the besieged city of Münster. He opens up the gates to the rulers and causes a frenetic wave of plunder and murder. He himself escapes with his life and finally becomes the star of the episcopal ensemble. Some unknown Anabaptist in Münster who faints from torture is presented to the people as the alleged Bockelson who will be executed. The real Bockelson, actor of a total theater, sums up the action in front of the victorious princes: "I played a king and theatrically recited a farcical text filled with biblical passages and dreams of a better world that the people dream about in their way."

At the end of the comedy there is the confrontation between the bishop, who returns home, and Knipperdollinck, who is dying, as in the original version. This time, however, Dürrenmatt gives the final word to the bishop and patron of the theater: "The man granted salvation is tortured to death; the tempter is saved; the tempted, butchered; the victorious, mocked by their victory. The court has been soiled by the judges; the crowd, made up of guilt and error, perception and frenzy, breaks up in disgrace. Now, Knipperdollinck, grace, trickling between the bloody spokes, points its accusing finger at me."

In true expressionist tradition this comedy conglomerate, which plays both with life and the theater, closes with an open question. However, it is not a cry like that in Wolfgang Borchert's *Draussen vor der Tür* (*The Man Outside,* 1947) but a soft comment spoken by an old man talking to himself: "This inhumane world must become humane. But how? But how?"

One is supposed to laugh about this story. This is Dürrenmatt's dramaturgical intent. But one is not supposed to be happy about the laughter. "Nothing is more comical than misfortune," says Mother Nell in her garbage can at one point in Beckett's *Endgame*.

At the end of *Die Wiedertäufer* there is a real-life torture and murder. However, the actor Bockelson returns to the stage after his monumental flight onto the world stage. This is a new Dürrenmatt. He has gone beyond Wedekind and beyond Brecht. Just as in the beginning of his literary career, the life substance seems to be penetrating his work more and more strongly—the relation between the man and his work. Along with this, we can see that a new qualitative change has become possible: from the worst possible turn of events to comedy, there is now a turn to a realm which allows for tragic situations. A new form of tragedy as the highest form of comedy thought to its finish. One will have to wait to see how it turns out.

Günter Grass and Thomas Mann:

Aspects of the Novel

"You can begin a story in the middle and create confusion by striking out boldly, backward and forward. You can be modern and do away with time and distance, or afterward proclaim or let it be proclaimed that you have finally, at the last moment, solved the space and time problem. Or you can declare at the very start that it's impossible to write a novel nowadays, but then, behind your own back so to speak, fire off a best seller, a novel to end all novels. I have also been told that you can look good and modest if you begin by saying: it is no longer possible for the novel to have heroes because there are no individualities, because individuality is a thing of the past, because man—each man and all men together—is alone in his loneliness and no one is entitled to individual loneliness, and all men taken together form a lonely mass without names and heroes."

As the ironic stance seems to indicate, we are apparently dealing here with another modern contribution to those popular television programs and panel discussions about the problem of the modern novel and the difficulties in writing faced by contemporary writers. The speaker—for the rhetorical tone is unmistakable —obviously does not believe that there is such a great crisis of the novel. He is even less prepared to admit that a theoretical debate about novel-writing can itself serve as a new form of the novel— "instead of a novel" as it were, or as "a novel of a novel."

However, the "easy" tone is deceptive, and the sentences quoted above are not taken from a symposium. The text continues in the following manner: "All this may be true and correct. But for me, Oskar, and my keeper Bruno, the facts are, however, different: we are both heroes, very different heroes—he on his side of the peephole, and I on my side; and even when he opens the door, the two of us, with all our friendship and loneliness, are still far from being a mass with names and heroes."

We have, then, the first chapter of *The Tin Drum* (*Die Blechtrommel*). Oskar Matzerath expounds upon his situation in the mental hospital, introduces his friend and keeper Bruno, shows himself to be superbly informed about the difficulties in writing prose narratives and about literary discussions, yet favors the position of the conservative narrator from the old school.

The ironical confusion is at its high point. Günter Grass has begun to narrate a story whose strange situation at the onset can only be compared with Kafka's *Metamorphosis* or *The Penal Colony*. Immediately after the literary theoretical introduction and exposition of the narrative framework have been concluded, we are told how the future Anna Matzerath came into being under the skirts of Anna Bronski. Since the author of *The Tin Drum* uses Oskar to proclaim the principle of a narrative tradition and to dismiss the talk about the crisis of the novel as mere brooding, he proves just the opposite—he reveals the justification of those misgivings about the traditional mode of narration, misgivings which do not trouble the dwarflike biographer and novelist Oskar Matzerath.

For Oskar, Oskar is a hero, and his keeper Bruno is one also. Individuals in the good old sense of the word. In the period of the Sturm und Drang one would have spoken about them as "original geniuses." Tradition demands that the hero of a novel must, however, correspond to epic probability. Whether one talks here about "inner truth" or makes an attempt with the vocables of realism, all the work is done according to the principles of mimesis, the imitation of live events in arts, whenever the hero of the novel is concerned.

Yet, will one be able to say that the story of Oskar (including his parents and grandparents) was composed according to mimetic principles? Doubts arise immediately while reading the novel. Grass intended this. It is part of his method of composition. Everything apparently flows in the mainstream of the tradition of the novel. In fact, it has been frequently asserted that a remarkable and charming amalgamation had originated in *The Tin Drum* consisting of a Bildungsroman and a picaresque novel. Hence, we have Oskar Matzerath as a follower simultaneously of Lesage's Gil Blas and Goethe's Wilhelm Meister. Yet the hero of the Bildungsroman takes a path through society, enters into it, sometimes climbs the social ladder, and even develops himself. After much too much contact with society, he expressly and decisively departs, as is often the case in the works of Hermann Hesse. No matter what the case may be, he is always viewed in a social sense.

With Oskar Matzerath, there is nothing at all like this. He has no conflicts with his environment and society, is actually a monad and locked off from it. As Leibniz would say, Oskar is a "monad without windows." There is no connecting path between Oskar and his environment. For society, Oskar is a monstrosity, and depending on the reader, one sympathizes with him, hates him, or makes excuses for him. In one of his remarks to the reader, he himself formulates it like this: "Never has a person—if you are ready to view me as a human being . . . experienced a more disappointing Christmas celebration than Oskar." On the other hand, society is for Oskar a mere object for reflection. It becomes a pretext for him to discover and bring out a new consciousness. No conflict between Oskar and the family. This is a relationship without anger and grief. As objective narrator, he calls his presumptive father simply Matzerath. When his mother dies, he writes: "I couldn't cry because all the others, the men and grandmother, Hedwig Bronski and Stephan, who would soon become fourteen, were crying."

Yet, this is not an incident of repressed feelings that come from a plan and design. Oskar does not feel in sympathy with the rest of the people. Also, Oskar's considerable estimate of himself cannot be trusted. His self-awareness is not exactly overpowering. For the most part he sees himself just as reified and objectified as all the others do. He continually changes his narration from the first person to a "report about Oskar." He depicts Oskar's history like the ostensibly impartial historian, just as Julius Caesar used to write about himself as Caesar.

A Bildungsroman requires that outer events transform themselves into causal factors in the development of a character. This is not at all the case with Oskar. He does not change. The stopping of his growth and the gratuitous toleration of a small increase in growth do not derive from experiences with society or reactions against it. Oskar imbibes parts of the social but owes nothing to society. He relates to it like a free-loader and pirate not like a *zoön politikon*. Since it proves necessary to learn how to read and write, he transforms Gretchen Scheffler into a teaching object. She is required by him only to open up the way to Rasputin and Goethe. He will achieve everything else by learning how to help himself.

Oskar Matzerath as a "monad without windows." As the self-reliant individualist who views society merely as an object. Oskar Matzerath without "faith, hope, and love"—to quote the horrendous title of the last chapter in Book One. It is all quite clear: the narrative account completely resists the attempt of a critic to take seriously the ideas of the literary theorist Matzerath and his role as hero of a conventional novel. Oskar is neither a hero nor a character of a novel as he himself understands the norms of the traditional novel. The essential meaning of the book will be missed if one wants to understand it—and in this way to be taken in by Oskar's ideas—as an epic account.

This is not what *The Tin Drum* is. And Oskar is not an individual in the sense of Tom Jones or Madame Bovary, Leopold Bloom or Baron de Charlus. Oskar is an artifice in a completely new and momentous sense. His existence in the novel is an artistic process that keeps itself as far away as possible from simulating any kind of "nature." The ingredients of this artifice gradually become visible. Above all, Oskar is pure awareness that can manage with a minimum of corporeality. To compensate for this awareness, he had already demonstrated a high capacity for reflection to protect himself while yet in his mother's womb, and most definitely from birth up to the present. The awareness intends to reveal as little as possible and to resist pressures of society. While

Oskar follows his precise plan with the help of a picture book about Rasputin to learn how to read, he feigns a childlike babble with Gretchen. Then, however, he talks to the Liliputian and musical clown Bebra in a refined, somewhat antiquated manner of speaking German.

The tin-drum language is an art language which Oskar learns and perfects because it allows him simultaneously to articulate the awareness, and yet to decline communication. Pure awareness almost without corporeality. The tin-drum language as the antithesis of human language. Robbed of his drum, Oskar falls constantly into danger, is forced to grow up and use human language. He knows that and writes: "How should Oskar be able to maintain his three-year-old face when he lacked the most necessary thing—his drum?" Finally, the shattering of glass with his voice as a form of destruction without a motivated feeling. The course of the novel shows how this grotesque gift of little Oskar is used only in the beginning as a means of protection, then as an emotionally motivated aggression that assumes the final form of pure artistry, that is, becomes an objective, aesthetically perfect act of destruction.

At this point of the analysis it seems necessary to include the author Günter Grass, to examine how he maintains the distance between Oskar and his author. The question here involves the function of the artifice Oskar Matzerath. Since Oskar does not have any emotions and, aside from small crises of the nerves and attacks of sensuality, would like to remain pure consciousness without communication with things social, it must be assumed that Grass is attempting to portray a special social pattern with the help of a supposed hero who is fit for neither the Bildungsroman nor the picaresque novel.

Oskar as an artifice is important chiefly as a location and standpoint, and this is at the far end of normal human dimensions. Oskar sees only the bottom of everything. He is the gnome, the perpetrator, who is neither seen nor heard. In this way he avoids (along with his author) the difficulties that the realistic narrator of the old school encounters, who can portray the actions of his characters only the way the general public is able to see. This is the reason that there are so many hotel and dinner scenes in the old novels, from *Tom Jones* to *Buddenbrooks*. The epic reality as social behavior in the outer world where all the figures in novels are completely clothed and had to be shown as members of society. Since the narrator pretended to be present at all the reported events, it was only logical to exclude scenes in which his presence would have been awkward. Marcel Proust suffered greatly under these rules of the game. At one point in *Remembrance of Things Past* he had to describe certain events which the narrator Marcel could not have experienced. Proust helped himself in this instance by having an older character in the novel tell the younger Marcel about these things. Then there were some scenes to describe between Charlus and Jupien at the beginning of *Cities of the Plain*, which by their nature did not allow for witnesses. This time Proust made his narrator into a secret eavesdropper and peeping Tom.

On the other hand the first person narrative of Oskar Matzerath demands that Oskar really experience what he describes. Here his shape as imp helps him. The bottom of a family, city, petty bourgeois class can be depicted only in a way that would not be possible for a normal Gil Blas or Figaro. For Grass, the function of the tin-drummer is evident: it allows a portrayal of the wicked look, the background, and the underground.

Something else is achieved by this. Since Oskar leads the existence of a monad and artifice, he is obviously free from all the taboos and prejudices of the society. He is just as far from shame as he is from vicious cynicism. Here it becomes apparent that, in writing the novel *The Tin Drum*, Grass wrote the satirical novel of a modern version of a man of the Enlightenment with the help of his grotesque artifice. Oskar's existence in the Danzig epoch before the war as well as in the Düsseldorf postwar period runs its course like the behavior of a modern Gulliver whereby it is not certain whether he feels himself a dwarf among giants or even, in regard to his awareness, a giant among intellectually underdeveloped dwarfs. Therefore, if one wants to speak about tradition in the first great novel by Grass, one is most compelled (as far as form is concerned) to think about Laurence Sterne, Jean Paul, and E. T. A. Hoffmann. Reading Oskar's report about the procreation and birth, one is reminded of the corresponding parts from *The Life and Opinions of Tristram Shandy, Gentleman.* Oskar's size brings to mind Klein Zaches, named Zinnober, in Hoffmann's fairy tale. Grass loves his Sterne and Hoffmann. Quite clearly, in speaking about the type of novel, *The Tin Drum* does not belong to the realistic convention of the picaresque novel or the educational novel of development but to the satirical novel of the Enlightenment.

It is most typical of the comic-satirical novel that the narrator, or rather the author, sets up a secret agreement with the reader by occasionally shoving aside the persona who is supposedly reporting the events as though he were a hindrance. This is done —behind the back of the chronicler—in order that the author may address the public himself. Günter Grass also makes use of this device at a decisive point in *The Tin Drum*. Here we are supposed to have a report of how Oskar, in contrast to his own statement, *really* behaved during the takeover of the Polish post office and the arrest of his presumptive father Jan Bronski. Therefore the chapter "He Lies in Saspe" in Book Two begins in this strange way: "I have just reread the last paragraph. If I am not too well satisfied, then it is particularly due to Oskar's pen. Writing tersely and succinctly, he has succeeded at times in consciously presenting succinct accounts which exaggerate, if not lie. However, I would like to stick to the truth and am going to attack Oskar's pen from behind by reporting that Jan's last hand, which he was unhappily prevented from playing out and winning, was not a grand hand, but a diamond hand without a two; in the second place, Oskar, as he left the storeroom, picked up not only his new drum but also the old broken one, which had fallen out of the laundry basket with the dead suspenderless man and the letters."

All of this is formulated in highly ambiguous terms. It is possible to be satisfied with the explanation. Oskar himself adds another correction to this, which ends with the confession of his guilt about the murder of his own father. As is well known, Oskar continually switches from the first person to the third person report about Oskar. Yet here the first-person narrator is suddenly the narrator Günter Grass correcting the commentator Oskar. But this is only a moment (of which there are more in the story).

Then the form of the novel is once again closed: the first person of the narrator once again becomes the ego of the small tin-drummer.

Grass employs here a typical artistic device of humor which belongs to the traditional novel. The forms of the grosteque and satire, of irony and humor, demand distance. They never allow the narrator to lose himself completely in the narration. Only a novelist who prefers not to use a narrator as function, and yet cannot do without one (as in the case of Flaubert), will strive to present the story by itself and nothing but the story, a narration without a narrator. But a novel such as *The Tin Drum,* which is concerned with functions, needs the interplay between narrator and reader—mostly with the help of a persona, often in contrast to the persona.

The situation is essentially the same in the late works of Thomas Mann. "Who then rings the bells of Rome?" is the first sentence of the novel *The Holy Sinner,* and immediately following this, there is the startling answer: "The spirit of the story." Thomas Mann even has this sentence set in italics. A few pages later the strange event is explained to the reader: "In that the spirit of the story has attached itself to my monastic person named Clemens the Irishman, it has retained a great deal from that abstract condition which enabled it to ring forth from all the basilicas of the city at once." The reader sees through the game and continually hopes to catch the eye of the narrator Thomas Mann while reading, unconcerned about the narrative doings of Clemens the Irishman. This can be further demonstrated by comparing Thomas Mann's last great novel, which remained a fragment, with the first great novel by Günter Grass.

Felix Krull and Oskar Matzerath—this combination seems to lead to a confrontation of two borderline cases. The highest sociability of the irresistible confidence man and the extreme lack of socialness on the part of the tin-drummer. The mythically transcendent seducer and god of lies as the antithesis of the representative of an "underworld" in every sense of the word. There are still traces of Hermes in Felix Krull. This is apparent not only to the writer Diane Houpflé, but to everyone. In Felix Krull's case, one should not draw the balance without the ironic Thomas

Mann. And the satire in Günter Grass's work is not at all far from the irony of the late Thomas Mann.

In *Journal on the Origination of Doctor Faustus* there are strange references to the connection between Faust and Krull, the German composer Adrian Leverkühn and the irresistible confidence man, right at the beginning. At that time, in 1943, Thomas Mann recalled his earlier drafts of Faust but was not so certain as to whether he should take the jump into the unknown or merely add a few new chapters to those he had already written about Krull, with the aim of finally finishing *Confessions of Felix Krull, Confidence Man (Die Bekenntnisse des Hochstaplers Felix Krull)*, begun more than thirty years earlier. Then there is the following passage in the journal: "One day . . . I opened the package containing the material on *The Confidence Man* and read the drafts once again.—With a strange result. It was an 'insight into the inner affinity that the Faust material had with it,' based on the *motif of loneliness,* in one instance tragic-mystical, in the other, comic-criminal. However, the former seems to me to be more relevant to our times, more pressing if it can be given shape . . . ."

It was evident from the beginning that the young confidence man from the Rhineland, reared in a "fine bourgeois home even if somewhat disorderly," had a connection with the favorite problem of the early Thomas Mann, that is, the relationship between the artist and the bourgeois world. Even in his first stories, such as *Bajazzo,* and later in *Tonio Kröger* and *Tristan,* the writer from Lübeck had anticipated a theme of *The Threepenny Opera*: the yearning of the outsider for the joys of the bourgeois commonplace. Naturally the beggars and the gangster king in Brecht were representatives of a social class of outsiders. In contrast, Thomas Mann always meant a spiritual aloofness, culminating in the borderline existence of the literary man. The constellation Tonio Kröger and Hans Hansen, Mr. Spinell before King Mark Klöterjahn. Hanno Buddenbrook battling the norms and rituals of the school hierarchy. In each of these cases, it is the life of the artist versus bourgeois life. These stories strive for the joys of spiritual humiliation everywhere by attaining unspirituality.

The original conception of the Krull novel was here. Krull, too, is presented as an artist in a field that no school of art teaches, namely thievery and fraud. Nevertheless, Krull is a genuine artist, skilled in the fine art of deception. He does not force himself out of the bourgeois sphere by his illegal acts because he never belonged there in the first place. He was a confidence man long before he committed his first swindle. His loneliness springs from this. His story has nothing to do with the trivial story about the son of a good family who does something wrong and is then rejected by society. Krull is the center not of a sentimental novel but of a comic novel. His position is antibourgeois from the beginning.

Mann held to this basic concept until the end. The third chapter in the third and final book of the Krull memoirs, written in the last years of Mann's life, begins with two short sentences of a retrospective nature. Felix Krull establishes the following: "My basic attitude toward the world or society can only be designated as contradictory. For all my eagerness to have a warm exchange, there was a considered coolness that was characteristic here, a tendency toward derogatory reflection which astonished even me." Felix Krull knows the loneliness of the artist and does not allow himself to be deceived by any of his erotic triumphs about the basic facts of his relation to his surroundings. Krull makes it seem as though he were the suitor and the taker in all situations. Actually the reverse is the case: he is in all instances the object of libido, sympathy, and trust. The charlatan can pretend in a magnificent fashion that he enjoys his existence. Whether he truly enjoys it is an open question. This means that Krull is a man of fictions. He lives in the webs spun by his imagination, naturally also in the lie, and he draws certain advantages from the most intrinsic part of his existence—from the play of the power of his imagination. He is an artist in the sphere which the paragraph about swindle in the penal code seeks to formulate as "under false pretenses." However, the false pretenses serve first and foremost an artistic self-purpose. Krull's existence is like one of *l'art pour l'art*. That this artistry also throws off something in the process is agreeably accepted, but it is not something that is intended.

It now becomes obvious why Mann unhesitatingly could compare Krull's loneliness with the loneliness of the artist Leverkühn: Krull, too, senses that each act is actually part of an artistic process. He is an artifice and moreover is constantly making himself into an artifice. When he goes out in Paris as a man of the world, he prepares himself for a theater appearance following the pattern of that irresistible operetta hero from *The Merry Widow* whom he might have admired as a youngster: "But, my new acquisitions—a tuxedo, a silk-lined evening cape which I unconsciously chose under the influence of my rather vivid recollection of Müller-Rosé as attaché and lady-killer, in addition, a slick silk-hat, and a pair of patent-leather shoes—I would not have dared to exhibit them in the hotel." The confidence man Felix Krull is the prototype of a *homo ludens*. He spends his life as an aesthetic existence. This is the reason why there are three great descriptions of artistic exhibitions at the core of the three books of the novel: the operetta, the circus, the bullfight.

The loneliness of Felix Krull the confidence man and artist brings him closer to the monstrous existence of the tin-drummer Oskar Matzerath. Oskar, too, follows the career of a successful artist. "Oskarnello" becomes an artistic attraction. The gap between him and his admirers, which is one of self-awareness as opposed to unaware vitality and the joys of the commonplace, does not close. But Krull yearns unsuccessfully for the bourgeois world and even risks a change of identity with the genuine Marquis— again unsuccessfully. He is and remains an object of the all-encompassing pity—of "the others."

If it could be noted that Günter Grass occasionally shoves aside the self-conscious literary man Oskar with a slight shrug of the shoulders in order—as though in his own interest—to communicate something to the reader, then it can easily be demonstrated that the same procedure takes place in the Krull novel. The late passages written by the old Thomas Mann work chiefly with this artistic device so that the reader feels that the change of gears in these late chapters by the confidence man is only a trick, that he is in reality having a permanent conversation with the real author. It is part of the artistic intent of the author that Krull's stilted prose in the first chapters serves to make the arch liar visible, caught by the seeming openness of all his revelations. Aside

from this, the reader has known from the outset that—even with
all the adroitness and ingenious eclecticism—the confidence man
Krull could never write so elegantly as the famous writer Thomas
Mann from Lübeck. In other words, we have a pretext here and
a means to characterize the figures.

At the end of Felix Krull a new artistic skill begins to emerge.
In addition to the characterization of the figure of the confidence
man through his speech, and the direct intervention of Thomas
Mann, who addresses the reader, as it were, in his own name, a
third manner of portrayal is tested: Thomas Mann parodies the
late style of Thomas Mann. The second book of the Krull
memoirs opens with the reflections of the confidence man, which
one can designate as the simultaneous play of the real narrator
with the stylistic manner of Krull and Thomas Mann: "These
papers have lain for a long time under lock and key; for at least
a year now, indifference toward the venture and doubt of my success have kept me from continuing my confessions, piling page on
page in faithful sequence. For although I have often maintained
in the previous pages that I am setting down these reminiscences
principally for my own occupation and amusement, I will now
honor truth in this respect, too, and admit freely that I have in
secret and as it were out of the corner of my eye given some heed
to the reading public as well; indeed, without the encouraging
hope of their interest and approval, I would hardly have had the
perseverance to continue my work even this far."

If one asks what is happening here, then one is chiefly confirm-
ing the abandonment of all epic illusion. No sort of reality is
being pretended. The late Thomas Mann most certainly had
nothing to do with the type of novel of the nineteenth century.
From the beginning the Krull novel was intended to demonstrate
the open form. Now, the objection could be made that this specific technique of contemporary narrative works, for example *The
Tin Drum,* presents a return to the epic models of the eighteenth
century, leaving out the realistic compositions of the bourgeois
novel of the nineteenth century. However, Thomas Mann and
Günter Grass withdraw from the reader at the very moment when
the artifices Krull and Oskar are removed, and when the reader
believes that he has entered a conversation with the authors. One

could formulate it this way: when the marionettes Krull and Matzerath are withdrawn, the stage becomes free for new artifices. This time their names are Thomas Mann and Günter Grass, but they are nonetheless artifices. In *Doctor Faust* "real" musicians and critics are periodically called upon: Bruno Walter and Otto Klemperer or the critic Willi Schuh. But the situation concerns *characters of the novel* with names taken from people who actually bear them. Brecht's phrase—"whomever you are seeking, I'm not it"—is applicable in each of these cases.

In the process a new element of contemporary novel-writing, not merely the German novel, takes on importance—something that has not been understood by many of the present-day readers and often causes misunderstandings. It is more difficult in contemporary literature than ever before to attribute any kind of idea, action, or answer of any artifice to "the writer himself." The bourgeois epoch of a literature which strives for the self-realization of an artist is at an end.

Wherever one turns, there is the interplay of artifices. The function of the novel and the actual motifs used by the author—it is possible to see that certain progress has been made here—are to be interpreted on the basis of the entire work and not to be drawn from the dubious identification of the author with particular passages or figures of the story. The striking preference of modern writers for the so-called fictional roles is related to this. The fiction of the omniscient narrator has been abandoned, and now any figure narrates the story in the first person, but in such a manner that the reader is prevented with ingenious tricks from falling into the trap of identifying or sympathizing with the narrator of the story. The modern novelist prefers more than anything to create distance as quickly as possible between the first-person narrator and the reader whether it be by having a shocking commentator or shocking events. In this respect *Felix Krull* anticipated the modern form of the novel from the very beginning and did not continue the tradition of the novel along the lines of Tolstoi and Flaubert. Oskar Matzerath belongs to the same family tree as the "hermetic" confidence man created by Thomas Mann.

There is someone else who belongs to this family even though he twitches nervously and becomes melancholy when any mention is made of family. As he says: "My parents, devout Protestants, subscribed to the postwar fashion of denominational tolerance and sent me to a Catholic school. I am not religious myself. I don't even go to church, and I make use of the sacred texts and songs for therapeutic purposes: they help me more than anything else to overcome two afflictions nature has saddled me with—melancholy and headaches." It is easy to recognize the style and the tone: the confession belongs to the clown Hans Schnier, son of the brown-coal Schniers, created by Heinrich Böll in *The Clown*.

For the third time, a state of affairs which already has a familiar ring to it: complete antinomy between the entire society and one of its supposed members. The monstrosity Oskar had stylized himself in such a way that he did not resemble other men. The confidence man did not live like a haughty delinquent in opposition to the legal, customary, and political norms which, after all, means a form of collective living but outside of all sociability. He was an object that was constantly desired but never possessed because he instinctively withdrew from all community. The frigidity of a man can be integrated into a society in an emergency, as we know. The loneliness of a "select individual," however, does not allow itself to be transformed into communication. This applies to the loneliness of the artist in Adrian Leverkühn's case as well as to the criminal and innate artistry of Felix Krull.

Hans Schnier also. He is the artist who remains lonely and, in contrast to the wicked culprit Oskar, can only react idiosyncratically as a sufferer. He lives in a society that is capable of including everything except the clown because he sees everything that occurs in society from the outside and imitates it in a burlesque manner without ever taking part in it for one single instant. He is the observer and the mimic. Whether it be good or evil, the society lives as a totality. However, the clown who stands outside and is not involved in the society experiences only the breakdown of the totalities in unexplainable and senseless moments. In a telephone conversation, Hans Schnier's brother Leo asks the decadent member of this Protestant family from Bonn the following question: "What kind of a person are you anyhow?" The reply: " 'I'm a clown,' I said, 'and I collect moments.' "

Each one of them, Thomas Mann, Günter Grass, Heinrich Böll,

has "overcome" the early form of the novel, and here one should avoid talking about this in terms of progress or decadence. The novels of our times are simply different from the narrative works of early times.

Krull and Matzerath are monsters, and the melancholy clown Hans Schnier is also a kind of monster, and not only in the eyes of society. The wicked imp Oskar presents himself to the reader in the guise of an ugly and awful villain. There is nothing human about him. This is something Grass knew and calculated. The strange quality of the dwarflike existence is employed by Grass for a specific artistic effect. He even allows himself the joke of having a confrontation between the artificial dwarf Matzerath and the "natural" Liliputian Bebra.

On the other hand, Krull is a somewhat decrepit half-god and is inferior to his archetype Hermes. He, too, is not human, and it would seem to him—this is continually the case with Thomas Mann—that some ingredients of the inhuman are always included in the artistic existence from the beginning. When Krull sees the daring circus act of the trapeze artist Andromache and also admires the other acts, he asks himself: "What amazing people these artists are! Are they really human beings? Take the clowns for example, those basically strange creatures, jokesters with little red hands, little thin-shod feet, red wigs under comical felt hats, their impossible lingo, their handstands, their stumbling and falling over everything, their senseless running to and fro and useless attempts to be of help, their hideously unsuccessful efforts to imitate their serious colleagues—in tightrope-walking, for instance . . . which bring the crowd to a pitch of merriment, . . . are they, I repeat, human beings, men who might conceivably find a place in the bourgeois and natural realm?"

Hans Schnier usually becomes furious if someone refrains from calling him a professional clown in order to endow him with a name more in keeping with a normal, bourgeois artistic profession. At one point he states—and he is probably correct: "I believe that there is no one in the world who understands a clown, not even a clown who understands another clown. There's always some jealousy or ill-will at work."

Three forms of the inhuman: dwarf, half-god, and clown. The

bourgeois novel of illusion (and even the novel of disillusionment) of the nineteenth century had usually worked with terrible sinners and criminals. Vatrin alone in Balzac's work, or the notorious criminal Valjean in Hugo's *Les Miserables,* stood outside the bourgeois world on account of his deeds and tendencies, and yet, these two consumed themselves in yearning for integration. Around all of them, the prostitutes and the artists, those favorite figures of European writers about 1890, there was an aroma of sentimentality. The author saw them with the eyes of the bourgeois world, and sympathy was what he had to offer them. *Tonio Kröger* was an ironical variation of this narrative scheme, but it still followed the scheme. Felix Krull is different.

Loneliness is portrayed in the contemporary forms of the novel through unnatural central figures, and it has nothing to do with the scheme of earlier novels about artists which Hermann Hesse was still accustomed to follow. The earlier pattern required boredom with the society, as in the case of Peter Camenzind, and this gradually led to inner worldly isolation. All of them remained within the given world. Even hermits and eccentrics have their position in a fully formed society.

However, Matzerath, Krull, and Schnier are not loners. Here is something new and different. Moreover, it is remarkable that they all embody an artistic talent of a highly unusual kind: Oskar through his shape, his innate and acquired gifts; Krull through the simultaneously sacred and profane sphere of beauty and imposture; Schnier in that he is never in a position to "conform" and can experience all the "engagements" of the others, the Catholics and Protestants, artists or Communists, only as negative irritations of the nerves.

Yet, in this way they join the great phalanx of artists, above all of the writers who have been accustomed to populate the modern novel. Oskar, Krull, and Schnier are artists on the far side of language. But next to them there are the many heroes of novels in which the noteworthy events usually consist mainly in their searching to transform life into literature. In the 1920's this was generally successful as long as one was willing to believe the authors. The writers in Lion Feuchtwanger's novels describe the events in Munich from 1920 to 1923 or the Jewish war against the

Romans, or the eve of the French Revolution. The real heroes are, however, the writers. Arnold Zweig's books about World War I are conceived in such a way that the writer Werner Bentin, the author's mouthpiece, consumes life in order to change it into a world of the novel. Even Marcel Proust's *Remembrance of Things Past* is conceived in a similar fashion.

On the other hand, the more recent novels about writers take pains with special persistence to demonstrate why life no longer allows itself to be transformed into literature. The dying Vergil in Hermann Broch's novel *The Death of Vergil* wants to see the *Aeneid* destroyed because he did not succeed in transforming life into poetry. The "man without qualities" in Musil's opus leads the existence of both a literary man and man of the arts who seeks to unite experience and description, ecstasy and exactitude with one another—in vain. In André Gide's work the novelist Edouard is hindered by an encounter with counterfeiters from writing a novel with the title *The Counterfeiters*. In one of Uwe Johnson's works a West German journalist by the name of Karsch travels to Leipzig to write the biography of a popular hero and bike-racer by the name of Achim. There are already two books about him. Now the third one is to be written. It does not come about. This is the substance of the novel *The Third Book about Achim*.

The perception and obstinacy of so many heterogeneous authors who want to portray the theme of unsuccessful creation time and again, specifically the impossibility of transforming the experienced condition into a work of art—this is connected to the relationship between the writer and society. It says something about the conditions where the authors believe that they are reproducing their own relationship to their surroundings only by producing the archetypes of the inhuman or reports about the unsuccessful attempts to report. Then the fool and the monster are, in fact, the most purposeful representatives of a literature of the lost language and the broken contacts.

Whoever seeks to characterize the production of novels by the new writers will naturally find a great deal of repetition of past forms, motifs, and substance. One can still make an impression with the repetition of the old stories with a slightly different point and an objective, godlike narrator—thanks to the manner of writing. Yet, it has nothing to do with desperate avant-gardism when this kind of story-telling has become absolutely too repulsive for the serious writers of the younger generation and even the older generation.

"Where does the writer actually know that from?" Alfred Döblin asked this question more than thirty years ago in reflecting about the traditional story-line of novels. In fact—where do the writers actually gather their knowledge for their stories? It is considered more honest to compose a work of the imagination based on familiar and artistically serviceable fictions. Then a figure begins to narrate, and from the first page on, the author has distanced himself from it. This is easy for the reader to recognize. The stories that the modern novelist writes are stories of lies. Now everything is in order. All writers lie. Even Plato knew this, and that is why he wanted them banned from the republic. *Stories of lies*—this is what Martin Walser has called some of his narratives. The boundaries between narrated and experienced reality are strictly laid-out aesthetic walls. Only the official aesthetics of Soviet and East German literary theorists is strangely enough directed against the construction of such walls. It is there that writers such as Erwin Strittmatter still cling to the type of novel in the tradition of Balzac and Tolstoi. It is most logical that they still seek to present that prototype of the positive, average, or negative hero that has long since been disregarded by the more astute writers in the world on the basis of aesthetical conscience.

These contemporary writers are not necessarily happier because of this, but they are more credible. One does not write a story about Felix Krull, Oskar Matzerath, or Hans Schnier in a merry mood or with a good conscience. The young Thomas Mann once hit upon a striking formulation for a writer: he is a man who finds writing especially difficult. We are experiencing today a splurge of novel-writing which seems almost to be a presumptuous burden for most of those who undertake it. To want to write about a reality which one is less and less confident of perceiving. To want to write in a language which one secretly no longer trusts. To hit upon a set of circumstances without distorting them. To write down stories according to the rules of a craft which no longer apply.

It is no wonder, then, that many of these novels resemble a book that first appeared at the decline of medieval German literature and has served as the model for Katherine Anne Porter's work with the same title: *Ship of Fools*. Psychotics, fools, criminals, monsters, artists of all kinds populate the world of the novel in the middle of the twentieth century. Does all this have to do with the fact that the art of the novel today presents a late type of artistic exercise, or do the novels imply something about the condition of a society?

Ionesco and Ideologies

Detective (in increasing terror): Everyone ought to write.
Nicolas: We have Ionesco and Ionesco. That's enough!
Detective: But, Monsieur, there are always things to be said.

EUGÈNE IONESCO, *Victims of Duty*

With the development of the Rorschach test in Switzerland, it has become a well-known practice in psychology to place ten cards with gray and colored inkblots sequentially before the subject who is to be examined. The subject is then told to explain what he has discovered in the figures. The psychologist classifies the answers in terms of whole answers and partial answers. A whole answer is one which "interprets" the inkblot as a whole, for example, as a butterfly. On the other hand, the subject who gives a partial answer usually "identifies" the parts of the inkblots separately and without consideration for the whole. In one place a finger is noticed; in another, a linden leaf. These answers help the psychologist judge whether the subject tends to experience or conceptualize.

If one examines the basic dramaturgical tenets of the so-called theater of the absurd, one is often reminded of the Rorschach test. The works are reminiscent of the cards with symmetrical inkblots. There are absurd plays which seem similar to the gray cards while others seem rather like the colored ones. All of them are symmetrical. The rules of theater demand this, and even the absurd play in the final analysis remains theater.

The comparison can be carried still further, and it will have to be if the peculiar structure, above all the structural fragility of Eugène Ionesco's theater of the absurd is to be understood. Supposedly the cards and figures in the Rorschach test hold no special significance for the psychologist. There are no right or wrong answers. Every statement, whether it applies to the whole or only to a part, is equally justified and valid because the test applies only to the subject, and everything depends on the subject.

By using his theater pieces as Rorschach cards, the playwright of the absurd theater sets himself apart from all previous dramatic theories, from the Aristotelian and the non-Aristotelian, from those demanding empathy and those demanding alienation. Ionesco is well aware of why he always attacks all previous world drama so sharply and contemptuously in his interviews. At most, he occasionally likes to claim that his plays are related to those of Shakespeare. On the other hand, his grotesque railleries against Brecht are not based on political differences alone but also on dramatic principles. It is precisely because Brecht attempts to destroy the drama of empathy and prevent any identification by the audience with the action and characters on stage that his place is further from the theater of Ionesco than from that of any other dramatist in the last hundred years—despite all apparent similarities. One may occasionally observe certain elements in Ionesco that can also be found in Ibsen and Shaw, in German romanticism, in surrealism, and even in the "station dramas" of the expressionists. However, between Brecht and Ionesco there is no common ground.

The balance sheet leaves us with the following result: Brecht's plays are not suitable for Rorschach tests. They have a meaning and want to determine the direction of the subject's reaction. There are right and wrong interpretations of Brecht's plays. Statements about his plays are not equally valid. The new art of audience participation must be learned. The behavior of some of Brecht's figures, for example the camp follower Mother Courage, may appear absurd, but the playwright himself did not write an absurd play. One can understand or misunderstand. Brecht became very angry when the original Zurich production of *Mother Courage* in the spring of 1941 was interpreted by the public and critics alike as a play about a Niobe-like mother who suffered a great deal of pain. Presumably Ionesco would never disagree with any interpretation of his plays whether it be a whole or partial answer even if he himself might never have conceived of such a possible interpretation.

Max Frisch gave his play *The Firebugs* the subtitle "A Didactic Play Without a Lesson." This does not at all align him with Ionesco. Frisch's subtitle has more to do with irony and is only intended to warn the theatergoer against "whole answers," which are much too superficial. Frisch definitely *intended* that this play also convey a message. In addition, the theme of the play fits exactly into line with the basic motifs of Frisch's other dramas and novels. This Swiss dramatist was not a student of Swiss Rorschach psychology.

With Ionesco the situation is somewhat different. In his case, it is altogether possible that his theater pieces will not contain a lesson nor "mean" anything at all. Inkblots of the theater, gray and colored. In the mixing of color effects, Ionesco has succeeded in making some charming inventions. Nevertheless, the limits of this Rorschach drama are quickly reached. Eugène Ionesco's development as a dramatist makes this most evident.

Just how fast these limits can be reached is interestingly illustrated by the reaction of the English critic Kenneth Tynan to the successive works produced by Ionesco. Since Tynan has published a collection of his reviews under the title *Curtains,* one can study the change that takes place in his critical opinion of Ionesco. The evolution of Ionesco's dramatic style has caused Tynan, who was at first so enthusiastic, to become more and more distant and reserved in his criticism of Ionesco's works. Naturally, in such a situation the critic himself may have undergone a change. Yet, even if this be the case, something becomes increasingly apparent in the situation itself, something that critics until then had overlooked or had not wanted to observe. Alfred Kerr, as a critic of Gerhart Hauptmann, was similarly very enthusiastic about Hauptmann's early works, *The Weavers* (*Die Weber*) and *Der Biberpelz* (*The Beaver Coat*). However, after this early enthusiasm, which took in *Hanneles Himmelfahrt* (*The Assumption of Hannele*) and Hauptmann's experiments with neoromanticism,

Kerr felt a greater need to make certain reservations in his praise as each new play was produced. All this despite the admiration he had for the playwright. The factors that changed Kerr's attitude sprang mainly from the dramatist Hauptmann rather than from a new development undergone by the critic.

The case of Ionesco-Tynan is similar. The critic Tynan greatly admired *The Bald Soprano (La Cantatrice Chauve)*; *Amédée*, concerning the vexation of the married couple Amédée and Madeleine Buccinioni, who are disturbed by the huge corpse growing larger in the next room and the mushrooms springing up in the living room; and *The Chairs (Les Chaises)*. Here was a writing style developed by a new and unique dramatist, extraordinary playwriting. Yet even then Tynan could not rid himself of the impression that Ionesco's originality as a dramatist was somewhat limited. Repetitions appeared. Shock effects no longer worked. These attractions had lost their appeal. The critic discovered that Ionesco's theater world consists of isolated robots who converse with another in "cartoon-strip balloons of dialogue" which are "sometimes hilarious, sometimes evocative, and quite often neither." They are, indeed, blurbs. Sometimes it is as though Donald Duck were speaking in a cartoon. After viewing three or four of Ionesco's early plays, one finds that the material becomes somewhat sticky during the fifth and sixth plays, or, as Kenneth Tynan has discovered, downright boring. This new effect and ineffectiveness is not so much due to the limited originality of the dramatist but due to his concern with the dramatic theory of the Rorschach cards.

In the case of the dramatist Eugène Ionesco, one can speak of a basic idea that is repeated and thus loses its effect just like a trick. In the early plays of Ionesco the underlying principle of this absurd theater actually has very little to do with absurdity. Ionesco's vaunted hatred of ideologies is itself of a purely ideological nature. In fact, it incorporates the double sense of the concept "ideology"—pure consciousness and false consciousness. Ionesco intended the absurdity in his theater to include a program, in other words, an ideology. The starting point of his thesis is that the reification and increasing meaninglessness in this society are most clearly revealed in the *speech* of contemporary man.

Hence, the blurbs and the Donald Duck dialogues. Whoever is meant to become a rhinoceros (to take an example from the most famous of Ionesco's plays) recommends himself for this fate by the style, form, and content of his speech while still in the shape of a human being that is not threatened. In the great dialogue between Jean and Bérenger in the first act of *Rhinoceros,* Jean shows himself predestined to become a rhinoceros with every sentence he speaks.

Ionesco's basic concept—consciousness and false consciousness in one—is wielded against the torpidity of society that manifests itself in linguistic torpidity. Here Eugène Ionesco, though seemingly anarchistic, is not so far from the Austrian Karl Kraus, seemingly conservative and traditional. Kraus, publisher of the remarkable magazine *Die Fackel,* used the grand bourgeois metropolitan press as his object of study. Ionesco appears to confine himself more to language, but he also concentrates on the torpid culture, the literature and science that have degenerated into meaningless industriousness. This can be seen in the preparations for the lecture in *The Chairs,* the scholarly nonsense in *The Lesson (La Leçon),* the poetic sterility in *Victims of Duty (Victimes du devoir).* Ionesco is also intelligent and witty enough to recognize the particular kind of reification which this absurd theater of reification (*Entdinglichung*) experiences amidst the culture boom.

In the first act of *Rhinoceros,* Jean, who is already in essence a rhinoceros, takes his friend Bérenger sharply to task for his total lack of culture: "Instead of squandering all your spare money on drink, isn't it better to buy a ticket for an interesting play? Do you know about the avant-garde theater there's so much talk about? Have you seen Ionesco's plays?" The man Bérenger, who up to the very end wants to be a human being and not a rhinoceros, must regretfully answer no. But apparently not very regretfully. Jean becomes more insistent. At this moment a play by Ionesco is being performed. One should take advantage of the opportunity. (This is a gag, but at the same time it is also a romantic theatrical device of disillusionment. "At this moment" a play by Ionesco is being performed: this is being discussed by two characters *in* an Ionesco play.) Bérenger, always polite, admits:

"It would be an excellent initiation into the artistic life of our times." One detects here not only Ionesco's self-irony but also his skepticism about the effectiveness of his dramaturgy in regard to the dematerialization of modern society and its "artistic life." In *Victims of Duty* the reference that is made to the dramatist Ionesco—"We have Ionesco and Ionesco. That's enough!"—is essentially even more apodictic.

A kind of cultural criticism that must be understood almost exclusively as criticism of language. Separation of language from the subject matter. Once again we have ideology. Moreover, in addition to the separation of language from its social substratum, Ionesco's early plays took on another element of reification and thereby placed modern society on the same level with French bourgeois society. They demonstrated the linguistic torpidity of modern society in general by using French clichés and stereotyped thought patterns. It is for this reason that nearly all translations of the first Ionesco plays have necessarily resulted in a significant loss of substance, seldom without distorting the author's original intent. It was only with *Rhinoceros* that Ionesco first achieved genuine international acclaim—mainly because he had broken free of the narrow confines of the French language through the basic idea of the play and the development of the dialogue.

The Bald Soprano offers the classic schema for depicting how eminently torpid French language and life have become. The first set of stage directions relates Ionesco's sense of irony, which is focused on French bourgeois life: "A middle-class English interior, with English armchairs. An English evening. Mr. Smith, an Englishman, seated in his English armchair and wearing English slippers, is smoking his English pipe and reading an English newspaper near an English fire. He is wearing English spectacles and a small gray English moustache. Beside him, in another English armchair, Mrs. Smith, an Englishwoman, is darning some English socks. A long moment of English silence. The English clock strikes seventeen English strokes." Then in the most refined style of French cliché speech, "Monsieur" and "Madame" Smith begin the conversation. The grotesque little "English" milieu depicted by the first sentences of the text suddenly brings to mind how close Ionesco is to the French Enlightenment writers who pur-

posely placed their criticisms of French life in foreign settings. Gil
Blas lived a rogue's life apparently in Spain. Similarly, Lessing
felt obliged to set the story of Emilia Galotti in the court of an
Italian prince. However, Ionesco transposes this evening conversation that is obviously French to an English setting not because
he is taking precautions as an ideologist but because he is playing
with a literary cliché.

The French language, the speech and style of the middle-class
French citizen, offers the most favorable conditions for Ionesco's
linguistic and cultural criticism. A language refined through centuries and adhering to strict rules of tasteful usage and aesthetic
beauty. Even the structure of the French sentence, so unlike the
free, rhythmic structures of English or German, is a contributing
factor. During the course of time a large number of well-defined
idioms evolved in a society that was very much interested in literature. These idioms may have been elegant, witty, and ironic at
one time, but unfortunately they have continued to be considered
as such while the times have changed. The average journalist in
France need not complain about a lack of flowery phrases. The
floridity of the language, however, reflects a reification of middle-
class life. For example, a middle-class family in the French prov-
inces has the corresponding linguistic formula at its disposal for
nearly every life situation, and these formulas were used to force
rebellious young generations back into the realm of middle-class
life. Ionesco treats this theme in *Jacques ou La soumission*
(*Jacques, or The Submission*), one of his most interesting plays.
(The linguistic peculiarities may be the reason why it is one of
his least successful plays outside of France.) The submission of
Jacques ends when the victim is led back into the traditional patterns of thought, life styles, and linguistic phrases. Also the writer
Choubert in *Victims of Duty,* an early model for the character
Bérenger, completes his phase of submission by learning to chew
and swallow the immense portions of cultural hash passed on by
bourgeois generations.

This all began in France with the moralists—in my opinion,
with Montaigne: maxims and reflections, proverbs and practical
adages, were gradually produced for the bourgeois society, and it
made use of these maxims. La Rochefoucauld's basic theory about

social egoism as the most important human impulse was recognized as belonging to the bourgeois class, and as this class adopted the maxims, it also adopted the equivalent linguistic expressions. In *The Bald Soprano,* this situation is brought up for discussion once again. Unbearable idioms determined by etiquette, traditional good manners, the desirable flow of congenial conversations. This time, however, it is carried to the point of inanity and insanity. The conversations run dry. Not only do they miss their mark so that the characters talk right by one another, as in the plays of Georg Büchner and later in the works of Frank Wedekind, the figures in Ionesco's works even talk by themselves. They merely articulate and repeat what they have heard in society. There is no feeling or thought behind their speech.

Ionesco was not the first writer to make this theme, the torpidity of language, into a theme for literature. Flaubert knew why he collected clichés of speech and "stupidities" as he called them. The druggist Homais in *Madame Bovary* was an Ionesco figure long before Ionesco arrived on the scene. Proust followed. Even though he was more interested in the process of the spiritual torpidity than in the social process which manifested itself in it, Proust cultivated the linguistic clichés and the meaningless journalistic idioms which he had heard at the reception given by the Duchess of Guermantes and which he had read in the cultural section of *Figaro.* Ionesco has the opportunity to view a later stage of a French bourgeois culture. His dramatic texts depict the moment in history when the greatest torpidity must necessarily turn into a new chaos, into a wild outbreak. Obviously his absurd theater works toward this goal. He employs Rorschach figures that mean nothing because even the speech of his characters no longer contains meaning. It has been drained of thought and feeling alike. Moreover, there is no will power, for all of Ionesco's important and typical figures are monstrosities who lack will power and submit.

This, then, is the basic position of the dramatist Eugène Ionesco. He is not so far from ideology as he would like us to believe. Also this position is not without tradition, nor can it escape the fate of becoming an element of reification. Cartoon conversations about Ionesco and the avant-garde were also possible, and

here is where the change took place that Kenneth Tynan, originally an admirer of this French-writing Rumanian, refused to
make. Nevertheless, the change was essential for Ionesco and his
career as a playwright. A new type of Ionesco drama originated
from this. Language and subject matter were fused together once
again. The world of babbling opponents was given an opponent.
This character had already been anticipated in the figure of
Jacques, who had been forced into obedience, and also in the
figure Choubert in the "pseudo-drama" *Victims of Duty*. This
character had already been given the name Bérenger for the first
time in the play *The Killer* (*Tueur sans gage*). When he appears
again with the same name in *Rhinoceros,* he is clearly to be understood as a type. Moreover, it is significant that the formal structure of the plays now changes with the appearance of this character in the role of opponent. Ionesco's first plays were more or
less long cabaret scenes. *The Killer* and *Rhinoceros,* however, are
regular plays with the usual three acts.

With the appearance of a hero, so to speak, a whole new configuration takes shape in Ionesco's dramaturgy. As the author
himself has occasionally revealed in reminiscences of his childhood or in self-interpretations, these protagonists, namely Choubert and Bérenger, have doubtless been patterned after the man
Eugène Ionesco. Both in their speech and thought, they relate to
their torpid environment with irreproachable humanity and
at the same time in a highly unique manner that is apparently
a weak will power but reveals itself in reality as moral strength.
It has been said that the typical characters created by the dramatist Ionesco are on the whole monstrosities who lack will power
and submit. This is the way it seems at first. However, this statement must be modified. The society that lives in clichés is not
without will power or without spirit and feeling. In fact, it is
not aware of what that is: spirit, feeling, will power. An object
that is hit and consequently driven forward does not reveal any
will power when it continues along its path. To use a phrase
from Brecht: "From the standpoint of a billiard ball, it is difficult to conceive the laws of motion." Whoever is naturally pre-
disposed toward becoming a rhinoceros may act with great energy
and strength of will, as does Mr. Dudard in *Rhinoceros*. How-

ever, he soon decides to become a rhinoceros in spirit and after that assumes the veritable shape of a rhinoceros. All this has nothing to do with true will power.

On the other hand, Choubert and Bérenger actually appear as monstrosities who have weak wills, are unfit for life, and are lost in dreams. They are much too polite and cooperative and offend the sensibilities of all well-meaning people. There is a deep fear of life and death hidden within them, a predisposition toward compromise, conscience and an attempt to escape from conscience, uncertainty and constant fear. Bérenger, who takes it upon himself to free the world of its murderer in *The Killer*, carries on a soliloquy of fear and cowardice in the darkest of nights, enumerating all the arguments that would induce him to return into hiding. Yet he does not turn back. In *Rhinoceros*, Bérenger is tortured by the conflicting feelings of a man who fears to lose his humanity, but who immediately thereafter desires to become a rhinoceros so that he may finally stand on the same level with his fellow man. Still, he does not become a rhinoceros. He remains Bérenger and eventually acknowledges himself by deciding to remain the last man to the end, to defend himself spiritually, not to capitulate.

The individual and his possession. His possession is his fear. His theme is the moral victory over this fear. However, for Ionesco, the fear that Choubert and Bérenger feel is connected to childhood. Nearly all the autobiographical documents that Ionesco has made public deal with his childhood. The peculiarly weak wills exhibited by his protagonists and always closely associated with tenacity contain some strange elements of infantilism. Jacques, Choubert, Amédée, and Bérenger are adults who are unfit for life and are under the spell of infantilism. This is both a strength and weakness.

Ionesco made a most remarkable statement in the *Lettres françaises* on April 10, 1958, in an answer to a questionnaire on avant-gardism. In defending himself against an accusation that linked his world view to that of the petty bourgeois, he replied: "Are children also petty bourgeois? Perhaps. Throughout the centuries I have found that there have been numerous 'petty bourgeois,' who have also held this world view. The petty bourgeois Solomon, who was, by the way, a king; the petty bourgeois Buddha, who was a prince; the petty bourgeois Shakespeare; the petty bourgeois St. John of the Cross; and many other petty bourgeois." Let us leave aside King Solomon, Buddha, Shakespeare, and Spanish mysticism as caprice. The important point is the reference to children. It helps explain what Ionesco had described earlier in this reply as the actual theme of all his literary work. Childhood memories of an endless street in the south of Paris, evening twilight, errands, bustling people as shadows. A remembrance of the past. Nearly all those people from the past are probably dead today. "I am overcome by dizziness, by fear. This is the way the world is: a desert in which shadows of the doomed move about. Can the revolutions change anything about this? Both the tyrants and the enlightened ones of the past are dead today." Furthermore: "Existence has always seemed to be this way to me. Everything I have always been since then has only confirmed this childhood vision: wild fits of frenzy and despair, screams that suddenly turn into silence, shadows that sink back forever into the night. What more can I say?"

In *Victims of Duty,* Choubert is forced again and again by both his wife Madeleine and the police, who represent society, to sink back into childhood, into the past, to dig up the shadows of the past. Bérenger is a being who lives in fear and in his lost childhood. For both of them, the seemingly moral resolutions they form against murder as a means of castigating the state and against the mischief caused by the rhinoceroses are not actually decisions which have been reached after weighing the pros and cons about good and evil. Rather, they stem from infantile obstinacy above all. Therefore, they can help only Choubert, Bérenger, and Ionesco in their fight against anxiety and the fear of death. If they succeed. This is, without question, ideology— an ideology that has nothing to do with morality. Ionesco's dramatic genre is not absurd, that is, not recently. It has a message. Admittedly only for Ionesco. Even *Rhinoceros,* no matter how it may be interpreted or staged, does not postulate maxims that could become principles of common law. Bérenger remains alone in a world of the rhinoceros. His position is merely negative. Nothing is said about the possibility of his being able to change the rhinoceroses back into men.

Perhaps this is not so much a psychological problem. The remarks about infantilism and anxiety are not to be taken as a psychological interpretation of the plays. Instead, they should make the original intellectual position of Choubert and Bérenger apparent with the aid of the texts of the plays, the autobiographical statements, and the self-interpretations. Presumably the matter does not concern the man and human being Ionesco, who need not interest the observer of his work, so much as it concerns the *writer* Ionesco. The actual problem of Amédée, Choubert, and Bérenger is a problem of creative writing. It is a question of writing in a world in which one feels oneself alone, a world whose reality appears to perish as the transition from hectic activity to sudden silence becomes visible. It would seem that there is neither an ideology nor a message here. One feels like the king, mentioned in Ionesco's 1958 statement, who spoke of *vanitas vanitatum,* or like the prince who preached that the world should be bypassed because it is nothing. Shakespeare's appearance in this context is probably due simply to misunderstanding. The real adversary is Brecht. Ionesco staked out his position much better in his later maledictions against the German playwright than he did in the report of April 10, 1958, when he even tried to include *Mother Courage* in the sphere of his own Ionesco world. He insisted that Brecht's chronicle of the Thirty Years War shows above all how "time kills and consumes" and how "man is lost in time, in existence." Brecht was already dead then and could no longer respond. What he would have said is already contained in his notes on *Mother Courage and Her Children.*

An individual with his obsession—the threat of anxiety and death. An ideologist who imagines himself to be fighting against all ideologies. A dramatist with a message, a message addressed to only one person. Yet, all those proud and free individuals who speak and write against the absorption by the masses consequently become an expression of the absorption by the masses. Ionesco's plays against reification become part of this very process of reification. Ionesco was not unaware of this. His constant play with the theater in the theater, the disillusionment, and the mention of Ionesco in Ionesco plays—all this belongs to the tradition of French comedy since Molière's *Impromptu de Versailles,* which was occasionally imitated by Ionesco. More important, this allows us to see the fate of a nonideology that has itself become an ideology. It is more than a gag, more than the romantic smashing of an illusion, when Ionesco proclaims: "We have Ionesco and Ionesco. That's enough!" In fact, it is enough. For Ionesco.

Observations on the

Situation of Sartre

"The Beginnings" *

Material for a novel. Through various circumstances, perhaps a denunciation or misinterpretation of the facts, a man finds himself in court and becomes the subject of investigation. He is a doctor whose competence is questioned by his patients and thus finds himself accused of deeds which he had never imagined possible. Appearances are against him—he relies nonetheless on his good reputation, friends, relatives, and his long record of good and irreproachable deeds. They will all stand up for him, eliminate the suspicion. However, things turn out quite differently. The suspicion that enshrouds him has now influenced the impression others have of his life and deeds. Suddenly they see him—also retrospectively—in light of the present pattern. Pictures and impressions may always be regrouped and reinterpreted. His existence was not secure and preserved, unchanged as a jewel which never depreciates. New pictures follow the old. The statements of the witnesses become uncertain where they should lend support. They doubt where they should be affirmative. Previous uncontestable actions are now shown as ambiguous. They become "indexes" which reveal a completely new "accused person" and effortlessly classify a "deed" in a completely different way than the subject had intended it and lived

---

* *The Beginnings* was written in 1943 in Zurich on the occasion of the premiere of Sartre's play *The Flies*. The article was one of the first studies of Sartre's work written outside of France.

it. He compares the portrait he has of himself with the one painted by the others, and he no longer understands anything. Where is the truth? The actual truth? The trial creates a totally different portrait of him than the one he actually had of himself. The transcripts of the trial unfold a new being—a work of art next to the "real" existence. Is it the real one?

This could be a theme for Jean-Paul Sartre. Naturally the plot is contrived, but it points to a central problem concerning this extraordinary writer and philosopher. His background can be briefly summarized. A schoolteacher, professor of philosophy, who publishes his first literary work as an adult in 1938. And then, nothing less than the novel *Nausea* (*La Nausée*). It is followed in 1939 by the novellas in the volume *The Wall* (*Le Mur*), and then suddenly a writer emerges who commands all the forms: horror and grim irony, formal and colloquial dialogue, dream conversations and the most precise philosophical analysis. Aside from this, there are his essays about Faulkner, Dos Passos, and Giraudoux, a philosophical novel about the power of the imagination—about the imaginary—and later a metaphysical work, *Being and Nothingness* (*L'Etre et le néant*). Finally, the philosopher and novelist publishes his first drama, *The Flies* (*Les Mouches*), which is performed in Paris with great success. It, too, is a masterpiece of craftsmanship, as is everything which has appeared up to now under the name of Sartre. One after the other, after such a long silence, the works and actions all strengthen the impression of the extraordinary, the incomparable. They are all internally connected without showing the slightest sign of popularized or trivial thinking. They are true works of literature which have an effect and disturb in those places where their true depth is unsuspected.

However, the abyss is wide open under this work. It is totally open because it is identical with existence itself. Even Nietzsche's hopeful nihilism appears played out in view of this relentless, disciplined objectivism of Sartre, who does not allow existence to become endowed with any meaning. Existence in and by itself is meaningless: there is neither the beautiful nor the good, neither the heroic nor the treacherous, neither the Christian nor the humanistic life. Life—existence as such—means contaminated, meaningless physical drives. Whoever seeks to find in these drives meaning and order, mission or foresight, selection or predestination, deceives himself and others. The humanistic antagonist Antoine Roquentin in *Nausea* is merely a sad pathologist. His love for man is in reality a fear of the herd which huddles together for warmth in the stall. The crime of Herostrates in the Rue d'Odessa of Paris reveals itself to be—instead of a signal which leads to an elevation of life—a small insane act found among the notices in small print. Worse yet—an existence resists meaning, it forgoes all illumination through thinking. Where man in rare instances beholds his mere existence beyond all his routine thoughts, he finds a dark abyss of vegetation. It is the true existential sickness, the nausea which increases at such a sight. And on top of all this, an intellect which chatters like a parakeet "I think that I think that I think" and cannot get further than this. It is because we are only able to think of ourselves as existing beings. We can neither conceive of our non-being, our death, nor of our existence other than as it runs its course—somewhat like a spirit without flesh or as an existence which unfolds itself with a totally different character, totally different habits from those it actually has. All this runs its course without meaning or consolation or mission. It is pure arbitrariness. This lesson is drawn throughout Sartre's novels in a variety of pictures and bright parables.

But, what should become of art and genius, creative life and experience, if our existence removes itself from all categories, the ethical as well as the aesthetic? Suddenly Sartre's work reveals a totally different face. Nihilism served to make a clear division of the spheres. It was far removed from all metaphysical despair. Pessimism was a necessity for thought, not an affectation. Next to the meaningless being came nonexistent meaning. Art. It recognizes necessity and meaningful form, laws and categories, beauty and greatness. But all for a price—that of being nonexistent. It is necessary because all that is created intellectually appears as unreal. It escapes time, chance, meaninglessness, which have mercilessly characterized all that which exists. One recalls Proust and his attempt to discover "lost time" in his works of art, in the word, in remembrance taking on new form. Even the young Proust did not want to exchange his dream Venice, which he joyously anticipated, for the real Venice. Sartre's Roquentin, too, finds in art, in melody (which is ''form,'' and is something totally different from the individual material tones out of which it is constructed) a *néant*, a disavowal of existence. This alone gives a meaning, which we can never wait for in our lives (because there is nothing to wait for). Instead we have to form and create through our actions. Thus, we create pictures of ourselves, for ourselves—and perhaps for others. That is why "naturalistic art" makes no sense; all creation of meaning is the creation of legends. Whoever has written a legend about himself and for himself that corresponds to the picture others make of him is fortunate. Not recognizing this would be the tragicomedy of the hero in our contrived novel.

"One has to choose: either to live or write." There are good reasons why Alexandre Astruc quotes this sentence from the novel *Nausea* in his essay on Sartre. Life and stories about life are irreconcilable concepts: the one is without spirit, arbitrary, meaningless; the other creates the necessary, a meaning, and laws for the price of its reality. Whoever tells stories, composes melodies, or writes stories offers form, perhaps consolation. However, only because the art works are fictitious.

Sartre's final word, however, is not this aesthetic ideality or imagination. The Atreus drama *The Flies* reveals a new aspect. Sartre combines his experimentation with a new form, the dramatic, with a new chapter in his interpretation of the world. Next to aesthetics, there is ethics. Here, too, he is concerned with Electra and Orestes, with the gods and the Eumenides—as in Giraudoux's *Electra*. A drama about the twilight of the gods, about the turning point in time just as in Giraudoux, where the last word is the double meaning of the word "dawn." Orestes frees the city from the gods. Through this deed man deliberately frees himself without remorse from a world ruled by the gods. The law of the gods is turned against the gods: the law gave man the freedom which he used to take his affairs upon himself. Here, too, existence is without a plan: the belief in a divine world scheme is pure illusion. Orestes proves this by his deed. The gods have been banished; fear is removed from man; the "metaphysical age" of Auguste Comte is replaced by the positive. In spite of all this, chaos does not emerge. The Eumenides pursue Orestes. The city is free of fear, but the individual is not free in his actions. The world of appearance and art alone cannot establish meaning. The world of action must also be included. Next to fiction stands action. Both leave behind an impression, a picture of that which they encounter. Everyone is followed by pictures and reproductions of his actions. In the final analysis, he "is" only through their reflection—as through the reflection of the art that he creates. The freedom of the act transforms itself into a necessary fiction of the picture that leaves the act for the outside world. Is this still ethics? Is it still aesthetics? Certainly the work, the act alone, conveys meaning to life, which would still be meaningless by itself. The difference between the works and the deeds alone is not of major concern. Beauty is ugly; ugliness beautiful. One is often reminded of André Malraux and his obsession with action as the actual substance of the human condition no matter what kind of action. A few steps deeper there is Henry de Montherlant, who believed that the deed filled with experience was more important than all doctrines. Saints as well as sinners, heroes as well as villains, can originate in this way. Is Orestes a hero or a criminal? He is a crossroads. But is that enough? The Negro woman sings for Antoine Roquentin. But isn't there a deeper, richer meaning of meaninglessness conveyed through art? Sartre gave no answer to this. Will he be able to find it in the experience of his awakening country to which he has remained faithful?

Philosophical Interim Statement, 1960:
Sartre's "Critique of Dialectical Reason"

A book of more than 750 pages.* A torrent of philosophizing

* This book includes the treatise called "Questions of Method" and Part I of *The Critique of Dialectical Reason*. The volume as a whole has appeared in English translation under the title *A Problem of Method*. Part II of the *Critique* has not been completed.

only occasionally channeled by paragraphs. The large sections are not subdivided. There is no thorough, carefully conceived arrangement of material, which had still been the case with the books of Bergson in accordance with the best French tradition. When Sartre makes a subdivision, it consists of more than one hundred pages in small print. It is practically a book in itself rather than part of an organic division. Even the part called "Conclusion" of the section "Questions of Method" does not actually offer a summary of the thoughts and their results but is a continuation of the stream of thought. Hence, it does not fulfill the purpose of providing an intellectual balance.

The outward appearance of the book—I mention it here because it is connected with the problem of the book—reminds one of the original French text in Proust's epic colossus *Remembrance of Things Past*. The formal similarity demonstrates an affinity between the novelist Proust and the philosopher Sartre, especially in the manner in which they treat the theme. This is not the case (another interesting facet) between the *novelist* Jean-Paul Sartre, who likes to try to characterize his figures through the original tone of their local jargon, and Proust, who achieved a completely different structure with his novels, that is, the "imaginary," as he called it in one of his early philosophical studies.

An epic philosophizing, as it were, which is just as distant from the French philosophical tradition of Descartes as—in the twentieth century—from Henri Bergson and Émile Meyerson. This new philosophical work of Sartre is inconceivable without German philosophy—without Hegel, without the early philosophical works of Karl Marx, without Kierkegaard's dispute with Hegel, or without Heidegger. A German reader, versed in philosophy, will have less trouble with the text of Sartre than a student versed in French terminology. Sartre uses numerous neologisms that either were introduced first into French thought during the last decades, or were invented by himself to fit his present mode of thought. It is impossible to understand precisely what he means unless one translates the new French terminology he created back into the German original: *Verfremdung* ("alien-

ation"), *Verdinglichung* ("reification"), *Warenfetischismus* ("fetish for goods").

There is a great bias in the choice of philosophical star witnesses, as well as those with opposing views. Hegel and occasionally Friedrich Schelling. Marx and Engels. Kierkegaard and Heidegger. Jaspers and Lukács. These philosophers have determined
the ingredients of the book. A discussion of the basic positions
of Marxist and existential philosophy. The entire book could be
entitled "Existentialism and Marxism." As noted in the preface,
this title was the one he had originally intended to give the work.
However, it was discarded and replaced by the somewhat more
general and less conspicuous title "Questions of Method." This
in turn became a treatise of one hundred pages which Sartre wrote
in 1956 in response to the question of Polish Marxists about his
philosophical position. This treatise proves itself—in good dialectical fashion—to be both an end and a beginning. A beginning
insofar as Sartre decided to think beyond the methodological
position already maintained, or rather, to think back. In other
words, to give a precise account of the path he had followed in
order to have reached his basic methodological principles. The
one hundred pages called "Questions of Method" were to make
an end. They were a result, a final point. More than that, however, they were also a starting point in that they applied the
methodological principles in a concrete historical context which
an existentialist with Marxist tendencies might continue to attempt to follow in the future. For example, in an analysis of
Flaubert or of the historical connections of the French Revolution of 1789, just to mention two areas that Sartre uses time and
again when he needs to illustrate a point in "Questions of
Method."

For the time being, Sartre has given only the first part of his
critical foundations. He himself considers the task successful
merely in "that he was able to establish the dialectical basis of a
structural anthropology." The presentation of the interplay between the different basic structures must be depicted in the second
volume. So much for the process of the work and the position of
the philosophical investigation up to now.

Thus, the volume contains two parts which, viewed superficially, have hardly anything to do with another. First we have the treatise, "Questions of Method," which actually presents a result: the result of a thought process which itself had never been completed. This thought process should actually be completed in the second book of *The Critique of Dialectical Reason,* a work that lays a foundation that is consciously linked to Kant's critiques but borrows the term *critique* more directly from the Young Hegelians, particularly from the terminology of Marx and Engels around 1845. The section "The Critique of Critical Experience" is obviously a reference by Sartre to the subtitle of the famous first book which Marx and Engels wrote together, *The Holy Family, or Critique of the Critical Critique.*

Any critical comments about *The Critique of Dialectical Reason* and its methodological conclusions should take into account that only the first part of the philosophical trend of thought was published. On the other hand, it is already easier today to judge the position that Sartre takes because the first book should be by all rights the conclusion of the entire investigation and the question of method, as he himself has rightly admitted. His thesis is expressed in the following statement: "These considerations enable us to understand why we can at the same time declare that we are in profound agreement with Marxist philosophy and yet for the present maintain the autonomy of existential ideology. Indeed, there is no doubt that Marxism appears today to be the only possible anthropology that can be at once historical and structural. It is the only one which at the same time takes man in his totality—that is, in terms of the materiality of his condition."

Basically a materialist position and nonetheless allowing autonomy to the existential point of view? According to Sartre, this is the way it is. His existential way of philosophizing is intended as an extension and enrichment of Marxist philosophy since the openness of the research in the present state of Marxist scientific scholarship, in particular the actual dialectics, has been lost.

As a historical conclusion there is a grain of truth to this contention. Sartre's sarcastic judgment is not without justification when he confronts the original method of Karl Marx with certain pseudo-Marxist treatises. Take the following sentences: "The Marxist method is progressive because in Marx it is the result of long analysis; today it is dangerous to proceed via the process of synthesis. The leading Marxists make use of it to constitute the real a priori. The politicians make use of it to prove that which has had to come. They can discover nothing by this method of pure exposition. Proof of this is that they know from the beginning what they have set out to find." This is correct and reminds one of a bitter comment by Kurt Tucholsky about the former Austrian Marxists who used Marxism only to determine after a defeat why the defeat had to come.

Sartre compares this mentally lazy application, or nonapplication, of the Marxist method with the following mode of work: "Our method is heuristic; it teaches us new things because it is at the same time regressive and progressive. Its first concern is, as with the Marxists, to show man in his context." According to this, the heuristic method appears to have the task both of overcoming the undialectical dogmatism of present-day Marxist philosophy *and* of opening up certain scientific areas for Marxist observations. In Sartre's viewpoint, this could serve to make the Marxist analysis of society more profound.

However, this standpoint is not new in the history of Marxism. In such cases Marxist terminology usually speaks of *revisionism,* which chiefly allows a tendency to be shown without attaching any value judgment to it. This basic goal is also not new to Sartre: namely, *the demand for a Marxist anthropology.* Sartre designates the lack of such an anthropology as the shortcoming of Marxist theory up to now. However, it quickly becomes apparent that this Marxist anthropology, which Sartre sets as his goal, exposes a basic premise of Marxism which Sartre by no means wants to expose: the thesis that every consideration of man in history must begin with the class position of these men. Yet Sartre wants to enrich the Marxist anthropology mainly with the help of scientific principles which, as he himself admits, are inseparable with the positions of international entrepreneurship. Sartre means specific research methods of modern American sociology, that is, microsociology. He himself remarks: "I remember, in fact, that this branch of knowledge favored the entrepreneurs in the United

States." However, he adds to this—rather naïvely for someone who is supposed to be a Marxist: "One should not take this as an excuse and immediately reject this knowledge because it is the weapon of a class in the hands of the capitalists." Actually it is not at all a question that concerns the scientific results of this microsociology. Sartre speaks about the questions of method. Here he reveals that he wants to enrich the Marxist doctrine with scientific methods whose social position is the opposite of the basic position of Marxism. The concept of comprehension (*Verstehen*) that Sartre borrows from Wilhelm Dilthey and incorporates into the so-called sociology of comprehension is so inextricably bound to specific forms of late bourgeois philosophizing that there is once again a syncretism of method, an eclecticism in all of Sartre's efforts. The attempt to enrich Marxist philosophy through psychoanalysis that is proposed by Sartre is neither new (as we can see from the works of Erich Fromm and Herbert Marcuse), nor is it demonstrated very convincingly.

Since the publication of his *Critique of Dialectical Reason,* Sartre seems to hold tenaciously to his effort to bridge the gap between Freud and Marx. This project is mentioned once again in an interview with the English literary critic Kenneth Tynan during the summer of 1961. Sartre explains: "I believe the Marxists have lost a great deal in that they have totally cut themselves off from psychoanalysis by refusing to recognize it. Of course, Freud used his theories to lay the foundation for many historical theories which are hardly of use to sociologists, not to mention Marxists. What counts is his proof that the sexual drive is not merely a sexual drive but something which encompasses the whole personality and has an influence on how one plays the piano or violin. I believe that this is his lasting contribution." There are, according to Sartre, two lasting contributions which Freud made. First his discovery that all which constitutes man is rational. (This interpretation is, by the way, more Sartre than Freud: it converts Hegel's famous statement concerning the rationality of the real back into the mere individual.) Therefore, chance is not conceivable in the life of man. "And Freud's second great discovery was that even in the realm of self-recognition, the progress of mankind stems from his needs. I see Freud as a superb materialist.

He did not place hunger in the forefront because he came from an environment where hunger did not exist; instead he chose sexuality which is equally necessary—not because man would die without it but because the lack of it can drive man to insanity."

However, this is mere play with terminology. A more thorough examination of the psychoanalytical point of view and of its therapy will be able to discover little of Freud's supposed materialism. On the other hand, it will discover much more about the idealistic ideas concerning the primacy of the intellect and cognition, about the uncritically adopted norms of life and order from the bourgeois society. One speaks of Freud as a man of the Enlightenment, an adherent of philosophical idealism, a fanatic with regard to education. But can one link him to materialism?

Behind all this, there is a process that no longer has anything to do with eclecticism but must lead to *the surrender of the basic position of Marxism*. In reality the matter does not concern an enrichment of Marxism through Sartre but a basic existentialist position tinted with a little Marxism. The philosophy of Marx and Engels is dialectical materialism that in part still adheres to Hegel. Hegel's system, which started from the principle of *Entäusserung* ("denial"), did not place man against nature antithetically. With Sartre there is a division between man and nature. Sartre rejects a dialectics of nature such as that which Engels had developed. For him dialectics exists only where man becomes an observer of nature. Sartre makes a distinction between "positive reason" and "dialectical reason." The latter he wants used for society and history. Actually, since Heinrich Rickert, this is the division of those methods used in the natural sciences from those of the humanities. In 1923 Georg Lukács, in his book *Geschichte und Klassenbewusstsein (History and Class Consciousness)*, had already endeavored to reach the position that Sartre holds today: rejection of a dialectics of nature on the grounds that dialectics is valid only in the observation of human conditions, and rejection of the basic position of materialism in the natural sciences. Like Sartre, he attempted not only to separate the dialectics of human history from the so-called dialectics of nature, but along with this, to separate Marx from Engels, since Engels had written a book called *The Dialectics of Nature,* whereas Karl Marx, as Lukács happily established, agrees with an idea of Giovanni Battista Vico's referred to in the first volume of *Das Kapital*: "For, as Vico says, human history distinguishes itself from natural history in that we created the one and not the other." However, Lukács himself turned away from this theme later never to return to it.

We are concerned here with a great deal more than a mere conflict between the "isms." Every decisive analysis in Sartre's book shows that it is only superficially connected to the basic position of Marxism. Occasionally one comes across the same terminology, but Sartre means by it something totally different. This in itself must not be considered a counterargument against Sartre, except perhaps from the standpoint of an orthodox Marxist. However, it proves that Sartre's attempt at a marriage of reason between Marxism and existentialist ideology leads to a watering down of the contradictions, which may affect everything but will not produce a dialectical synthesis.

What becomes clear in the treatise "Questions of Method" is confirmed in the course of the actual *Critique of Dialectical Reason*. Socioeconomic factors are transformed in good idealistic fashion into psychological problems. Sartre's Marxist anthropology turns from Marx and investigates only the consciousness of man, not his social being. Economic and social antagonisms are transformed, as we know from Sartre's plays, into conflicts between the individual and the others. Twenty years ago in his play *Closed Society*, Sartre wrote, "Hell is what the others are."

The official philosopher of the French Communists, Roger Garaudy,* rejected Sartre's book completely—as can be well understood. He readily admitted that he makes the criticism of Sartre easy for himself. However, he is perfectly correct when he objects thus to Sartre's thesis: "When one isolates alienation and reification from their economic and social foundations, they resemble the theological concept of sin more than the concept of fetish of goods (*Warenfetischismus*) in Marx." A public confrontation between the theses of Sartre and Garaudy took place at the end of

---

* Garaudy *was* the official philosopher. He has since been ostracized from the party because of heresy.

1961, the same year that the interview with Kenneth Tynan appeared. On December 7, 1961, in a packed auditorium in Paris, Garaudy and the Marxist natural scientist Jean-Pierre Vigier debated the French expert on Hegel, Jean Hyppolyte, and Sartre on the topic "Is dialectics solely a law of history or is it also a law of nature?" In the course of the debate Sartre returned to the thesis of his latest philosophical work and explained his rejection of all dialectics of nature—according to a detailed account in the newspaper *Les Lettres Françaises*—with the following words: "The basis of history is a totality. Hence, our knowledge is a knowledge of the totality. Our thought undertakes totalization. Here man really finds the basis, and thereby he finds himself. Here one can speak of dialectics as being intelligible, illuminating. One is dealing with the thought of a being, and a thinking being. For Marx as for Hegel, both of whom start with the idea of a totality of human events, every moment of history can be explained. Thus, on the basis of this totality one can set up comprehensible laws of dialectics. History makes man in the same way as man makes history. History can only be understood through all this, through our being and doing."

However, all these facts that could be used in favor of a dialectics of history speak against the possibility of a dialectics of nature. According to Sartre, it is—and Garaudy protested against this—merely a play of analogies if one wants to discover this human historical totality in the realm of nature, in other words, independent from man. Sartre asked his adversaries two questions in reply:

1. Do totalities also exist in nature?
2. Can one imagine a totalization of the whole that would be identical with nature itself?

The atomic physicist Vigier answered in the affirmative. It appears, however, that he did not convince Sartre. Of course, the philosophical mass meeting ended in a draw. Apparently this evening did not move Sartre to interrupt his work on the second volume of his philosophical study as he had done in the past with the third volume of his series of novels *Roads to Freedom*, when he stopped writing the fourth and concluding volume of the series. At that time he had a sense of failure.

The term *failure* is valuable for an existentialist. Sartre failed as a *romancier* with the concept of freedom. He gives the reason for this in his interview with Tynan. "It would be much too easy to write a novel in which the hero dies in the resistance movement because he was committed to the idea of freedom. Nowadays it is hard to define the commitment." On the other hand, the criticism of his treatment of the problems of dialectical reason in his book seemed to have had little effect on Sartre.

The large-scale ambitious attempt to create a scientific synthesis. Extravagantly planned, burdened by an abundance of repetitions and historical and literary digressions that are interesting in themselves but do not exactly make the reading easier because they are not always pertinent. The result is a philosophical eclecticism that would like to be dialectical without being so. In addition, a nonhistorical consideration of man in this anthropology that replaced all concrete economical problems with the very abstract concept of "lack of goods." Out of this Sartre wants to explain man's modes of relationships and group formation so that he can finally land in the middle of the seventeenth century at Thomas Hobbes. One should not speculate in scientific fields, but it is improbable that the second part of Sartre's *Critique of Dialectical Reason* will have an essentially different result.

Situations, or "What Is Literature?" (1947)

Three years after the liberation of France, Sartre undertook to answer the question, What is literature? His comprehensive essay reads as though one were climbing a mountain: excursions and digressions and a mixture of sociological, psychological, and aesthetic observations allow us to recognize the author of the philosophical treatise *Being and Nothingness* and also the Sartre who wrote the *Critique of Dialectical Reason*. His essay on

literature goes around in spirals to its summit. First, Sartre studies
what literature has to do with the work of an author. Then Sartre
asks why a writer writes. Here he is already half way up the
mountain. The next problem to be studied concerns the audience
of a writer. This is the last steep incline before the summit. As
the essayist reaches the summit, he has an unimpeded view from
above. Now he can see near and far. The reader who has followed
Sartre's path from the beginning will hardly be surprised that the
view from the summit of the essay *What Is Literature?* means a
view into time. Sartre entitles the report of this view "The Situation of the Writer in 1947." A reference to time, the word *writer*,
the term *situation*.

This balance of the records by Sartre concerning the principles
behind his work (this is nominally what it is about) is indeed remarkable. One of the finest works by Jean-Paul Sartre. He is
possibly at his best as an *essayist*. The term is understood here
not in the narrow sense of a cultural or literary critic but in the
broad traditional sense which he may claim to have developed out
of the tradition of Montaigne. The essay sections in Sartre's
philosophical treatises are always the high points and represent
for some a compensation for "weaker parts." Both the dramatic
works of the 1950's, *Lucifer and the Lord* and *The Condemned of
Altona*, are actually dramatized essays by a philosophical writer
who is not very critical in his selection of dramatic devices since
the action on stage is not of great importance. Whoever knows
Sartre's theories will recognize in his later plays and also in the
framework of the three books of *The Paths of Liberty* mere ex-
emplification of philosophical and literary theories. When a
writer of this type writes about the basis of his writing, he reveals
himself more completely than through a drama or novel.

The term *writer* is the decisive point. All Sartre's literary works
are demonstrations of his philosophical theories. All the figures
in Sartre's stories, dramas, and novels are exemplifications and
hardly have a right to exist "in and by themselves." The figure
of Orestes in *The Flies* or Mathieu in the novel cycle or Franz
in *The Condemned of Altona* corresponds respectively to a
particular part of Sartre's theoretical writings. *Thus, the literary
theory of this philosophical writer forms the basis of his entire*

works. It is hard to determine which comes first in Sartre's theories, philosophy or the literary essays. Sartre himself would say philosophy.

The writer, the year 1947, the situation. Three years after the liberation of occupied France. The period of German rule gave the strongest impulses to the man and author Sartre as a complex of experiences. The intellectual and literary evaluation of this historical pattern lasted until 1950. It was followed by years of sterility. Sartre had become fashionable. Saint-Germain-des-Pres became a place of pilgrimage for people from the other side of the Atlantic. The mandarin of Paris. Literary production consisting of repetition and unsuccessful projects until the wars in Vietnam and Algeria created a new center of experience for Sartre. The novel *Nausea* and the stories in the volume *The Wall* contained the quintessence of Sartre's prewar development. Sartre was thirty-four years old at the outbreak of World War II. *The Flies* was an intellectual and artistic highpoint of his creative powers during the occupation. The treatise *What Is Literature?* represents the end of this creative period in Sartre's life.

We are speaking of the writer in 1947. From the very beginning, Sartre placed all his essays under the heading and the title *situations* (not merely this one section of a single work). His observations about the basic problems in literature clearly state why the term *situation* is so important. In order to understand the insistence of the essayist about this point, one must remember that Sartre likes to speak of historical totality but does not want to recognize any kind of historical law. As a result of this position, we find the strange and often striking structure of the dramas and novels, which consciously renounce the consistency of the characters in order to present man continually in the epic and dramatic realm with amazing incongruity—in decisions that usually dispense with any deeper motivation, seem to be causeless, and often reveal a frightening discontinuity of behavior.

In Sartre's novels and plays, man lives in a world that is unrecognizable to him, one which appears to him to be illogical, incomprehensible, completely meaningless. There is neither a law of history nor a transformation of reality through common efforts. Each action has a significance only for the one who acts. The narrator or the dramatist is in no better position than his characters. Since he does not know more than they do, he cannot think of assuming the attitude of the director or the omniscient narrator. To use Sartre's own words: "Since we were situated, we could think only of novels of situation, those without an internal narrator and without omniscient witnesses. In short, if we wanted to give an account of our epoch, we had to move from the novel techniques of Newtonian mechanics to generalized relativity. We had to fill our books with minds that were half lucid and half overcast. We might sympathize more with one or the other, without, however, placing one of them in a more advantageous position in regard to himself and the action; we had to present creatures whose reality was a contradictory web of phenomena." In another part of this situational report about the position of the writer in the year 1947, the essay completes the analysis by focusing on the dramaturgy of situational thinking: "More authors are returning to situational theater. No more characters: the heroes are, like all of us, freedoms caught in a trap. How do they get out of this trap again? Each figure becomes merely a choice for a way out and is worth no more than their quality as a chosen way out. It is to be hoped that all literature will become moral and problematic like this new theater. Moral—not moralizing: it should show simply that man *also* represents a value and the questions that he asks himself are always moral."

An artistic contradiction arises here. A contradiction that seems to be insoluble, and even Sartre, an extraordinarily gifted man, could not overcome it with all the means of his talents. He demands that the theater once again become a moral institution. This conception belongs to the theme of the Enlightenment that can be constantly observed in Sartre's thought and work. Thus, nothing would be more absurd than to bring Sartre's plays together with the so-called theater of the absurd. Sartre is the opposite of a thinker and writer of absurdity. *His opposition to Camus is based on this.* He is a moralist and cannot conceive of literature without a function.

However, the moralizing of this author with his conception of mere life situations in an unrecognizable world continually falls into conflicts. A literature with a moralizing function must strive to involve the theater audience as well as the reader with the action of the figures. Either through identification or distance. There is empathy and alienation. In both cases the author determines the nonliterary effect of his work. However, moralization and functionalism are not possible when there is only a world of situations and abrupt actions that are not based on the nature of character or causal events. Either the situational concept of a freedom in the incongruous individual action that is valid for no one else but the one who is acting, since no one else goes through the same situation, or—literary moralizing. Both together are not possible. Thus, it becomes clear why Sartre's dramas, stories, and novels, though always captivating because of their intellectual intensity, can never lead to any kind of non-literary life decision by the reader and spectator the way Sartre seems to wish they could. Sartre's heroes always live in a unique situation especially prepared for them. The way in which they cope with the situation cannot be accomplished by anyone else or repeated by anyone else. No matter what Sartre might introduce, their way must remain without a function.

Sartre has a mania for constantly portraying man as hermetically sealed off from others in a godless world without common ideologies or beliefs. Man is not able to break through this barrier even in "erotic" intimacy. All this is not presented merely as "existential" but is linked to the historical situation of the bourgeois society in 1947. A new contradiction, which was unavoidable given Sartre's theory of situations, opposes his own honest efforts to understand historical relationships and to avoid everything that could seem like bourgeois apologetics. Sartre is completely familiar with the relationship between literature and bourgeois society. He states: "Thus literature in the nineteenth century risks becoming the good conscience of the oppressed classes after having been the bad conscience of the privileged classes in the eighteenth century." Sartre also points out that this process eventually contributed to making the most important literature a literature without an audience. He also makes the formulation that contemporary literature has, to be sure, readers but no audience: "Since the bourgeoisie gained control over man and possessions, the spiritual was once again separated from the temporal, and once again a form of priesthood sprang up: Stendhal's public was Balzac; Baudelaire's public was Barbey d'Aurevilly; and Baudelaire, in turn, made himself the public of Poe." As the process of alienation between bourgeois literature and bourgeois nonapologetic literature continues, the situation of the bourgeois writer becomes increasingly difficult. "Watchdog or buffoon . . . these are the alternatives." Here Sartre contradicts his philosophy of discontinuity completely—as a philosopher of history and as a sociologist who studied Hegel and Marx. Such observations really expose the term *situation* for what it is.

Sartre has noticed this himself and has attempted to eliminate some of the contradictions. However, this leads to eclecticism. Sartre's answer to his own question of the theory about literature ended in the same theoretical dilemma as did—thirteen years later—his philosophical attempt to create a dialectical synthesis out of existentialism and Marxism. What Sartre formulates as "a task" is actually an act of theoretical desperation: "Compelled by circumstances to discover the force of history, we have a task for which we will perhaps not be strong enough. (This is not the first time that an epoch has failed its art and philosophy because of a lack of talent.) That task is to create a literature which once again unites and reconciles the metaphysical absolute and the relativity of historical events and which I call, for better or for worse, the literature of relationships."

This is the task. It is an absolutely impossible one. Sartre has no success with it in his treatise *What Is Literature?* nor in the later *Critique of Dialectical Reason*. Certainly not in his literary works after 1947. The theoretical eclecticism often became political incongruity. The play *Dirty Hands* was readily accepted by anticommunist institutions, which in turn quickly led to Sartre's displeasure. The farce *Nekrasso* was a dramatic satire about this kind of anticommunism. The unique "situation" of *The Condemned of Altona*—and the highly concrete historical situation of a German "Grossbürger" in the Third Reich. Sartre attempted everywhere to force a union between the "metaphysical absolute" and the relativity of historical events, and this never came to fruition.

The writer Sartre seeks a literature of "not only/but also."

Yet from this it becomes a literature of neither/nor because "the class of oppressors has lost its ideology; its self-consciousness is uncertain; its boundaries are no longer clearly recognizable. It is no longer seclusive and calls upon the writer for help. The oppressed class is organized into a party, prides itself on a strict ideology, and becomes a closed society in and for itself." This confirmation also describes a situation. It is the situation of the author Jean Paul Sartre.

"The Words" (1965)

On a first reading of Sartre's account of his development as a youth and the origins of his decision to turn to writing, it becomes evident that the basic situation that was of such importance for his entire life was not engendered by related words, that is, by words that coordinate themselves into texts—for Sartre, into sacred texts—but by something else. What? Apparently by the consuming and spellbinding magic of individual words that had the power of driving him forward.

Sartre describes the reading stage of his career as a writer: lying on the carpet, before him Fontenelle, Aristophanes, or Rabelais. In other words, good and genuine reading for children. But he does not read in the usual sense of the term; instead he is always engaged in a quest in the manner of such renowned adventurers as the great Magalhães or Vasco da Gama. The child's expeditions do not lead to foreign lands and foreign peoples but to an encounter with peculiar words: *heautomorphism, idiosyncrasy, chiasm.* One monstrosity of a word was discovered in an Alexandrine-verse translation of Terence, another in a history of comparative literature. However, for the young Sartre, words assumed a strange form. In retrospect, Sartre calls them "impenetrable and repulsive fellows." They were reified and represented the world. More than that, they meant the world to the beginning reader. His path to reality was filled with endless encounters with word images. In the beginning were the words. This is to be taken literally. It was not the word in the sense of Logos that stood at the beginning for Sartre. His path led from words to phrases, then from phrases to things. It is in this sense that one has to understand the meaning of *words* in the book by the sixty-year-old Sartre.

The story of Sartre's youth is portrayed here as a path toward idealism—idealism in the precise philosophical sense, not in its typical bourgeois distorted meaning where idealism stands for the decision to become a Sanskrit scholar rather than manage the father's firm. Since the time of Plato, idealism has been postulated on the primacy of unrecognizable ideas. According to this, our reality is a weak reflection, a colored reflection, of truth, in other words, of ideals. As a child Sartre thought of all reality as a dim reflection of the world of ideas since he compared it to his own reality, which he saw as being pitiful. However, reality meant for him the world of books. From the very beginning, reading had been an expedition into the wonderland of words. The youth's picture of reality was gradually completed as his map of unexplored regions was reduced, and it became possible to "name" even the rarest of words. Reality was presented as the world of texts, as Logos, as literature. Sartre's world was based on the laws and hierarchies of the world of books.

An incredible idealism for a child who could not really sense what it was—idealism. Aside from this, it was a neurosis. Sartre describes this situation of his youth in great detail: the word is absorbed in order to be absorbed simultaneously by the image. This was a double poisoning. The only antidote was to let the two poisons neutralize each other. With careful attention to small points, Sartre describes that the situation reached such an extreme that sounds in the room became interjections, as if the squawks of a parakeet were in quotation marks. In the beginning were the words.

An idealistic conception of the world. A childhood neurosis. Above all a sacred process. Sacred in the sense of a substitute religion. This is the reason why Sartre uses the German word *ersatz*. The actual religious experience was omitted, or rather it was hindered by external circumstances. A young Catholic grew up in a Protestant environment and appeared predestined to become a believer, perhaps a monk. However, he lost his taste for this course of life because of the dull Christianity stemming from the good situation of bourgeois tolerance. His religious ardor found a new object in the world of books. "The man of the pen appeared as a 'substitute' for the Christian I could not be." Therefore, literature became a sacred realm. The encounter with God the Father—Sartre describes this episode of his childhood—was unfruitful. The redeemer role of the Son was barred to the child who—here he unknowingly anticipated his entire late philosophy—was bent on self-redemption since the beginning of his conscious life. The Holy Ghost remained, and it took possession of him at the early age of eight.

All the holy truths of various religions, particularly those of Christianity, were brought into the child's world by the Holy Ghost in a secularized form. The young Sartre decided to become a writer. His grandfather Karl Schweitzer encouraged him but not with real sincerity. Still, a writer was a priest of the sacred sphere of literature for him. The writer stood in the service of holy words. Aside from this, he was a born martyr because his life on earth had but one goal: literary posterity. However, you had to be predestined to become a writer. You were chosen and had posterity from the very beginning as a guarantee. The young Sartre decided to become a writer and meant by this a martyr in the service of a belletristic substitute religion.

Yet, at the same time he knew that his belief in the miraculous power of literature was dangerously similar to the comic affectations that he had so often "put on" in excess for his grandparents and mother during his first "wunderkind" phase. His early decision for the chosen life as writer and martyr had its theatrical side. Moreover, in reading his autobiography one can understand why he was so fascinated when he later encountered the criminal writer Jean Genet and why he gave his remarkable book about Genet the seemingly blasphemous title *St. Genet: Actor and Martyr*.

"I have caught the Holy Ghost in the cellar and driven him out. Atheism is a terrible and tedious venture. I believe I have carried it to its end." This passage is on one of the last pages of the book *The Words*. A second break became necessary from his belief in literature, and the book concludes with a retrospective glance— actually it is a view toward the future. Sartre writes in his narrative about his encounter with words as a youth and how "the normal religion" quickly became—through external influences and the fate of a child growing up without a father—a secularized substitute religion of literature. Still, it was just a substitute religion. The Holy Ghost had buried itself deep in his soul. It played a definite role even when the realistic author Sartre wrote his novel *Nausea*. According to Sartre, this was still theism in the form of a religion of literature. Here, too, a new process of secularization became necessary. The Holy Ghost of belles lettres also had to be banished. The gruesome venture of total atheism led Sartre into a "situation," and the belief in literature also had to be dismissed as heresy. Nonetheless, Sartre continued to write. He wrote the essay on the origins of a substitute religion that had to be denied. There are certain inferences that allow us to assume that the account of the banishment of the Holy Ghost of literature which then followed and was due will be told in the future.

There is still the question as to how this total atheism can be reconciled with Sartre's thesis about the committed author. One of Sartre's best stories, which is filled with black humor, depicts the childhood of a boss. A student from a good family for whom puberty is a process fraught with boredom experiments with various patterns of existence. He begins to test the Oedipus complex because Freud had just come into fashion and ends with the attitude of a vicious anti-Semite. Actually he has nothing against the Jews. He hardly knows any, but this role proves to be highly successful among the upper middle classes. This pattern is a hit and is assumed only after puberty.

As a youth, Sartre read the entire classics in his grandfather's library as well as countless penny novels in secret. His career as a writer is the culmination of a role as a child prodigy, which he had successfully played for a long time. This writing—the real beginnings of Jean-Paul Sartre—is both a role and an emotional necessity. The role consists of having others stand and watch as a smart aleck fills page upon page at his desk, and once the pages are filled, he is no longer concerned with his writings. Only the act of writing (and having others observe him while he writes) is important. (He does not think at all of rereading his material.)

This means imitation, mimesis, as with all roles. Of course, real people and their deeds are not imitated here—this is related to the sacred sphere of literature in his grandfather's house—but rather books with their descriptions of life, in other words, books by well-known authors. Sartre imitates what he believes to be the actions of Corneille or Musset.

The young Sartre writes not only to complete a role as part of a process of repetition and mimesis, but he is also driven by an infantile, compulsive idea of redemption. He is a fatherless child who, as a prodigy, has to act on the stage of the family theater. Yet, he is secretly aware that these theatrical successes cannot last. Above all, there is one thing they cannot produce: meaning in an existence that is felt to be superfluous, and, in fact, *is* superfluous. Behind all the mimicry, the young Sartre recognizes again and again that his existence lacks "legitimacy." In spite of all the pampering, this existence is felt to be unnecessary. Everything depends on the cultivation of some necessity through one's own energy, and in the process one simultaneously creates and redeems oneself. A delicate child, without means or heritage, ugly and apparently without any pronounced talent, he sees writing as the only means for self-redemption.

Here a thorough understanding of adventure stories, magazines, and comic books is beneficial. Sartre knows two types of heroes: an invincible book hero and a movie hero. The sheriff in the Wild West film defends innocence and defeats the bandits; the three musketeers spite even the king and his ministers in order to bring about the cherished triumph of justice; after many setbacks the courageous white man conquers the natives and frees the famous explorer from the stake. The hero is always a redeemer. He is necessary because injustice would win without him.

The young Sartre does not read for the sake of suspense. His reading, as the beginning of all reading, leads rather to identification. While reading, he himself is the hero and redeemer. Yet how is this possible when all heroes on the screen and in books are handsome and rugged? This is certainly not the case with the reader. How then is it possible to create this identification? Once again, through literature. There are famous writers who have emerged as redeemers of mankind—if one can believe books. For example, Voltaire, Hugo, Zola. There are also others. Apparently mankind needs great writers in order to preserve the continuity of existence. At least this was the case with the literary substitute religion of the grandfather, and his grandson was of the same opinion. He needed this kind of justification for his existence through writing, books, works. A self-redemption through the written word.

The glorious Pardaillan,* ostensibly a heroic synthesis of Dumas and Karl May, was the favorite object for identification. As always, there was also Pierre Corneille. "I dressed up Corneille as Pardaillan . . . . Then it was mere child's play to transform myself into Corneille and assign myself the task of protecting mankind." Writing as action from heroic epics. The great author became a hero of humanity and a world redeemer for the youth who was looking for a model in life. Young Sartre was also determined to become such an indispensable savior of mankind. Through his writing. Through literature.

It becames apparent why writing could initially be nothing less for Sartre than literature of commitment. Moreover, one senses here why the great essayist Jean-Paul Sartre later had to dismiss the opposition between "pure" and "committed" literature as an artifical antithesis. This was because the choice of a seemingly nonmissionary literature was understood as a special form of commitment—thus Sartre's passionate interest in Baudelaire. As is known, Sartre remained true to this basic position, which called for existential options. The complete works of this philosopher, sociologist, dramatist, politician, and novelist are rooted in a strange amalgamation of Corneille and Pardaillan.

However, what happens to an author who gradually catches himself at his own tricks and must recognize that the beloved Pardaillan and the somewhat less beloved Michael Strogoff, famous courier of the Czars, are slightly degenerate epic heroes in keeping with their literary genres while they play the role of substitute redeemers in an existential sphere? After such a reali-

---

* *Translator's note:* Pardaillan was a knight who appeared as hero of a serial written by Michel Zévaco for the newspaper *Le Matin.* As a boy Sartre read this serial with great enthusiasm and Pardaillan came to represent for him a champion of the people.

zation, a second secularization is due. In the process the belief in a religion of art is dropped as well as the belief in the possibility and necessity of literary commitment. In anticipation of later events, Sartre accomplishes this double expulsion in the last pages of *The Words*: he banishes substitute religion and commitment. Nonetheless he continues to write. He continues to commit himself.

One can interpret the situation of the man who wrote the last pages of *The Words* either as a joyous one without illusions or as one of deep disappointment. Yet, here one might object (if one refrains from any identification with Sartre) that we are given a situation as a final situation, as total atheism and renunciation of all substitute religions, while in reality it means a new substitute religion. A total atheist who continues to create and who constantly commits himself goes through a phase in which the work ethic takes on the function of conceiving a new substitute religion. Thus, a third secularization can take place. Atheism was never entirely enough. One can obviously assume that Sartre will complete this process only when he no longer wants to write or no longer writes. Fortunately, for the present there is no indication of this.

It is entirely possible that Sartre would accept this conclusion. This is because it is related to a basic premise of his philosophy and literature. The author of the book *The Words* describes most impressively how he conceives of his life and creativity as a permanent result of self-denial and renunciation. He even points out that the heroes in his novels and dramas never make their decisions in the form of a spiritual transformation but abruptly renounce all behavior up to that time. The philosopher Sartre has endeavored to generalize about these individual acts: "Transcendental consciousness is impersonal spontaneity." This means that the sphere of "I-ness," to use Johann Fichte's term, is not merely a dialectic correlative to the world but has a character of its own. The "I" for Sartre is "with the world at the same time." Permanent spontaneity is characteristic of this world sphere of the "I." Hence, Sartre states: "Every moment of our life reveals to us a *creatio ex nihilo*. Not a new pattern, but a new being." These lines stem from a philosophical study called "Transcendental

Character of the Ego," written in 1937, and it can still be considered valid from a philosophical point of view.

If this is the case, then a new spiritual creation out of nothingness can also mean the renunciation of all redemption through a work ethic and lead to a new stage. Thus, the third secularization would be "spontaneously" completed.

Sartre takes his philosophy absolutely seriously. Therefore, it becomes apparent once again why, in spite of all his efforts to create a synthesis out of Marxism and existentialism, he could never really come close to Marxism. His ontology and eschatology reject the basic Marxist principle of a dialectic subject-object relationship as well as the materialistic thesis of the "primacy of the external world." Aside from this, it becomes evident in *The Words* that Sartre also had to disavow Marxist dialectics in the relationship between theory and practice. Theory as ideology, as false consciousness, is understood under the negative aspect of total atheism. A theory of history can never accept this thesis of consciousness as impersonal spontaneity. Philosophy of history and *creatio ex nihilo* cancel each other out. In other words, practice without theory. Practice in and of itself. But also, practice as a substitute religion.

The freedom, which the last pages of *The Words* appear to proclaim, proves to be a new metaphysical bond. It is merely a condition, a "situation," and therefore, it can be resolved— abrupt in action, absurd in substance—by a new decision. This is because it became clear that the situation of being totally without illusions also represented a form of commitment and, along with this, institutionalization. Sartre is well aware of this.

The Views of
Witold Gombrowicz

Basso Ostinato

In his diary of 1954 Gombrowicz wrote:

"Say to yourself: people dream about getting to know you. They want you. They are curious about you. Lead them with force into your affairs, even those which would not interest them. Force them to become interested in that which interests you. The more they know about you, the more important you will be to them.

" 'I' is no obstacle in your relations with men. It is the 'I' that they demand. But this 'I' must not be smuggled through like contraband. What won't the 'I' endure? Indecision. Fear. Bashfulness."

In *Ferdydurke* he wrote:

"For—but frankly I don't know whether the time has come yet to mention this to you—it is false to postulate that man should be definite and determined, that is to say, unshakeable in his ideas, categorical in his assertions, clear in his ideologies, decisive in his tastes, responsible for his words and actions, completely rigid in his way of being. Look more closely at the false picture postulated. Our essence in life is eternal immaturity."

Real Poland, 1938 (Ferdydurke)

Real? Is the novel *Ferdydurke*, which first appeared in 1938, supposed to deal with the Polish reality in the thirties? The author, Witold Gombrowicz, would indignantly deny this and would write another entry in his diary treating the ignorance of critics. In his diary of 1954, he had already confided a few recipes from his literary kitchen to those writers "who are interested in my writing technique." The most important of these provided this advice: "Enter into the realm of dreams." Following this, he supplied an additional rule of thumb: "And write not with a view toward reckoning with reality, but with a view toward satisfying the needs of your imagination."

So is *Ferdydurke* real? Is it a picture of the Polish realities in 1938? Contrary to what you might at first believe, it most certainly is. Admittedly everything seems completely dreamlike and fantastic: a writer has just crossed the thirty-year turning point and is suddenly transported back into school and puberty by an internal psychic compulsion and the superior power of a critic and pedagogue who embodies literary authority. A thirty-year-old boy, then, who is given food and lodging and placed with a modern, tolerant, enlightened family of an engineer so that he might learn to bow to the supreme daughter of the house with the respectful feelings of a grammar school boy. A duel between representatives of noble feelings and those of harsh vulgarity. A counterduel between world famous authorities of analysis and synthesis. An unsuccessful attempt by the urban intellectual to become a brother to "the people" ends in a comic fight. Everything depicted as the consequence of associations. The language (actually, the words) are arranged musically like leitmotifs not according to their meaning—as in the case of Thomas Mann—but according to their tonal and emotional power of expression. One is reminded of E. T. A. Hoffmann, of the etchings by Alfred Kubin, of the eery dream scenes in Kafka's novel that take place in courtrooms located somewhere in an attic.

All the literary, musical, and visual associations which the reader of *Ferdydurke* feels welling within himself convey a dream world.

And this is what Gombrowicz would have wanted. As a writer he entered the realm of dreams, created dream pictures. He abandoned himself to the flow, creation, fables, and associations in order to bring about new dream worlds for the reader—not merely to bring about the reproductions of his own visions, but to allow for the free associations of the reader and those to whom the work is addressed. The work is certainly written in Polish and appears to take place in Poland, in a village not far from Warsaw, in the manor of a country gentleman. The action takes place during the 1930's, about 1935, for in this year Witold Gombrowicz, born in 1904, crossed the fateful turning point between maturity and immaturity. A novel written in the first person by a writer who has turned thirty and gives voice to his "I." Of course, Gombrowicz guards against endowing the narrator with too many autobiographical traits. His first name in *Ferdydurke* is not Witold but Jozio. In contrast, the first-person narrator of the novel *Pornografia,* which was published in 1960 and has the imaginary Poland of 1942 as its background, is expressly called "Witold Gombrowicz." The author conceals his identity in a 1938 novel that is set in Poland at a time when Gombrowicz himself was in his home country. In the other novel published in 1960 and set in an imaginary Poland during the war, the author seems to reveal his identity, and yet he also informs us in his preface that he is writing about a Poland that he no longer knows. Gombrowicz left Poland in 1939 and never returned home. Convex mirrors and funny reflections. All of them.

Nevertheless, we have a real Poland in the novel *Ferdydurke,* and the title remains entirely enigmatic right to the end. The word "Ferdydurke" is neither a name nor does it impart meaning. It belongs to the language of dreams and also to the language of children. Therefore, it is perfectly suited to introduce us to a work which is simultaneously supposed to be the realm of dreams and the middle realm between childhood and adulthood. The word "Ferdydurke" functions immediately as the formula "step into the realm of dreams." We still have a Polish reality of 1938. (When one writes about Gombrowicz, one is drawn almost naturally into the mire of a narrative style that moves along with the aid of leitmotifs and tonal pictures and even orgiastically enjoys the principle of the repetition of words and ideas at times. The compulsion to repeat is a basic element in the thinking of children. Repetition is an element of propaganda and also infantilism.) In the realm of dreams there is no absolute. The dreamer, dreaming, still lives in the real world. His visions and emotions may be spaceless and timeless. They may dispense with all causality. However, they can only produce something that has not been experienced from the reproduced bits and pieces of past experience. The old dreambooks distinguish themselves from the new Freudian ones by their relation to this phenomenon. In the former it is dream as anticipation, as preexperience of the future. In the latter it is dream as a strange and unsuitable reproduction of past experience. The epic dreamworld of Witold Gombrowicz would like to be both: the interpretation of dreams in a double sense—according to the biblical Joseph and Professor Sigmund Freud. Planted between past and future. In the hollow of the present.

The prognosis for the future remains vague, and this is not at all surprising. In his diary written during the fifties, the author pokes fun at those critics who would categorize his books according to theories and didactic views, claiming in effect, "In *Ferdydurke* Gombrowicz wants to say." On the other hand, the reworking of reality that has been experienced is different. All the frills and arabesques of the narrator belong to life situations that can be fixed in precise terms of place, time, and event. The real Poland of the thirties. This remarkable novel would not be understood for the most part without this background. In his homeland Gombrowicz had been somewhat successful as an author ever since 1933. *Ferdydurke* first appeared in Warsaw in 1938 and caused a considerable sensation. Then, however, the circumstances of the war diminished the success, and it was not until 1956 that it reappeared and was translated into numerous languages for the first time. When Gombrowicz had worked on *Ferdydurke,* the heirs of Pilsudski ruled a Polish Republic that was allied with France and England and busily engaged in industrialization. In the country itself, or better, in the countryside itself, the feudal forms of a aristocratic ruling class of landowners were maintained by brutal measures. Since Gombrowicz belonged to this landowning class, he knew the connections quite well. Decisive scenes in both *Ferdydurke* and *Pornografia* take place in the homes of the rural and ruling landowners. In the diaries, too, mention is constantly made of this class and its manner of behavior.

The theme of immaturity as the basic motif is modified in *Ferdydurke*, Gombrowicz's first novel. As a matter of fact, in one of the chapters, "Introduction to Philifor Honeycombed with Childishness," Gombrowicz even sets up a complete catalogue of the different forms of immaturity which all beget agony: from the agony of the old-fashioned to the agony of the modern. Naturally the term *immaturity* can be applied to the situation in life of the aging person and to the methodological problems of the prospective writer. Yet, as the decisive force behind it all, there is the *immaturity of a country*, the Polish state in 1938. Approximately one hundred years before Gombrowicz, Karl Marx had pointed out in an analysis of the conditions in Germany that there were actually no estates (*Stände*) nor classes in Germany but merely perishing estates and unformed classes. The Polish world of *Ferdydurke* also portrays an unstable world. Feudalism and a patriarchal hegemony that could be maintained in form only, and that with brutality. This is just as grotesque as it is illustrated in the detailed example of the landowner Edward and his family. "We had awakened the beast! We had unchained the impudence of the lackeys! During that dreadful night, lying sleepless on my bed, I grasped the secret of the manor house, the secret of the rural aristocracy and the townspeople. The numerous and disturbing symptoms of the secret had from the outset given me a premonition of the approach of facial terror, of face! The secret was the servants. The secret of the rulers was the common people." What is more, Hegel had long ago written about this, and it was expressed in a society that was similarly immature and in a transitional phase at the beginning of the nineteenth century. "The servant is the truth of the master."

However, a society that made the effort to stabilize itself went to pieces in 1939 exactly because of this effort, and inevitably it produced a condition of immaturity everywhere, one of transition, a provisional state in which the past and the turbulent present were amalgamated inorganically with another, entirely without connection. In the countryside, the feudal world of Uncle Edward; in the capital Warsaw, the urban technological capitalist world of the tolerant engineer's family which knows all the catchwords from Berlin, Paris, and New York, but which is overpowered at the decisive moment by the despised spiritual atavism. Social immaturity and social maturity rubbing elbows with one another. This is true of the unresolved relationships between the city and the country, the feudal world and the bourgeois world in Poland of that time. This is also true, however, as the novel demonstrates, of the corresponding ideologies and "superstructures."

Viewed superficially the schoolyard duel of making faces which leads to the defeat of the idealist seems merely to be a grotesque dream that is superbly narrated. However, what Gombrowicz intended to represent was the two extreme doctrines that were set against each other at that time in Poland: official messianic and ecstatic idealism ostensibly derived from the Polish romantic writers Mickiewicz and Słowacki versus the exaggerated popular trend of the urban intellectuals and ideologists who, like the nineteenth-century Russian Narodniki, wanted to become brothers with the common people, above all the peasants. In this duel between two philosophical principles, the popularist who seems to be a realist answers the idealist's "radiant expression" by mocking his ecstatic countenance "with a benumbed look of a cow full of dumb enthusiasm." The idealist is defeated in the duel, and the victor Mientus gets beaten when he makes the real attempt now to become a brother of the common people. A beating from his brothers—the Polish peasants.

The duel between Philifor and Anti-Philifor has the same meaning—this time in relation to the realm of science. Even this science was formalistic, consequently immature. The narrator must suddenly realize something that applies likewise to both the great philosophical antitheses: "And then I understood what I had feared so much: it was the symmetry. The situation was symmetrical, and therein lay its strength and also its weakness."

For Gombrowicz, the writing of *Ferdydurke* constituted a severe mental shock. This indicates that it functioned as a kind of catharsis. The author seemed to speak only of himself. He seemed merely to be giving form to the transition from a preliterary to a literary existence, from the preludes of a writer to artistic originality that had been achieved with great effort. In reality, however, he also described the situation in his fatherland during that time. Here the author's own situation bespoke the state of his nation and also—as it seemed—the literary situation in that country. It is for this reason that Gombrowicz continually links the permanent theme of self-confession as a counterpoint to the theme of permanent discussion concerning Poland and Polish conditions.

Sixteen years after the publication of *Ferdydurke*, Gombrowicz was living in Argentina and noted in his diary that the writing of his first novel had severely shaken him. This is understandable, since that novel offered neither a theory nor a solution. Everything remained open. To be sure, the narrator appeared to have returned to the reality of the thirty-year-old, to have discarded the second puberty phase that had been forced upon him. But, did he now find his way to maturity and form? This is doubtful. In recalling the period of 1938–1939, Gombrowicz reports: "I was still completely benumbed by the poisons of this book. I myself did not know in my heart whether the book wanted to be 'young' or 'mature.'" In another place in the diary of 1954 the same conflict is transposed from the *individual* to the general, corresponding to the structure of *Ferdydurke*, which seeks to treat the theme of maturity on a personal and a social level. The writer of the diary disputes the idea that the primary conflict in modern culture will be decided between the forces of civilization and those of savagery, between enlightened science and ignorance: "On the contrary, the most important and most drastic and incurable struggle is the one that goes on within us, between two of our basic drives: the one which yearns for form, shape, definition; the other which defends itself against shape, which does not want form." But a human being or a social group that struggles against development, that would maintain a condition of immaturity or immature conditions, *adheres to a position of conscious infantility*. Like the French-Rumanian Eugène Ionesco, Witold Gombrowicz demonstrates the ambivalent attitude of an artist toward the seductive song of the infantile that resounds whenever romantic things are supposed to be happening. In this instance, one searches for the way home, the way into the land of dreams and children, naturally with a bad conscience. Gombrowicz in his diary also fights with intractable fury for his natural rights as an individual. Ionesco is in no way outdone by him, and they are not alone in this endeavor. The demand for recognition as an "original genius," as it was once called by the Sturm und Drang writers, can become a characteristic attitude in certain historical periods. Witness German literature about 1770, the literature in Paris about 1890, the American "Lost Generation" about 1925 as well as after World War II.

Imaginary Poland, 1960 (Pornografia)

All this can be observed in the strange misfortune of Witold Gombrowicz. Though it seems to him to be a misfortune, it is actually not one. That is, time and again he was forced to see the themes and ideas in his works (which he rightfully considered his own hard-won possessions) simultaneously appear as reflections of other, more famous writers who, moreover, had the advantage of writing in an international language and were less dependent on translators and the art of translating. The connection between the chain of thought in *Ferdydurke* and the philosophy that one generally associates with Sartre is quite amusing and once again points up the peculiar misfortune of this complex and troublesome Pole Gombrowicz. The book *Ferdydurke* is, in fact, Sartre before Sartre, or rather, simultaneous with Sartre. Both novels, *Nausea* and *Ferdydurke*, appeared in 1938, completely independent of one another, one in Paris, one in Warsaw. Sartre's "autodidact" could also have appeared in a work by Gombrowicz. The theme of "the other" had at that time begun to dominate Sartre's thought more and more. Simone de Beauvoir relates in her memoirs that he originally thought of giving the play *No Exit* the title *The Others*. This same theme is treated and developed in Gombrowicz's first novel, completely independently of Sartre. In his diary Gombrowicz defends himself against the hints of Polish critics that his works bear a likeness to Pirandello and Sartre. He does not deny these similarities, and he himself draws connections between *Ferdydurke* and Sartre's works, but he adds defiantly: "In no instance do I want to be like anyone."

Nevertheless, he cannot escape this misfortune even though he becomes angry with the critics who prove such similarities. His last novel *Pornografia* not only brings new elements that are reminiscent of Sartre and that parallel certain Ionesco themes, but it also contains considerable chunks of narrative, and the raw material seems to have been supplied by Jean Genet.

In spite of this fact, the reader who is familiar with Gombrowicz's earlier works will immediately recognize the author's peculiar thematic structure in *Pornografia*, which is unmistakably a counterpart to *Ferdydurke*. The real and the imagined Poland. The yearning for immaturity of one who is in the process of maturation—the yearning for mature age of one who is immature and young. The story of *Pornografia* takes place in Poland around 1943 while it is occupied by a foreign army. An informative preface by the author explains that an event is depicted here, and it is something that the author never experienced. Gombrowicz had arrived in Argentina shortly before the outbreak of World War II. He had been sent there on a cultural mission as a Polish writer. The outbreak of the war caught him by surprise in South America. Poland was occupied by the German army. Gombrowicz remained in Argentina. After the war he decided against returning home. He lived as an emigrant but not as an exile. Nevertheless, his books, the novel *Trans-Atlantyk* and *Pornografia,* deal with Poland.

The occurrences in the imaginary Poland are contrived. The narrative depends on the climate of the war, which attracts him even though he did not experience the real war in Poland. "It is, then, an imaginary Poland—and do not be upset that it is sometimes confusing, sometimes fantastic because this is not important and is totally without meaning for the things which happen here." What does happen in the novel is murder. There are four murders altogether. The good Catholic wife of a landowner is stabbed by a young boy at night in her home. Was he a burglar? Did he act in self-defense? Gombrowicz mixes the motives with great artistry, leaving all possibilities open, even the spiritually remote ones. Then there is a matter that concerns the commanding officer in the Polish resistance army, Simian, who is to be killed on the orders of his fellow fighters because he had obviously lost heart for further illegal acts, wanted to quit the resistance, and thus endangered the security of "the others."

The home of a Polish landowner during a war occupation. Every person is a good Pole. The order to murder the commanding officer who has lost his moral strength is demanded by the circumstances. In a prefatory remark, Gombrowicz indicates that the situation does not revolve around an exceptional case but rather around an event that could possibly occur in any such organization. Therefore, it has symbolic meaning.

In *Ferdydurke*, dreamlike tales of absurd duels, the processes of infantilism, and grotesque spiritual antitheses were related. However, behind it all stood the real Poland of 1938. Visions of immaturity both general and specific as representative of the real environment in Poland. On the other hand the novel *Pornografia* describes scenes that are, to be sure, gruesome, agonizing, and repulsive (all these adjectives are actually meaningless, for there are no corresponding values), but all these scenes are possible, conceivable, even probable. Apparently a "realistic story," artfully constructed besides. Composed like a play. Unity of place determined essentially by the landowner's house and its environs. Unity of time that is maintained by the passage of only a few days. Unity of action in which five men "in their best years" are confronted with three young people about seventeen, two boys and a girl. A novel in two parts which both end like the final act of a play. The first part ends with the murder of the landowner's wife Amelia. The novel ends with three murders, and only the murder of Simian has a rational basis to it.

Everything depicted with precision, blood, horror, and agony. Presented in conformity with the classical unities, which can be fixed and repeated. Nevertheless, as Gombrowicz correctly explains, an imaginary Poland. The complete opposite of *Ferdydurke*. This time an apparently realistic story that can say nothing about the real Poland during the period of occupation.

This is not because Gombrowicz had been away from the country. Nothing prevented Gombrowicz in distant Argentina from reconstructing a real wartime Poland in his narrative. He just did not do it. In the apparently real narration of this book he entered the dream world once again.

Nevertheless, *Pornografia* is a counterpiece to *Ferdydurke*. Moreover, to dispel immediately any ideas to the contrary, it has nothing to do with "pornography" in its traditional sense. Anyone who is somewhat familiar with Gombrowicz's clowning would already suspect as much from the first glance at the title *Pornografia*. Nowhere is there even a realistic sexual situation depicted. If one can speak of intellectual obscenity (which is entirely possible here), then it lies precisely in the fact that there is not one *natural* sex act described among the young people, nor is there one between the young and the old. No sexual *reality*. Everything remains in a condition of sexual potential. It is exactly this that Gombrowicz calls pornography. The narrator at one time observes the young people, Henia and Karol, and secretly hopes that there will be a union between them. But they do not desire one another. The narrator is left only with the possibility and imagination. There was nothing between them. "Nothing but my pornography, which was feeding on them."

Again we have the theme of maturity and immaturity. Gombrowicz has created a remarkable character in Friedrich, an enigmatic, almost incredible figure who seems to be a Mephistopheles and an Alberich all in one. A man possessed by the demon of evil and ungodliness, who kills faith, hope, and love. Friedrich "stages" erotic situations, which he thus prevents from having natural conclusions. He turns life into art. It would be impossible to argue that Gombrowicz has made this figure convincing. He obviously intended to create a mythical character. Elements of Polish romanticism of the 1830's become visible, no matter how strongly Gombrowicz may deny such imputations. Mephistopheles, Alberich, Antichrist. But at the same time, an artful dialectician. Not only that, he is evidently insane. In trying to concoct a character with ingredients from Polish romanticism, from Mickiewicz, more likely from Zygmunt Krasiński, and to combine them with a figure from Sartre's works, Gombrowicz has produced a figure who has not contributed to his intentions of investigating the transition from the real to the imaginary but has hindered it.

The five adult men in the book destroy themselves by longing for youth and its immaturity. The central theme of the book forms the antithesis to *Ferdydurke,* but here immature youth does not desire itself or seek fulfillment in another youth. Instead it strives after union with age, with maturity. Both efforts fail and even lead to a grotesque distortion and a horrible restlessness just as the brotherhood between the urban intellectuals and peasant youths in *Ferdydurke* had once failed. In Gombrowicz no one can help the other. Each appears damned to his own existence: youth to youth, adults to adults, the common people to the common people, the literati to literature. Once again, this is really a thought from Jean Paul Sartre, who, not without reason, chose the theme *The Time of Maturity* as the title of a novel.

The theme of the *coward* and his exoneration before the others also belongs to Sartre's inventory. The cult of betrayal and the betrayers personified by Simian and Friedrich undoubtedly has a literary correlative in the plays and novels of Jean Genet. Basically it is an insignificant question whether Gombrowicz somewhere in Argentina had read and digested the books of these two French writers. The novel *Pornografia* is and remains authentic Gombrowicz. If his fingers think and act like those of Sartre, if an element of absurdity surrounds the three murders of the finale as often happens in the works of Ionesco or Dürrenmatt, it has nothing to do with literary "influences" but mainly with philosophical positions. And this is not a matter of unique positions but representative positions. Man cannot help man. The relationships cannot be changed. There is no road from youth to age, from immaturity to maturity. "Henia plus Karol returned to what they were, to their perfectly normal youth. But, we, the older ones, recovered our sense of maturity, and we suddenly found ourselves so firmly and so eternally immersed in it that there could no longer be a question of any threat from them, from below."

The Diaries of Witold Gombrowicz

Someone like Gombrowicz, who is in love with immaturity and at the same time strives to reach maturity and form, finds the ideal medium for expression in the literary genre of the diary. This form does not allow for the completion of anything, for anything to reach maturity. Everything remains in progress, everything is provisional, noted down always with the possibility of being retracted later by another note. In extreme cases the diary form recommends itself as an escape from really giving shape to ideas. What is once committed to a diary will in all likelihood not be resurrected in another artistic form. There are, of course, diaries —for example, those of Max Frisch—which are treated as reservoirs of fables, themes, thoughts, and impressions. In Frisch's case it is quite possible that *Graf Öderland* and *Andorra* took shape first in a diary and only later were converted into dramatic form. As a diary writer, Max Frisch is not at all lyrical. Thus, he succeeds in the novel *I'm Not Stiller* in writing an extreme anti-lyrical form of the diary. Stiller does not wish to be Stiller. Therefore, he takes notes in a completely objective manner recording the meetings with people who were once close to Stiller and who believe him to be Stiller. In truth, he is Stiller, but as stated before, he does not want to accept his identity. This form of diary means a maximum of reification. A man notes down what is done to him. In the process he is like a mere object. This is the epic diary of a dramatist.

On the other hand, François Bondy, who was the first to call attention to Witold Gombrowicz and the book *Ferdydurke* in Paris after World War II, labeled Gombrowicz a "lyrical clown" and added that Gombrowicz was a clown "who stumbled about in his own circus." A clown? Then possibly there is a circus with a very earnest man who behaves himself in such a way that people laugh at him. He wants this laughter. To be sure, it is more than just an interest in pure artistry when someone chooses the profession of clown. If man's strong comic talent becomes evident, he can confidently decide to appear as a comedian. But the comedian and the clown are two different sorts. One does not take to the profession of the clown without also having clownlike traits in "real life." What Brecht had Herr Keuner say about the relationship between the "I" and the "others" does not hold for the clown: "It is useful to take other people's opinions of yourself and make them your own. Otherwise they won't understand you."

But Herr Keuner, who adapts himself to this maxim, is not a clown. With Gombrowicz, the situation is different. His relationship to others smacks of the ambivalence of a man between maturity and immaturity. In his writings and diaries he wants to explain to others his own immortal, permanent individuality *and* at the same time to conform to the rules of life in the world of the others. To modify the words of Herr Keuner: he does not want in any way to take other people's opinions of him and make them his own; instead, he wants to induce others to see him as he sees himself. Despite this, the others should understand him. This cannot and does not succeed.

The diaries of Witold Gombrowicz are consequently not suited for a discussion concerning ideas or conditions. One does not learn much from them about the intellectual views of the author. To be sure, he continually analyzes everything that he does not like in great detail: Catholicism, communism, existentialism, Oscar Milosz and Sartre, Camus and the various factions of contemporary Polish literature, the Jewish question and psychoanalysis. But all the objections raised are simply subjective attempts to differentiate. The apparent argumentation in the diaries is a defensive position and does not lead to objective knowledge of great value. For example, what Gombrowicz has to say in his criticism of Dionys Mascolo's book about communism is neither new nor substantial. It is more aversion than argumentation. The diarist is not wrong when he occasionally confesses that he rarely thinks and, if so, then unwillingly. He prefers to gape. This is true, and it should not be held against Gombrowicz even though it may be difficult to comprehend why he fills page upon page of a diary with philosophical and literary discussions that are not discussions at all. The deluge of aversions often carries with it intelligent and novel observations, but they can serve only to stimulate greater perceptions. They themselves are not perceptions. One can fight over the literary positions taken by André Gide in his diaries because they are positions, crystallized experiences. With Gombrowicz there is never such a crystallization. Everything remains in process, in a state of discussion. This is both a strength and a weakness. It is for this reason that Gombrowicz never achieves, in Stendhal's sense, a crystallization of feeling, and hence, love. Here, too, everything remains in the middle phase of indecision. The sexual direction of the feelings is undecided, the relationship to youth and age, the question of readiness for closer ties with any other person. If one modifies the formula from one of Ionesco's plays, then the essence of these diaries seems to indicate: "We have Gombrowicz and Gombrowicz. That's enough!"

Naturally the diarist is right in asserting that the Freudians cannot discover much about him with their psychoanalytical method since most of what he depicts is obvious, and the real problem only begins with the obvious. This is correct. Gombrowicz is an unusual figure in contemporary literature, and the ingeniousness of this artist cannot be understood by going back to the man Gombrowicz nor by a detailed dissection of his theses and thoughts. The literary phenomenon of Witold Gombrowicz lies beyond all assertions and biographical facts.

It is a continuing process. Yet, again, it is to be understood differently from Brecht and his Herr Keuner, who, under the motto "Error and Process" made the following realization about life: "When one only thinks of oneself, one cannot believe that one makes mistakes, and therefore, that one does not progress. Consequently one must think of those who will continue to work after oneself. Only in this way can one prevent anything from becoming finished." Nothing should be finished because history goes on and there can be no final positions in the course of time. In Brecht, the work of the individual limited by space and time stands, however, in a tense dialectical relationship to the activity of the past, present, and future worlds. With Gombrowicz, nothing gets finished because he simultaneously desires and fears the connection between the "I" and its present world. He would be a loner who nevertheless achieves harmony with others. In the diary of 1954 this is said very clearly for once: "So then, I want to speak. But I must say this about what I say: none of it is cate-

gorical. Everything is hypothetical. . . . Everything is contin-
gent—why should I keep it a secret?—upon the effect it produces.
This feature circumscribes all of my literary production. I try
different roles. I take different positions. I give the most diverse
meanings to my experiences—and when one of these meanings
becomes accepted by people, then I fix myself in it." But immediately he adds: "Not only do I give myself meaning. Others also
give me meaning. Out of this collision of interpretations arises a
third interpretation which characterizes me."

Because of this, there can only be unresolved questions in the
relationship between Gombrowicz and others, including his
critics. He will never admit that a critical analysis interprets him
correctly. On the other hand, literary critics must avoid equating
their final judgment of Gombrowicz with Gombrowicz's judgment of Gombrowicz. This situation is also not unusual. It applies more or less to every significant artist and every attempt at
interpretation. The uniqueness of Witold Gombrowicz in literary
history lies in the fact that this warped relationship between
artist and critic, between the "I" and its surroundings, was made
into the peculiar theme of his literary work. Into the peculiar
theme of Witold Gombrowicz. Into his only theme.

Doctor Zhivago

The Anticipation in Painting

After the success of the October Revolution in 1917, Anatoli Lunacharski, who had worked with Lenin, was named to the post of People's Commissar for Public Education. Lunacharski was a writer and a cultural philosopher, a man with a solid education and broad views. He proved this by appointing Marc Chagall as minister of arts in the Vitebsk government and as director of the local academy of arts. Chagall accepted these appointments and tried as best he could to place his art at the service of the new social order and the revolution. He and his students provided the placards for the festive May Day rally of 1918. At the demonstration—as was to be expected—large transparent signs with green and blue cows were to be seen. Furthermore, several of the cows were standing on their heads. Most of the demonstrators, who were workers from White Russia, were reportedly pleased by the sight and welcomed the idea. However, the experts in these affairs were dissatisfied for political and cultural reasons. In the aftermath, Chagall was dismissed from his post and reinstated several times until he was finally, upon his own request, granted permission to leave the country and make a new home for himself in Paris.

Twenty years after the revolution, in 1937, Chagall painted a large-scale picture with the title "The Revolution." Then he himself destroyed the painting. Only a study in oils remains, and in Walter Erben's monograph *Marc Chagall,* there is the following description of "The Revolution": "People are hustling and bustling on a village square covered with snow. They carry candles, staffs, lamps, and musical instruments. With them are the village animals. In the background the flags are flapping. We see the painter twice: before the easel with his wife and muse Bella beside him; and then on the roof of a house covered with snow. . . . The Jew, who once fled through Vitebsk, leaves the house in the foreground, blinded by the burst of spring and the light of the sun which has come down upon the earth with its rings of light. A genius playing a flute is trapped in the whirl of the sun-wheel. A table stands in the square. On the top of the table a young man executes a daring hand-stand. The crowd applauds. . . . What is above is suddenly below. . . . Sitting at the side of the table, an old man meditates. He is indifferent to the momentary tumult. Beside him lies a small open book."

It is unfortunate that Chagall took it upon himself to declare this painting meaningless. It would be presumptuous to deduce from the painter's act that he felt he had not mastered the theme through his art, or that he had the impression that his painting had failed to attain its object, the revolution. From the description of the painting, it is not difficult to recognize the most important motifs from Chagall's earlier works. The Jew, who flees through Vitebsk, is the painter quoting himself. In this vision Chagall obviously wanted to represent the *simultaneity of continuity and change* which the revolutionary events produced in his White Russian world. The stark juxtaposition of the most diverse worlds, the old and the new society, is not just a peculiarity of expressionist art and literature, which used such means in its early stages to try to capture a complexity of life that mocked all causality. Chagall's painting was produced long after this period of expressionism—in 1937—and it must be approached from the standpoint of the stylistic technique employed in his other works of that time. Obviously he intended "The Revolution" to be a retrospective work. The painted memories of a revolutionary past. The prerevolutionary Jewish milieu of Vitebsk. The familiar milieu. Continuity of meditation in the Jewish *schul*. Books that remain. Wife and muse. Man and animal celebrate the revolution as they would celebrate the coming of spring. The daring acrobat receives the applause of the crowd. Up and down are turned around. Juxtaposition and simultaneity of persistence and staggering change. The painter himself takes part in both: he continues to work on his paintings, but he also stands on the roof of his house to establish harmony with the sun that melts the snow.

More can scarcely be said about the painting and the intention behind it. A work of memory and juxtaposition. It was neither a revolutionary nor a counterrevolutionary painting. Certainly not a work of "partisanship." Chagall painted what he had seen and experienced. As a painter who can never be completely involved, his emotions must constantly take on a form which in turn can never be completely uninvolved.

Boris Pasternak's novel *Doctor Zhivago* is also a work of memories. In September 1956 it lay in manuscript form in the editorial office of the Soviet newspaper *Novy Mir*. An official certificate from the editorial board signed by Konstantin Fedin, Konstantin Simonov, and Boris Lavrenyov explained why the paper refused to publish the novel, a decision that also prevented it from being published later in book form in the Soviet Union. Pasternak was sixty-six years old at that time. Almost forty years had passed since the February and October revolutions of 1917. The rest is common knowledge: publication of an Italian translation, a tremendous success, followed by translations in English, French, and German; the award and refusal of the Nobel Prize; Pasternak banned from the League of Soviet Writers; a grotesque quarrel not even concerned with the real cause, namely the story of Doctor Zhivago; praise and criticism without, in many instances, the novel having been read. Boris Leonidovich Pasternak died on May 30, 1960. He had suffered from an incurable lung disease and had a weak heart just like his Doctor Zhivago.

When one reads this large-scale controversial book, it might appear that Marc Chagall's "Revolution" was an anticipation in painting of what Pasternak had intended with the story of Doctor Yurii Andreievich Zhivago: a book of reminiscences, a portrayal of continuity and change in juxtaposition, a completely impartial record of what was seen and experienced. How successful a painter can be in such an attempt can no longer be determined.

Chagall destroyed his "Revolution" himself. The question remains whether a similar attempt by the lyric poet and narrator Boris Pasternak could succeed artistically. What is evident is that it concerned a rejection of all historical philosophy, even simple social causality, that Pasternak regarded splicing, with no attempt to identify cause and effect, as an adequate form for describing pre-World War I days, the February Revolution, the October Revolution, the civil war, and the emergence of the Soviet Union.

When Zhivago is abducted from his Siberian refuge by Red partisans and taken to their camp to tend their wounded, he finds himself forced into endless conversations with Liberius Mikulitsyn, the leader of the partisans and the son of a wealthy bourgeois family. These conversations are boring for the doctor. A civil war is being waged between the Reds and the Whites, and the end seems as remote as the end of the doctor's sequestration and the intellectual argument. Mikulitsyn makes a derogatory remark about Zhivago that is not far from the mark: "You have an atrophied social sense, just like the illiterate peasant woman or an incorrigibly indolent petty bourgeois. And yet, you are a doctor. You are well-read. I believe you even write. How do you explain all this?" Zhivago answers with some horribly ironic "self-criticism": "I can't. There are probably no connections to make. Nothing can be done about it. You should be sorry for me." Naturally Mikulitsyn recognizes the mock tone and justifiably answers: "Resignation is worse than arrogance."

The whole problem of the novel *Doctor Zhivago* is essentially revealed in this dialogue. Zhivago's recognition and acceptance of coexistence, of impartiality, of the apparent absence of causality in social events demonstrate at the same time the secret creative principle of Pasternak's novel. In essence the accusations that Mikulitsyn makes against his hostage physician correspond exactly with the arguments that were later made by the Soviets against Pasternak and his novel. The author was not surprised by them. In this passage of the novel he had already anticipated them, even though he never allows the arguments of Zhivago's enemies and intellectual adversaries to be expressed in the remainder of the book—a definite artistic weakness of the novel.

Liberius Mikulitsyn—Yurii Zhivago. Partisanship and impartiality. "An atrophied social sense" and the incorrigible indolence of a petty bourgeois who at the same time wants to be a writer. The reply: an avowal of the discontinuity of behavior and character. "There are probably no connections." Zhivago's life, work, and poetry as consciously cultivated coexistence. The similarity between this confession by Doctor Zhivago and Marc Chagall's painting of the revolution is unmistakable. Pasternak's novel as self-confession and simultaneously as an objective and critical diagnosis of his life of discontinuity and indecisiveness. Liberius Mikulitsyn's critical accusations against Zhivago as the anticipation of everything which the Soviet writers, represented by the editorial board of *Novy Mir,* had to raise against the author Boris Pasternak, his novel, and his protagonists.

Yurii Andreievich Zhivago: An Antihero of His Times

All the discussions about Pasternak's novel, the hymnic panegyrics and the embittered rejections, always refer to a scene from the fourth chapter of the second book. The principal conception underlying the figure of Zhivago can be easily understood from this episode. Here it is relatively insignificant whether one interprets the doctor's actions at that moment of his life as counterrevolutionary or deeply human.

Doctor Zhivago was abducted and lived in the woods with the partisans. His family had to assume that he was lost or perhaps murdered. He tends the wounded partisans unwillingly and submits to the orgies of ideological discussion which are forced upon him by the leader of the partisans. Suddenly he is even compelled to take part in the battles since the Red Cross has no authority in the Civil War. White troops advance across a broad barren field. The partisans have the Taiga to their backs and lie under cover on the edge of a small wood. A scene follows that had been portrayed occasionally in early Soviet films: a heroic but senseless quixotic charge by White Russian officers without the slightest hope of success. Zhivago is lying on the grass with the partisans "without a weapon and watching the course of the battle. All his sympathies are with those young men who went to their deaths like heroes. With all his heart he wished they would win. They belonged to families which were probably akin to his in spirit. They were educated like him and had the same moral stance and notions." But the feelings remain vague and the notions unclear. "Once he had the idea of leaving his position, running out into the field and giving himself up to gain his release. But that seemed to him too dangerous. Before he would have reached the middle of the field with his arms raised, he would have been shot down from both sides, struck in the breast and in the back—by the partisans who would punish him for committing an act of betrayal and by the Whites who would not know his intentions."

"But that seemed to him too dangerous." Pasternak's critics on the editorial board of *Novy Mir* naturally focused on this scene because the reluctant Zhivago is compelled to fire a gun, and though he tries to miss, he cannot prevent wounding two White soldiers and killing a third. The people at *Novy Mir* in their letter to Pasternak draw the following conclusion about this scene: "In a short space of time your protagonist commits manifold treason: he sympathizes with the Whites, and his sympathy runs so deep that he wants to desert to the Whites. But he does not dare to do it and begins to shoot—at first only pretending—at the Whites with whom he sympathizes. Then he transfers his sympathy from the Whites to the telephonist whom the Whites have killed. Next he takes the part of a member of the White Guard whom he himself has killed, and he asks himself: 'Why did I kill him?' and when it turns out that the White soldier is not dead but only wounded, he hides him." This is all true. This is how Zhivago behaves, and Pasternak does nothing to play down the almost unbearable ambiguity of the situation.

The question arises whether the word "treason" accurately describes the situation. Objectively it does. The subjective side of the case is, however, more difficult to explain. When someone speaks of treason and traitors, he is presuming an ideological commitment which demands loyalty and can be broken by disloyalty. The peculiarity of Zhivago's behavior is caused precisely by the fact that he never inwardly completed such a commitment, least of all in regard to the partisans who abducted him and held him hostage to perform medical services. Nor did Zhivago "betray" the Whites, for he did not commit himself to them either. At that one moment he was filled only with vague sympathies, mere social affinities. The problem concerning Zhivago lies exactly in the division between the subjective and objective sides of the case. One misunderstands the complexity of the character Zhivago and the consistency of the author Pasternak if one views this episode in the civil war—Doctor Zhivago in the battle between the Whites and the Reds—as an isolated event which is important but breaks from the structure of the narrative and the portrayal of the character. Zhivago's so-called treason, or rather his inability to commit himself to a cause and to identify fully with a thing or idea, proves to be his most intrinsic trait. The story of Doctor Zhivago is simply a story of a fundamental noncommitment. Unless one understands this basic trait, the story of Zhivago's life becomes incomprehensible. On the other hand, if one recognizes this trait in the man Zhivago, then his story will become incomprehensible for a different reason: the reader will time and again demand logic and results from a life that has expressly refused both.

It is for this reason that Western critics of Pasternak's novel fail to comprehend the theme as clearly as do the editors of *Novy Mir* who call this episode treason. These western critics seem to see mere ideological abstention in the behavior and noncommitment of the doctor, poet, and intellectual Zhivago when confronted by the October Revolution and the Soviet power. They do not recognize that Zhivago has shown himself to be a man of inner reservations in nearly all the events of his life, a man who cannot commit himself, who cannot be tied down. A man who knows only momentary intellectual or emotional ties that are repeatedly severed. Zhivago's relationship to his wife, or even to Lara, not to speak of his grotesque second marriage, which was arranged purely for reasons of self-preservation—these relationships do not appear to be essentially different from that of the partisans' doctor in the attack of the White troops. Zhivago's conversations with Lara about his wife Tonia indicate

the same predisposition. Should one also speak here about manifold treason?

One can carry this analysis even further. For Zhivago, noncommitment and the compulsion for inner reservation characterize the most real and important aspects of his life: poetry and
science. At the very beginning of the last chapter of the novel
Pasternak endeavors to summarize the "brief story" of Yurii
Zhivago's last eight or nine years of his life. A horrifying sentence:
"His knowledge and skill as a doctor disappeared, and he also
suffered the loss of his creative talent." To be sure, we are told
that shortly before his death in Moscow he wrote something, but
it seems that here, too, noncommitment had impaired even his
intellectual and artistic abilities. Zhivago was well aware of his
condition. Since he was a doctor, he was able to make a self-
analysis that astutely diagnosed the connection between the
physical (heart disease) and intellectual malaise. He explained his
condition to his friends who were ennobled by the exile and
persecution they had suffered for their ideology, and this condition was not only his own: "Nowadays microscopic forms of
cardiac hemorrhages are quite widespread. They do not always
have to lead to death. It is possible to cure this condition, which is
typical for our time. I believe that its cause is of an ethical nature.
The majority of people today are forced into continual hypocrisy
which has been perfected into a system. One just cannot live
day-in, day-out doing exactly the opposite of what one feels,
taking a stand with body and soul for something one doesn't love,
rejoicing about something which causes misfortune. All this has
grave consequences for one's health. Our nervous system is not a
fiction, it is not an illusion."

It should be immediately added that the word *hypocrisy* that
Zhivago uses here to describe himself belies the actual facts, since
it defines them merely from a moral perspective. The last sickness, which leads to the doctor's death, may be attributed to the
continual contrast between thought and action, words and feelings. However, the extent of this hypocrisy, or rather of this
basic contradiction in Doctor Zhivago's character was not determined by the external conditions in which he had to live, speak,
and act. The dialectical formula of Hegel about changing quan-

tity into quality, which is often misused to explain unconnected events in life, proves useful here to summarize the story of Doctor Zhivago. This fatal illness, both organic and ethical in nature, leads to the death of his heart, but not before it has already caused the withering away of his professional skill and his artistic powers. It is a qualitatively different form of those innumerable large and small noncommitments of which Zhivago's life consisted. Indecisions and inner reservations wherever one looks. In Zhivago's profession, in his intellectual life, in love, in marriage, in politics, and in war. When a sufficient quantity had accumulated, this life had to end. First comes the intellectual death, then the physical.

There is no doubt but that Pasternak saw, described, and wrote down all of this. Nearly all the critics were ready to identify Yurii Zhivago with Boris Pasternak. Nevertheless, the comparison does not hold. Admittedly Zhivago himself is a master of self-diagnosis. He proves this in the conversation with Gordon and Dudorov in the final stage of his life. But Pasternak did not end like his Doctor Zhivago. Where in the novel the sum of the reservations and indecisions leads to the death of the heart and an intellectual decay, there is the poet Pasternak standing behind all the noncommitments, writing the novel *Doctor Zhivago*. The case cannot be dismissed with the formula of Zhivago's manifold treason. This touches only the objective, or let us say the civic, side of his behavior, not the actual structure of his character and consequently his career.

The basic theme of Pasternak's novel is *the total noncommitment of a man*. This is the topic of the last conversation between Zhivago and his so-called friends. This attitude, however, is not a peculiarity of Yurii Zhivago, but a characteristic of a human and social type: the total ideological abstention of men who in a particular period of their lives and in an epoch of history are resolved to be the nonheroes of this time. To a certain extent, this makes them into typical phenomena, into "heroes of their times." The conflict in the life of Zhivago was made more sharp (the controversy about Pasternak's novel has underlined this fact) because the doctor's own noncommitment occurred at a time that seemed to demand and force commitment more strongly than any epoch of bourgeois saturation and historical calm. So it happens that the doctor and writer Zhivago does not only come into conflict with his contemporaries who have committed themselves to action either by entering on the side of the revolution or, like his wife and father-in-law, by leaving Russia and going into exile, but he also falls off the course of history. Zhivago's noncommitment means a decision for a nonhistorical existence at a moment in the world of greatest historical significance.

Zhivago's fate is actually predetermined in its progress; it is determined in spite of (or because of) his refusal to commit himself to anything. Pasternak as narrator has attempted to make this process clear with remarkable symbolism. Zhivago's step-brother Evgraf appears in the novel in two forms: once as the puzzling, cautious brother, the patron and executor of the will, and the other time in the curious form of *an angel of death.* The appearance of Evgraf in the novel demonstrates that Zhivago's refusal to live in harmony with his environment and with the course of history means intellectual and eventually physical death for him. In the decisive epoch of the year 1917, between the February and October revolutions, an especially melancholy banquet in Moscow is attended by members of a perishing social class. Zhivago is one of the guests that evening. Sadness prevails. "They sensed that only a life which was suited to the environment and dissolved into it without a trace is real life, that a separate isolated happiness cannot be real happiness." Soon afterward the Bolsheviks seize power. At the time that Zhivago reads the newspaper containing the first decrees of the Soviet powers which—"in this way of ruthlessly driving things on to their end"—move him deeply, he meets a young man of eighteen with narrow Kirghiz eyes who looks at him in a friendly way. Everything is suddenly transformed for the doctor into a poem that should be written down. The progress of the successful October Revolution and the new social beginning, the meeting with the young man with the Kirghiz eyes, his own indecision. The poem is to be called "Turmoil." "Only now and then a boy got in his way, a boy with narrow Kirghiz eyes in a reindeer coat like the one worn in the Urals or Siberia. It was completely clear to him that this boy was the spirit of his death or, to put it more simply, that he was his death." In relation to the concrete events of the novel, the young man is simply Zhivago's stepbrother. But at the same time he is the angel of death. When Zhivago lies in state and Lara meets the stepbrother and angel of death at the coffin, the union of life's destiny and the symbol of life is complete. Lara is the incarnation of everything in Zhivago's life that was destined to fail; the man with the Kirghiz eyes who first appears when Zhivago encounters the October Revolution means the historical constellation of this failure. Naturally there are similar prototypes in novels written before Pasternak's. The peasant child who meets Anna Karenina time and again and finally in the railroad station before her suicide is also a death symbol. In Thomas Mann's *Death in Venice* there is a similar connection between being and meaning as there is here in Pasternak's work. By raising the figure of Yurii Andreievich Zhivago to a symbolical level, Pasternak does not merely succeed in "elevating" the occurrence, but he also eliminates the fictitious equation that Yurii Zhivago equals Boris Pasternak.

The Contra-Account:
The Skin, the Type, the Christ Figure

Naturally one can also view the doctor's case in an entirely different manner. Pasternak depicts a life without logical consequence. Zhivago's death came after a period of long physical and intellectual torment caused by permanent indecisions—the torment which grew out of the distance between an individual and his environment that had become much too great to bridge. The Soviet writers who rejected the manuscript explained this differently, but their explanation is, to be sure, inadequate because they never examined the possible spiritual drives of the protagonist. This interpretation is thoroughly conceivable in regard to Zhivago's life—considered from the outside.

The result of the official interpretation (taken from the letter of the editorial board to Boris Pasternak) is as follows: "You speak quite nobly about 'divided feelings,' but for a man who waits in ambush with those he hates and who shoots at those he loves, and all this to protect his own skin, that is truly a very weak expression." One's own skin. The writers of this letter return to this point later and compare Zhivago's conduct to that of "every subjectively honest man who only once in his life has valued his conscience above his own skin!" At this point the conflict between Pasternak and his critics seems to become material belonging to a literary theme from Jean Paul Sartre's works. Certainly Pasternak sees his character objectively and avoids a trivial identification between the novelist and the protagonist in the novel. However, he also had to experience the character internally in order to acquaint the reader with the character's motives and conduct. The editors of *Novy Mir* are "the others," in Sartre's sense, who know nothing of Zhivago's motives and create an image of him based on his actions. For Zhivago, the image is the way of life of a man who feels himself talented and, therefore, is out of step with the times and is even asocial. For Pasternak, the image is the career of a man who cannot make a decision. For the others, the image is a talented man who is like the nonswimmer before the swift-flowing stream of great historical events, who continuously refuses to give his useful skills to society in order not to run risks, in order to save his skin.

It cannot be denied that Pasternak's report allows for such an interpretation. Naturally Zhivago is not a coward in any simple form. He demonstrates his bravery in both the war and the civil war. But he tries to "survive" everywhere and—wherever possible—to avoid the centers of historical actions. The great trip of the Zhivago family from Moscow to Varykino is expressly motivated by the common resolve to escape the feverish political activity in the new Soviet capital and to find peace on the far side of the Urals, a life without politics, with more food and fuel. Of course, the reason behind all this is Zhivago's expressed disinterest in the historical events taking place all around him. The small emotional involvement that he felt when he first read the decrees of the new Soviet power had long since dissolved. "The others," however, can explain this logically consistent attitude of noncommitment in terms of the "skin."

Although the emphasis is different, there is a remarkable similarity between the reasoning that leads to the Soviet writers' appraisal of Zhivago and certain famous theses that Curzio Malaparte propounds in his novel about the end of Fascist Italy and the Allied invasion. As is well known, his novel carries the title *The Skin*. Malaparte is often asked by Allied officers what it was that put Italy and the Italians in such a position. Was it hunger? Bombs? Political parties? Executions? Malaparte says no: " 'It wasn't those things that affected us.' 'What was it then?' asked General Guillaume in a slightly husky voice. 'The skin.'— 'The skin? Which skin?' General Guillaume asked.—'The skin,' I answered with a quiet voice, 'our skin, this cursed skin. You have no idea what a man is capable of, what heroic deeds, what secrecy, just to save his skin.' " Much can be said against Malaparte and his novel. However, the theme that he used as the title of his novel is legitimate.

The question remains as to whether one, from the standpoint of "the others," could also give Pasternak's novel the title *The Skin*? The letter of the Soviet critics reveals the contrast: consciousness versus skin. Yet, a man's conscious decisions which allow him to disregard mortal danger first demand a certain harmony—of feeling, of conscience, of conviction. Harmony means an agreement with oneself, but above all, it means an agreement with some group from the realm of "the others." For a long time Malaparte's Italians had missed the harmony with the Italian Fascist regime, which had been declining. Only the skin remained. As writers of the October Revolution and the Soviet Union, Konstantin Fedin, Konstantin Simonov, and Lavrenyov had a feeling of complete unity with the people, the state, and their world. Boris Pasternak's position remains uncertain. The matter does not concern the author but the protagonist of the novel. Yurii Andreievich Zhivago did not live in harmony with "the others." Only the skin remained. Moreover, something else remains which the critics did not wish to see but which alone might be decisive for the doctor: *harmony with oneself,* with that which he considered his genius and, in Pasternak's opinion, something that he justifiably considered to be his genius. Thus Malaparte's diagnosis applies to Zhivago only in a very limited sense. The essential part remains untouched by it.

It is precisely this singularity of a man who stands under Daimonion that is contested by Pasternak's enemies and critics. Where the author intended to create an unforgettable individual, an exceptional case, "the others" see a type: Zhivago as a prototype. This viewpoint must have particularly disturbed the author, since Zhivago himself once declared: "To belong to a type is the end of a man. It is his death sentence." Fedin and "the others" reply: "We don't mean to assert in the least that such men never existed or that Doctor Zhivago's fate is not typical. It is our opinion that Doctor Zhivago is the incarnation of a particular type of Russian intellectual during those years, a man who spoke quite warmly and intelligently about the sufferings of the people, but who unfortunately could not heal this suffering, neither in the practical nor higher sense." The critics do not condemn Pasternak for depicting such a—in their view—typical life history. Such condemnation would not have been permitted, since many of the most important works of Soviet literature deal with the theme of the bourgeois intelligentsia in the proletariat revolution. The novels and dramas of Maksim Gorki, *The Road to Calvary* by Aleksei Tolstoi, and not to mention Konstantin Fedin's *An Unusual Summer,* which exhibits several motifs that are similar to those in the Zhivago novel, which was written by Fedin's neighbor (and former friend) in the writers' colony Peredelkino near Moscow. In general, then, there were no objections to the portrayal of such a social type. But Pasternak in his novel seemed to have "unreservedly defended" this type. Here again is a misunderstanding, as in the case of "the skin." It is entirely possible that Boris Pasternak intended such a defense of Zhivago. Nevertheless, the objectivity in the novel makes the case different. To be sure, this does justify Pasternak's detractors insofar as it allows them to judge Zhivago's permanent indecisiveness more as socially typical rather than as unique and original. Cultural history is constantly providing new examples of a strange dialectics between uniqueness and typical behavior. The timely untimeliness of Nietzsche, the proud esoterics of Stefan George, Karl Kraus's alleged untimely proximity to the source. Time and again it has been proved that a historical moment completely favors such express singularity.

The story of Doctor Zhivago can thus be read as the history of a representative of the prosperous bourgeoisie, the son of a wealthy father with good connections, talented and cultivated, a man who eventually finds himself a member of a state for which he must perform useful work, a state to which he has neither social nor intellectual ties. A large portion of the bourgeois intelligentsia shared this fate with Zhivago. The portrayal of this conflict was not new in Soviet literature. It was, if anything, a popular theme. Still, Pasternak violated what had been up to then considered a valid literary convention. Such conflicts had to end either with an ideological change in the hero or with his quick decline. He was either destroyed as an enemy or accepted into the new community. Neither occurs in Pasternak's novel. Zhivago is not destroyed like an enemy. Instead he continues his existence until his death, which is the qualitative outcome of a slow process of corrosion. Here Georg Büchner's remark about the playwright Lenz, who is withering away, can also be applied to Zhivago in the final stage of his life: "And so he lived away . . . ." No mention of any sort of change. On the contrary, Zhivago makes cruel fun of such rehabilitation in his last conversation with Gordon and Dudorov. In this connection, something was said that caused the Soviet critics to suspect their colleague Pasternak: "I found it difficult to listen to you, Dudorov, when you told us how you were rehabilitated and became mature in exile. It was as though a horse wanted to tell how he broke himself in." Neither a quick decline, nor a slow change. In spite of this, it is perfectly correct to find the behavior of the doctor typical, his talent and character aside. Indeed, Pasternak violated long-standing taboos when he described the results of noncommitment as slow death and not as catastrophe or purification. As has been correctly observed, his narrative contains only a thoroughly realistic report of the typical condition and behavior of men belonging to the Russian intelligentsia in the first decade after the revolution.

In the last moments of his life Zhivago himself senses something of this sort, and from this it can be deduced that Pasternak wanted to see this aspect treated as well. The narrator reports the last clear thoughts of the doctor, who is now suffering very seriously from a heart disease. They occur as he is riding in an overcrowded streetcar in Moscow. Zhivago's death is hideous and trivial and is purposely described as such: "He thought about the course that the lives of adult people take, and how these people move on different tracks, and he wondered at what moment fate would raise one above the other and who would survive the other. He understood that there is some kind of principle of relativity which has a decisive effect. But then, he found that his imaginings became twisted, and he stopped indulging himself with these observations." Here the principle of relativity must certainly be understood as a *principle of selection,* presumably not in Darwin's sense, but as the basis of a selection between men who are in harmony with their environment and those who are forever indecisive in all their relationships.

The poet Pasternak has reserved for himself the last word in his novel about the fate of Doctor Zhivago. After the epilogue there is a small collection of lyric poems entitled "Poems of Yurii Zhivago." Here, as in Hermann Hesse's *The Glass-Bead Game,* this collection of poems, which is seemingly appended to the narrative, is meant to give a final explanation of the events in the novel. At first glance Pasternak's novel appears disjointed, inarticulate, sometimes helpless. In reality it has been very carefully constructed. Therefore, this lyrical conclusion must be as carefully considered as the internal arrangement of the group of poems. They begin with Hamlet and lead, in a language that becomes more and more veiled, to Christ. The star of Bethlehem together with the description of Zhivago's childhood in Russia, Lara together with Mary Magdalene, his own life together with the Passion. Finally the garden of Gethsemane. The last verses of this poem form the conclusion of the novel:

> Seest thou, the passing of the ages is like a parable
> And in its passing it may burst to flame.
> In the name, then, of its awesome majesty
> I shall, in voluntary torments, descend into my grave.

I shall descend into my grave. And on the third day rise again.
And, even as rafts flow down a river,
So shall the centuries drift, trailing like a caravan,
Coming for judgment, out of the dark, to me.

The equation of Zhivago-Passion is completed. Lara's declaration in the great love dialogue between her and Zhivago provides a strange counterpoint to this equation: "You and I are like Adam and Eve, the first two people on earth who at the beginning of the world had nothing to cover themselves with—and now at the end of it we are just as naked and homeless. And we two—you and me—are the last remembrances of all that indelible greatness and power which has been created in the world in the course of thousands of years between them and us . . . ." Occasionally, when annoyed, Zhivago would declare to his friends that their only significance for posterity will be that they were contemporaries of Doctor Zhivago. Pasternak did not see this as arrogance on the part of his protagonist but rather as a part of his protagonist's imitation of the Passion. It is remarkable here, too, that the uniqueness of this imitation of Christ, which increases most strongly in the closing verses of the book, becomes a literary cliché. Considering his great command of world literature, Boris Pasternak was definitely aware that Dostoevski would be detected here as well as the Passion dramas of the expressionists.

Zhivago's passion, however, is a non-Christian one, a secularized passion. Pasternak knew the poet Rilke well and had great admiration for him. Pasternak's autobiography, *Safe Conduct*, which first appeared in Moscow in 1931, begins with an event from his early childhood: on a summer day in 1900 the child Boris Pasternak boarded an express train with his parents in the Kursk station of Moscow. His parents greeted two acquaintances, a man in a black Tyrolean cape and a woman with whom they spoke German. Rilke was traveling with his companion to visit Leo Tolstoi. The closeness of the lyric poet Pasternak to Rilke is obvious and has never been denied. But both the lyric poet and novelist Pasternak (there are also remarkable connections between *Doctor Zhivago* and *The Notebooks of Malte*

Laurids Brigge) share with Rilke the practice of misusing Christian symbols for artistic and arabesque-like effects. The Christian motifs in the novel are part of a non-Christian aesthetic, like Rilke's "angel" in the *Duino Elegies*. It may be that the poet Pasternak in a deeper level of his personality accepted a synthesis formed from his calling as an artist and the idea of an imitation of the Passion. The transposition from Boris Pasternak to Yurii Zhivago, however, did not succeed.

The critics on the editorial board of *Novy Mir* are not entirely unjustified when they interpret the figure of Doctor Zhivago in the following way: "Basically the doctor does not in the least prove his claim of being a Messiah. He distorts and does not follow the path of the evangelic prophets he adores. Not the slightest trace of Christianity can be found in the dim path of Dr. Zhivago. He worries least about humanity and most about himself." The skin, the type, the Christ figure. Three accusations by "the others" against Zhivago. Never do they completely miss their mark, but neither do they fully hit upon the true situation of the doctor, or, for that matter, of his author. Certainly there are great political differences here, in the evaluation of Czarist Russia, the bourgeois intelligentsia, the October Revolution, the civil war. But the actual conflicts are mainly of an aesthetic nature.

An Artist Beyond the Bourgeois World

The aesthetic theory of socialist realism that was formulated and accepted during Gorki's lifetime by the First Congress of Soviet Writers demands the historically concrete representation of realities that change dialectically. Moreover, a work of art should serve to educate the people toward socialism by virtue of such a representation. The reflection of reality and the political-pedagogical function should be brought into harmony with one another in every new literary work. Of course, Pasternak's novel intentionally disregards the principle of functionalism. This principle is violated not by the choice of a central figure like Zhivago but by the way the doctor lives and dies. Zhivago is not an internally and externally defeated man, like Melekhov in Sholokhov's *The Quiet Don*. Decline and decay do not bother the doctor and poet at all. He sees in them only a symptom of his loneliness. In no way does he view them as an expression of a defeat that he must accept.

The representation of reality in Pasternak's novel, with its conscious discontinuity and lack of causality, also has nothing in common with the structural principles of his colleagues the Soviet writers. Had Chagall remained in Vitebsk or Moscow and had he painted his "Revolution," the embittered critics would presumably have reviewed it just as they did Pasternak's novel. Whoever demands pedagogical goals from a literary work must necessarily strive for logical causality in his representation, be it according to Tolstoi's principles of representation or be it the use of dialectical techniques of alienation developed by Brecht. Yet, among the notebooks from Zhivago's late period, there is the following idea: "The seemingly incongruous and arbitrary jumble of things and ideas in the work of the symbolists (Blok, Verhaeren, Whitman) is not a stylistic caprice. This is a new order of seeing, of reflecting impressions that stem directly from life and nature. Just as these poets have their series of images rush by us in their poems, so too does the busy bustling street of a city undulate with its crowds, carriages, and carts that are being replaced before our eyes by the streetcars and subways at the beginning of our century."

Pasternak names three poets for very good reason: Aleksandr Blok, Emile Verhaeren, and Walt Whitman. The parallel to the lyric poetry of German expressionism is also unmistakable. Georg Heym, Ernst Stadler, Alfred Lichtenstein. In each instance we have the new principle of unorganized coexistence, which must be understood as a new organizing principle necessary to bring about an adequate reflection of the big city world of the modern industrial society. It is for this reason that Zhivago sardonically adds: "There is no room here for pastoral simplicity." Chagall understood the organization of his painting of the revolution in a similar way. Discontinuity, lack of causality, the seeming nonfunctionalism of the works: Chagall's painting and

Pasternak's novel. Both men understood their works as appropriate artistic expressions of a new order.

Boris Pasternak's aesthetics results in another affinity between *Doctor Zhivago* and the great bourgeois novels of the first half of the nineteenth century. In Stendhal's novel *The Charterhouse of Parma* we find the hero of the book, Fabrice del Dongo, in strange circumstances: in a uniform that does not belong to him, with papers bearing the name of a convict. He is a soldier at the battle of Waterloo. Although completely different in type and motivation from Voltaire's heroes, he is a Candide who is suddenly flung into the stream of world history. Fabrice does not know how to use weapons. He does not even know what is happening. When he asks who the general is who is using such coarse language, people stare at him, for he obviously does not even recognize Marshal Ney. Stendhal proceeds—in a narrative form totally unheard of at that time—to present the battle of Waterloo completely through the eyes of this unsuspecting young Italian who has no interest one way or the other in what is happening. The result is, of course, a confusing succession of disconnected scenes. The decisive historical events are viewed not from the hill where the commanding officers stand (along with the historian) but through the eyes of a man who seems to be down there in the midst of it, yet who is outside of it. In the thick of the battle that means disorder, arbitrariness, and danger to him, Fabrice can see nothing but scenes of senseless haste. Since the conflict does not concern him in the least, there is no intellectual or emotional debate. In this battle of Waterloo, Fabrice cannot take a side, nor does he even consider it important to do so.

When the historical-philosophical current carrying the idea of the hero ran dry, Stendhal's method of portrayal received the attention it deserved and was imitated by the novelists of the late nineteenth century. Even Georg Büchner, a contemporary of Stendhal, had already declared that he would not allow himself to be impressed by the "parade-nags and loafers of history." In *War and Peace* the de-heroization of the campaign of 1812—with a definite emphasis against the hero-cult surrounding Napoleon— is carried even further than in Stendhal's portrayal of the battle of Waterloo. Yet, in its place we have Tolstoi's peasant-democratic sympathies for everything that concerns the "people."

Pasternak's novel stands at the end of this development. He knows neither the heroic protagonist nor the heroization of the people. Lenin is mentioned only once in the novel—and the Soviet critics found considerable fault with this. From the artistic standpoint this criticism was certainly unjust, for the mistake was not that he kept silent about this historical figure but that he violated the great artistic principle of silence by mentioning him in one single spot. Nowhere in this novel about an epoch filled with wars and revolutions do the well-known names appear that every history book records, no matter what its bias may be. Neither Lenin nor Trotsky, neither Kerenski nor the family of the czar. Very seldom is a name like Milyukov's mentioned even in conversation. This is a sound literary principle because it attempts to divorce the reader from all associations derived from newspapers and allows the reality of the novel to enclose the reader completely.

The result is naturally that the story of Doctor Zhivago can never take place in an environment where important decisions of the war or the civil war are made. The Kremlin appears just as rarely as the commanding headquarters of the White Army. At most Pasternak shows a figure such as Strelnikov or Galiullin, some lower rank commanding officer of the Red or the White Army. This occurs only because they are both figures in the plot of the novel aside from their high positions. Hence, we have a rejection of all historical protagonists.

Nevertheless, there is no imitation of Tolstoi. Pasternak is far from making the people into heroes. He pictures the poor people and the simple soldiers of the war and civil war as impulsive masses. It is as though he were transposing the modern investigations of mass psychology into novel form, but it is more than just a structural principle that we have here: it means an indifference to the possibility of collective historical decisions. This literary method becomes questionable only at that moment when the author stubbornly refuses to allow the representatives of views that oppose Zhivago's convictions even to present their case. A serious disproportion arises when only Zhivago is actually allowed to speak and expound his views while his partners are given the floor only occasionally to mouth unimportant stupidities. This is probably why so many critics simply equate the character Zhivago with Boris Pasternak. When the action on the part of the protagonists and the masses and a genuine intellectual dispute between the average people of those times cannot be experienced, then the reader should abandon hope that the novel *Doctor Zhivago* will lead to understanding the conditions in Russia between 1910 and 1929. This is exactly what Pasternak intended. All the misunderstandings that his book caused have their source here: every reader feels himself cheated when reading this story of a man in a world and a period of great historical importance because the world and the period serve merely as a backdrop to set the time and place. The principle of *partisanship* so constantly demanded by the Soviet literary theorists was disregarded. But also those readers of Pasternak who had expected an anti-Soviet tract were bitterly disappointed. We have, then, Zhivago alone before a huge panoramic backdrop painted according to earlier drafts by Stendhal.

An anachronistic book—and not merely in the eyes of the Soviet writers, for whom it had to be inconceivable that a citizen of the Soviet Union would describe the creation of his nation without joy or sympathy, as a senseless event so to speak. However, Pasternak's novel is an *epic* anachronism. Methods of a bourgeois novel form are employed here which hark back to Stendhal and Tolstoi, but which also find precedents in Flaubert, Dostoevski, and certain experiments of the expressionist novelists. Originally they were used in the presentation of events that were to lead the way out of the entire bourgeois world. The bourgeois novel form of epic realism fused with the lyrical experience of the symbolists and expressionists. Pasternak's refusal to employ the principle of partisanship had to lead to artistic regression—to an unintentional divergence between the form and content of the book.

That is, *Doctor Zhivago* is a novel about the artist (*Künstler-roman*) in the eminently bourgeois literary tradition. Therefore, one should not compare it with the great fictional social frescoes of the nineteenth century or the novels about the revolution and civil war by Gorki, Sholokhov, or Tolstoi, but rather with the numerous stories about artists which appeared at the end of the nineteenth century and the beginning of the twentieth century. And just as these artist protagonists run the danger of becoming slightly comic, this is also the case with Zhivago. This danger arises when the author has to describe great intellectual and artistic achievements without using words to give the impression that the literary hero has created great art. Gerhart Hauptmann's Michael Kramer ostensibly creates a great mural, but the author's description makes us smile. Rolland's Jean Christophe writes great musical works, and at least the structure of the works described by the music expert Rolland implies this. But when we read these descriptions, we cringe with discomfort. Perhaps only Gide and Thomas Mann succeeded in avoiding this dilemma: The Counterfeiters parodied the theme of the artist and the author of Doctor Faustus exorcised the ironical arpeggio with thorough, scientific, musical scholarship.

Pasternak did not escape this danger. The originality of Doctor Zhivago is only postulated by the author. Zhivago has (and betrays) his inspirational calling. Of course, the author seems so captivated by the theme of the genius' mission that he presents Yurii Zhivago as "genius itself," so to speak, without the necessary specialization of his mission. Pasternak has arbitrarily designated Zhivago as an important lyric poet, a deep thinker, and an extraordinary doctor. But Doctor Zhivago is shown to be a betrayer of his medical calling. What we learn of Zhivago's historical-philosophical and sociological discoveries, for example the principle of social mimicry, seems trivial and causes us as readers a feeling of discomfort.

What remains is the lyric poet Zhivago. The critics of Novy Mir make the following reproach: "You give your chosen hero the best part of your own poetic talent just to elevate him in the eyes of the reader." This is correct. And here we have something evasive: a mixture of artistic production and reality that is hard to justify, especially since Pasternak had been so anxious to avoid it in the structure of the rest of the novel. Zhivago's poems are and remain for the reader unmistakably Pasternak's poems (especially in the Russian original). It is this relationship that first led critics to equate Zhivago with Pasternak even though this equation was not intended in the objective structure of the novel, nor is there anything in the events of the novel to convey this impression.

To be sure, the poetry of Josef Knecht in *The Glass-Bead Game* is written by Hesse, but the content of the poems belongs specifically to the life story of the *Spielmeister* Knecht. Moreover, Knecht is not actually presented as a poet. His poems are comments on his life, nothing more. Zhivago's poems, however, are verses by Pasternak. The poet lends his hero his own position as a poet, and thereby blurs all the contours of the character as depicted in the novel. A desperate solution to a dilemma in all the novels about artists of the bourgeois world. The creativity of Boris Pasternak as the borrowed creativity of Doctor Zhivago, whose artistic calling would not otherwise have stood so well with the reader. The verses of Aleksandr Blok are referred to once in the novel: "We children of Russia's worst years." The poem from which Pasternak took this line might contain the poetic essence of his novel, which he may have intentionally modeled after the lyric experiments of Blok, Whitman, and Verhaeren. If so, he demonstrated in the end only that the structural principle of the poem is useful mainly in the realm of lyric poetry. Blok's poem appears in the collection *Homeland,* which contains poems written between 1907 and 1916. It is a poem concerned with the first period of the war:

> Whoever is borne by stifling times
> Does not know how to find his way here.
> We children of Russia's worst years,
> We are without power to forget.
>
> Years, reducing to ashes our daring!
> Was it insanity, it could perhaps be hope?
> From war to the days of freedom,
> On us bloody reflection lay.
>
> There is a silence—the rumble of alarm bells
> Forces each mouth to mute arrest.
> In hearts in which beauty burned
> An emptiness yawns like fate.

Rise up cawing swarm of crows
Even above our dying here—
Your kingdom, Lord, will still be seen
By those, Lord, more worthy than we!

The chiliastic hopes for the future are far more appropriate in the closing verses of Blok's poem than in Pasternak's novel. It is a question of the prefigurement of the Passion, not one of actual imitation of Christ, as with Pasternak's Zhivago. Of course, Aleksandr Blok wrote his poem before the year of the revolution. Pasternak's novel is a work of retrospection. Blok gives the quintessence in a poem; the lyric poet Pasternak tries to offer it in a novel. Chagall rejected his painting of the revolution that had been created according to the same maxims of discontinuity.

Literature and Daily Life:

Everyman in the Soviet Union

and the United States

On April 7, 1952, *Pravda* published an extensive and apparently official article called *Overcoming the Stagnation in Drama*. Stalin was alive at this time, and consequently one was well supplied with his quotations. The article was just as dull as its title and was directed against the principle of drama without conflict, against drama that tried to avoid the portrayal of tensions between men in the contemporary situation. The article stated that "some dramatists believe that they are forbidden to criticize bad and negative elements in Soviet society . . . . Whoever acts this way shows cowardice and sins against the truth. Not everything is ideal in the Soviet Union. We, too, have negative types. There are many evil and dishonest people in our life." Later in this critical article about the situation of Soviet drama in 1952, the anonymous author deals with the predominance of factual descriptions and work methods that noticeably displaced the concern with the fate of man and his conflicts in the theater. In other words, the fear of presenting social conflicts led to reification, to the alienation of man, to a dramatized still life.

It is difficult to determine retrospectively whether the author was aware of the causal connection between the lack of conflict and reification. It would be presumptuous to conclude that the problem of reification in the theater was a more or less accurate reflection of the reality of that time. Only two years later—Stalin already lay in the glass coffin—Ilya Ehrenburg returned to this theme in a long critical study, *Concerning the Task of an Author,* and made the following ironical assertion: "The writer who wants to find out about the stages of metallurgical production or about present construction methods would do well to turn to an expert rather than a writer who collects material, that is, to one who has more or less conscientiously acquired that which the experts explained to him. An experienced agronomist will be better able to report on the progress in agriculture than a writer of novels." He, too, seemed not to want to concern himself with causalities. In any case, the article in *Pravda* reported on the play *Where the Pines Rustle* by D. Shcheglev, which takes place among the lumberjacks in Karelia. Apparently the author found it important to assure himself of a success by presenting a milieu on stage which no other dramatist had already portrayed. (The challenge: the fishermen of the Arctic still have not received "their" drama or "their" novel!) What was presented on the stage—and has long since been forgotten—is described in the article as follows: "The thoughts of the characters in the play are concerned only with wood-cutting. Whether they are visiting one another or sitting together at the table or celebrating a wedding, the only topic of conversation is chopping trees, hauling and transporting the logs, and the rationale behind the work methods." The author of the article even takes the trouble to render parts of the scenes in dialogue. In fact, we have a complete fetish made out of lumbering. The maiden who waits for her lover utters in her monologue: "Perhaps he is coming only because he wants to tell me something about the work, about the wood?"

That was seven years after the end of World War II, which the Soviet Union defines as its "great war for the fatherland." The three great impulses that contributed to the most important epic, lyric, and dramatic works in the Soviet Union were exhausted by then: Revolution and Civil War, the first Five-Year-Plan, the defense of the country during the invasion of July 21, 1941. In spite of all the horrors of the war, the Lenin period had offered a hope even for the individual, and so it was sufficient to determine the substance of literature until the 1930's. Sholokhov's *Quiet Flows the Don,* the poems of Mayakovski, the *Optimistic Tragedy* of Vsevolod Vishnevski. During these times all work seemed to be dominated by the unusual. History itself seemed to want to raise the commonplace to something heroic. Literature became heroic because it appeared, at the same time, to be the reality in man's consciousness.

This heroic view became exhausted in the 1930's. World War II was directed by Stalin, Beria, and Zhdanov. Life and literature fell apart. Only the language of the daily editorial was heroic. Man's daily life spoke of fear and infringement of rights. Literature, and in particular, drama, seemed to have only the choice of producing heroic rhetoric—even an important dramatist such as Vishnevski wrote a miserable play about the "unforgettable year 1919" shortly before his death in March 1951. And here Stalin, the man from Gori, was enshrouded in all the glory of the perfect statesman and military leader—in other words, this was done to avoid the reified world of the lumberjacks.

This literary pattern was not new. We find such a phase also in the history of bourgeois literature. What took place in the Stalin era after World War II—a daily life of disillusionment, a decline of historical energy—had already happened in the bourgeois literature of the nineteenth century after the beginning of the secularization of 1800 and particularly in the period of restoration after 1815. The betrayal of Rousseau's ideas, the contrast between the *citoyen* and the *bourgeois,* between the Roman pathos in the Jacobean tradition and the *juste-milieu* of the bourgeois king Louis Philippe. There were those poets fortunate enough to live where the rise of a national liberation movement protected them from the general bourgeois disillusionment that prevailed elsewhere. The Poles and Hungarians, as well as the Italians and the Russians, still stood at the threshold of a bourgeois world. Their literature at that time was still permitted a heroic aura: the rise of the national, the literary amalgam of romanticism and revolution. It was worse for western European bourgeois society. Before the outbreak of the Revolution of 1830, Stendhal demonstrated in the story of Julien Sorel (*The Red and the Black*) how the daily life of disappointments appeared to those who still intended to carry on the Jacobean or Bonapartist heroics anachronistically during the restoration. The bourgeois monarchy of the 1830's meant a daily life of sudden turmoil and quick money. Balzac described both: the heroic impulses and the failure in daily bourgeois life, heroic asceticism and cynical conformity. *Danton's Death,* by Georg Büchner, described the slow process of the bourgeois revolution with regard to the experiences of a stabilized bourgeoisie. ˗

Gustave Flaubert's entire work concerns itself with the problem of giving form to the unheroic daily life—the monotony of a seemingly static, crystallized way of life that allows for excitement only on state and religious holidays—and thereby bringing it under control. The author of the Norman provincial novel admitted that he himself *is* Madame Bovary. Like Emma Bovary, he longed for the great extraordinary moment. Poetry in things, great feelings, the glory of history and the countryside. Literature that seeks an adequate portrayal of such exceptional conditions is generally referred to as *romantic*. Emma Bovary was a romantic within a provincial daily life without the possibility of flight. Thus her romantic flights became small scandalous escapades. Here romanticism had to remain paltry. Flaubert relished the romantic exceptional condition. Whenever possible, his works flee into the past, the exotic, the grotesque. The temptation of St. Anthony or the revolt of the mercenaries against Carthage—these were the themes that could satisfy the romantic in Flaubert. In the story about Madame Bovary he does indeed depict himself: a romantic attitude within the bourgeois daily life and its misery. The daily life in Flaubert's novels has such a horrible effect because the narrator, who is filled with anger, continually attempts to portray the contrast between a stagnant reality and the need of unheroic mediocrity for intellectual and spiritual "elevation." If a daily life is to be made heroic by its inhabitants and its nature does not allow for this, the process originates that had to be confirmed secretly by Soviet literature about 1950: the daily life drained of pathos. The pathetic word without the pathos of the matter deteriorates into the phrase. Flaubert was probably the first writer who attempted to show the dominance of the phrase, of the linguistic and conceptual clichés in a society that had become static. There is a straight line from Flaubert's writings to the dialogues in Ionesco's plays and farces. Wherever a society is determined to combat all change as a matter of principle, then the central theme of a writer becomes the phrase, stupidity, and conceptual clichés.

Flaubert helped himself in this conflict by seeking to force the impetus which he needed as an artist, and which reality actually owed him, from literature, language, and style. When he speaks about *L'Éducation sentimentale*, his great novel of disillusionment about the Revolution of 1848, he clearly reveals this: "Every work of art must have a point, a summit, must form a pyramid, or the light must fall on one point of the globe. But nothing of all this exists in life. On the other hand, art is not nature." In other words, art as an alternative.

The prevalence of this approach came to an end in European literature about 1900. The choice of language and objects became more and more exquisite and esoteric as the bourgeois daily life became more and more ugly, with its tenements, trains, and festivities carried to the point of absurdity. Amethyst and Roman boy-emperor, Hawaii and St. Francis of Assisi, Byzantine icons and fairy tales from Flanders: this could not be continued indefinitely and transformed into ersatz poetry. Hofmannsthal's comment on the selectivity of words and literary forms in the *Lord Chandos Letter* is appropriate: "They fall apart in your mouth like rotten mushrooms."

The earnestness of early expressionism lay precisely in its determination either to describe the ugliness of the modern world as ugliness or to view it as a reason to call for spiritual elevation and renewal, which in turn should lead to a new congruency between a life of "action" and an activist literature. The art and poetry of the expressionists meant an amalgamation of romanticism and revolution again. War and civil war as the vital substance of the movement at its height. When the bourgeois order was once again stabilized at the end of 1923, a daily life without the possibility of flight began anew for a generation of writers who produced a literature of disappointment, scepticism, and cynicism.

Neue Sachlichkeit ("new objectivity"). It was here that the gene-
alogy of all the excessively average "heroes" in the German novel
and theater began: all those insignificant people whose "fate came
upon them," Alfred Döblin's Franz Biberkopf and Erich Kästner's
Dr. Erich Fabian; all those helpless ones from Hans Fallada's
works to Heinrich Böll's; Ernst Wiechert's ex-ship captain who
retires to the "simple life" as a hunter and fisher in Masuren, as
Wilhelm Raabe's *Hungerpastor* had done in his parish at
Grunzenow on the Baltic Sea seventy-five years earlier in 1864.

"To live away." This phrase that underlines the fragmentary
element had already been used at the end of Büchner's story about
the dramatist Lenz. "Thus, he lived away . . . ." A daily life
without impetus, with sufficient provisions, that is, without needs,
with organized free time and a culture that has been preserved,
with an aversion to change as well as experimentation, moved
by an underlying secret fear and striving for security. A literature
that does not provide great romantic flights because its language
is derived from the travel prospectus. In a different setting, a
socialist daily life at the close of wars and revolutions topped
with portraits of Stalin on every wall seemed to have hardly any
other course in literature but to choose between, on the one hand,
the historical cliché that was distributed for revolutionary romanticism as if one were still at the stage of Isaak Babel and Vladimir
Mayokovski, and on the other, a grotesque reification of the
production processes without lumberjacks from Karelia who apparently know nothing else but the scores of the wood-cutting
contest.

What is it like, however, when the concept of "hero"—an
archaic notion stemming from feudal times or the pioneer years
that has been transformed into a phenomenon of citizen-feudal-
ism—moves from the era of the captains of industry and the
"royal merchants" into an era of automation and industrial culture? After all the speeches from the balcony of the Palazzo
Venezia and the Reichskanzlei, one became suspicious of the
heroic attitude. After the much too frequent imitation of em-
perors, condottieri, and Bonapartes. "Woe to the land that needs
heroes," says Galileo in Brecht's play. In any case, the concept of

the hero—in real life as in theater—presupposes the possibility
of going beyond the boundaries of daily efficacy and playing fate.
To become "fate" was very important for Nietzsche. He became
it in a way he did not desire. The followers of Nietzsche are
always in need of possibilities—increasingly so. No "renaissance
man" without a renaissance. The sound film attempted to draw
the concept of the hero from the military and political sphere and
to claim it for the great natural scientists or physicians and, at
the same time, to democratize it: Robert Koch, Paul Ehrlich, and
Ignaz Semmelweis playing the character of a Caesar or Napoleon
on the screen. The film battles of Pharsalus and Austerlitz took
place from then on in the form of faculty or academic meetings.
This course, too, has been exhausted.

A heroic literature without heroes still? Better yet, *the routine
of daily life understood as heroic.* This was neither new nor
original. Goethe said at the end of his life that if one has grown
very old, one has also accomplished something. This reutilization
of the concept of the hero is of major concern in the dramatic
works of Thornton Wilder. The great "man of deeds" is no
longer praiseworthy and the center of attention on stage. Now
it is the mere average man. Wilder clearly intends more than a
literature of average heroes. The American dramatist is serious
about reutilization. This is not simply "de-heroization" but daily
life understood as real heroism.

Thornton Wilder explained what this means at the beginning
of October 1957 in his speech "Culture in a Democracy" at St.
Paul's Church in Frankfurt am Main—the same place where the
National Assembly of 1848 convened. He criticized T. S. Eliot
and those who still believe today that only an elite "can produce
outstanding works." He attacked the fiction of an intellectual
feudalism. "Feudal fiction was strengthened through God's grace,
the position of the Father, and the laws of gravity. The feudal
life has impressed itself deeply upon our language: noble, sovereign, gentleman." Wilder calls for an end to all this and with it
also the end of the dramatist Thornton Wilder. "Now—the great
masses of mankind have been talked into believing a thousand
times a day that they are God's stepchildren, that God has his
favorites, and these favorites are above them. Democracy is not

only a striving for social equality of men but also the striving for equality in God's grace—they are not sons and not subjects and not low-born. This effort will take some time." Then the final thesis: "Democracy has a great task, namely to create new myths, new metaphors, and new images and to show the state of new dignity which man has entered."

Without question, this is Protestant philosophy. Nothing less than a middle-class American one. In 1931 Wilder had already showed how this was to be portrayed on stage in his play *The Long Christmas Dinner*. Here ninety years of a family (1840–1930) are presented as a single dinner made up of all the Christmas dinners they have sat through—always the same conversations, relationships, ceremonies. Wilder rejoices in this continuity, which at the same time has something paralyzing about it and falls all too easily into grotesque comedy. The pattern of everyday clichés celebrated by Wilder are not far from Ionesco's presentation of a grotesque comedy of similar content or Heinrich Böll's satire *Not Only at Christmas* which, perhaps unwittingly, is a parody of Wilder's play.

The best plays of the American dramatist, *Our Town* (1938) and *The Skin of Our Teeth* (1942), are intended to complement one another. We see in the later work that the path of average people like Mr. George Antrobus and his family leads through a world history of catastrophes. They survive by the skin of their teeth and are endangered most by what Wilder defined in his 1957 speech as the feudal way of thinking. George's son Henry and the maid Sabina are representatives of this master class of men and women. Sabina expresses this: "Listen, George: *other* people haven't got feelings. Not in the same way that we have—we who are presidents like you and prize-winners like me. Listen, other people haven't got feelings; they just imagine they have. Within two weeks they go back to playing bridge and going to the movies. Listen, dear: everybody in the world except a few people like you and me are just people of straw. Most people have no insides at all. Now that you're president you'll see that. Listen, darling, there's a kind of secret society at the top of the world— like you and me—that know this. The world was made for us. What's life anyway? Except for two things, pleasure and power, what is life? Boredom! Foolishness." According to the will of the author, Mr. Antrobus knows only one retort to use against this expression of a feudal mentality, which simultaneously wants to mean elitism, lack of ties, lack of spirit. This retort remains a mere postulate and cannot foretell the inevitable "final victory of democracy," as did Thomas Mann about the same time that *The Skin of Our Teeth* was written. Mr. Antrobus is of the opinion that there are three things that have always been together when he was able to see things clearly: "The voice of the people in their confusion and their need. And the thought of you and the children and this house . . . . And . . . Maggie! I didn't dare ask you: my books!" Once again it is evident here that Mr. Antrobus and Mr. Wilder have to recognize the principle of hierarchy if they intend to call on the great guiding lights in opposition to Henry and Sabina. Plato and Aristotle, Spinoza and Kant, Homer and the Old Testament.

In *Our Town* the author is also compelled to justify the heroism of daily life by choosing a point of view that allows average daily life, with joy and sorrow, first love, marriage, children, and death, to be understood as true "democratic" heroism. In *The Skin of Our Teeth* Mr. Antrobus acknowledges the way of the people, the daily life of the family, the great books of the past, the founders of religion, and the philosophers without ever admitting that the contrast between average and hierarchical was introduced again along with the democracy. Wilder must have noticed this himself because he finds it necessary fifteen years later to quote Walt Whitman in his Frankfurt speech, Whitman who believed that all the poetic masterworks are irreconcilable with the spirit of American democracy. Worse yet—each of them has an undercurrent that disavows and slanders democracy. Wilder puts forth this thesis and uses Whitman to question whether the *Iliad,* Dante, Shakespeare, Milton, or *Faust* really "slander democracy." In other words, his 1942 play questions that *Iliad* which was sung from the beginning by the blind beggar Homer with a guitar during the first catastrophe of mankind in the Ice Age. In his speech, Wilder talks about the inner contradiction of the relationship between culture and democracy without being able to solve it. In the play about Mr. Antrobus and his family he had made this contradiction disappear theatrically. Democracy was understood as the eternal recurrence of the same thing—as in the Christmas dinners of the Bayard family, as in the play *Our Town*. At the end of the play, one was once again at the beginning. At the end, Sabina had the same cue as at the beginning of the play. One survived by the skin of his teeth. Everything repeats itself. Does everything repeat itself?

It depends on your point of view. The principle of democracy in Wilder's Frankfurt speech is not sufficient. Not even the educational ideals of *The Skin of Our Teeth*. We are left with the "planetary mind" from the play *Our Town*. It is not by accident that Wilder achieved his greatest international success with this drama. A play about daily life, about the simple people, about the "heroism" of an average daily life. However, everything is seen from the same planetary point of view. Mr. Antrobus had merely quoted Spinoza. This time daily life is literally viewed *sub specie aeternitatis*. If one looks closely, Wilder's eternity is represented by the dead. The play begins on May 7, 1901, in Grover's Corners, New Hampshire, U.S.A., and ends in 1913, in other words, just before the outbreak of World War I. Everything is seen as completed past. The actual interpretation of daily life comes from the conversation of the dead. The young Emily who died in childbed at the age of twenty-six may now speak: "Do any human beings ever realize life while they live it?" The stage manager answers as the universal guide between the two worlds, as the chorus leader of the dead, as Mr. Wilder: "No. The saints and poets, maybe—they do some." Once again the same exception like the great books of Mr. Antrobus, like the answer to Whitman in the Frankfurt speech. Only after death does Emily recognize how men are plagued and must finish their entire lives in darkness. The dead have the task of forgetting that life. They wait, as the stage manager says: "They're waitin'. They're waitin' for something they feel is comin'. Something important, and great. Aren't they waitin' for the eternal part in them to come out clear?" These words assume a meaning only when they are understood as a Christian promise. The minister says approximately the same thing, only with other words. Wilder is able to heroize daily life only by reaching back to Christianity. Unfulfilled existence and heavenly fulfillment.

The planetary point of view results from the contrast between an infinite world of stars that are merely limestone and fire and the planet Tellus, which tries to make something out of itself in every way possible. On top of this, the contrast between the innumerable kinds of men on this planet and the importance which each one gives to his drives and life. With this, Wilder is actually as near to Kant as he is to Spinoza, for this is once again "the starry heaven over me." Here Wilder understands the moral code from a Protestant point of view, not from a Kantian. This is actually a mere rationalization.

Wilder's planetary point of view is a mere Christian appendage to his concept of *social statics*. The same Christmas dinner ninety times. No talk about catastrophes from which one survives by the skin of his teeth. For *Our Town* Wilder has to use a historical artistic device in order to produce the ahistoricality of daily life which he needs for his thesis. He must place the play in the first decade of the twentieth century *and* in a small American town. He carefully avoids the year 1914 because he wants to carry out the idea of the heroization of daily life. The heroics of this daily life lies in the apparently uneventful American small-town life at the beginning of the century. Before this, in 1920, Sinclair Lewis cynically and sardonically showed in *Main Street* what Wilder in the 1930's presented as a system of social statics equipped with all the dignity of eternity and limited to the period between 1901 and 1913: desperate monotony on the "main street" of an American small town. Satire, elegy, idyll, no matter how the sentimental poets of America in the twentieth century have attempted to portray the world of their small towns and middle-sized cities, this daily life is now almost past. Since time immemorial bourgeois thinking has pressed toward reification and toward viewing itself and the middle-class world as most absolute and planetary. This presupposed a social statics but eventually required that this statics be protected from all threats. Certain instances and institutions of American life in our time do not appear in Wilder. They would disturb the daily life.

Daily life was not known on the stage in the first decade of Soviet drama. The theater continually dealt with the behavior of man in war and revolution, in civil war and in the transitional period that led to a new economic politics. White and Red, the bourgeois and proletarian fronts, wartime communism and a sudden interspersion of capitalism within the proletarian dictatorship. This was to be dealt with on stage only as a heroic fresco. This treatment was even more to be required because the new members of society also appeared in the audience and wanted to view themselves. The old theaters—for the time being the new ones were inconceivable—which had been designed for aristocrats and the upper classes (Czarist Russia was very conscious of class distinctions, and "petty bourgeois" was a social designation stemming from the civil registry) often offered a grotesque contrast to the action that took place on stage in the turbulent style of the "liberated theater." Max Reinhardt had the "chamber theater" constructed for the "mood pieces" of the late Ibsen, Strindberg, and Sternheim, which dealt with the lives of middle-class heroes: all this for a couple of hundred spectators from middle-class circles who were especially fond of melancholy, hopelessness, and total distrust of ideology. After 1920 the most important literary premieres in Munich, Frankfurt, or Hamburg also took place in "chamber theaters." Of course, Reinhardt had the Grosse Schauspielhaus modeled after the "chamber theaters" built in Berlin by Hans Poelzig for a new monumental art for the masses. Historical frescoes, battles, expressionistic civil war paintings, migration, and sea battles. In Berlin the pluralistic theater was still for the middle class who enjoyed "atmosphere" as well as the theatrical revolts.

When a currency change was made at the beginning of 1924 and Neue Sachlichkeit began, Reinhardt's Grosse Schauspielhaus also had to change, and it introduced an era of operetta-revues with a grand format and young stars like Marlene Dietrich. One went to see comedians, artists, and "a thousand beautiful legs," as was advertised on the revue poster pasted on a billboard near the subway at Friedrichstrasse. The chamber theater continued to perform the plays of Strindberg and Wedekind and also produced Pirandello's theater questions about reality and illusion.

However, it was embarrassing. The heroic mass theater for the middle class came to an end, as did the "mood pieces" of the early twentieth century that had begun by celebrating Wilde's *Salome* and Hofmannsthal's *Elektra* in the chamber theater twenty years earlier.

In Soviet Russia (as one still called it at that time) this dualism of bourgeois chamber theater and liberated stage heroics was no longer possible. At the end of the Czarist regime, Anton Chekhov constantly presented daily life on the stage. Always the same jokes, a life of seeming social stability, above all, life as predictable. There are no surprises. At the most, an evasion. All that remains is a longing for it. "I want to go to Moscow. To Moscow, to Moscow!" cries Irina, the youngest of the three sisters in a dull provincial city. Then the curtain falls. A Chekhov ending. The poet's instructions clarify what hardly needs to be underlined: "Irina (left alone, filled with longing)." One became accustomed to the late productions of Konstantin Stanislavski and his followers, who produced such figures as Irina or Nina Michailovna in *The Sea Gull* as emotional heroines who want to break out but break down under the power of the stable daily life. Such fragmentary heroics seem quite inappropriate for a poet who was also a great humorist. A like-minded humorist, Thomas Mann, tries to pinpoint this in his essay on Chekhov (1957): "He did not look like a person who would take you by storm." Furthermore, "his artistic ability has captivated me. His irony about fame, his scepticism about the meaning and value of action, his disbelief concerning greatness—all this bespeaks a quiet, modest greatness. 'Dissatisfaction with oneself,' he wrote, 'is the basic element of every true talent.' "

In Chekhov's plays, all of which are essentially comedies, daily life appears on the stage, but it is not heroic. Much is desired but little is actually accomplished by the characters. Once again, to quote Thomas Mann, who understood a great deal about such situations, they are plays "which live from a feeling for the life which is perishing, for the existence which has become impossible, is possible only as fiction." Maksim Gorki learned a great deal from Chekhov. He continually depicted the downfall of the Czarist regime in his plays and quite wisely never developed his themes beyond the October Revolution. In contrast to Chekhov, however, he did allow representatives of the future revolution, and consequently the postrevolutionary society, to appear on stage. These things are treated rather strangely in Gorki's dramas. Some forms of the rebellious manner of speech used by a character in *The Lower Depths,* in *Smug Citizens,* or in *The Enemies,* that is, in plays written before 1914, would remind the average reader and theatergoer of the usual senseless chatter and bragging of Russian poet-figures from Dostoevski to Chekhov if it were not for the year 1917. The successful revolution allows itself to seem a heroic-pathetic anticipation which before this—according to the will of the author—must have been felt merely as a verbal revolt that would obediently become part of daily life.

Gorki's later plays, written after 1917, did not profit by this attempt to portray the daily life of the perishing Russian bourgeois world through the spotlight of the revolution. Gorki originally depicted Vassa Zheleznova as a figure who felt both sympathy and revulsion for the middle class. Yet, the later version gives her a counterpart who comes from the illegal struggle but is, however, not successful against Vassa, the representative of a fictitiously existing society, as it were. The daily life of a society that has reached the end of its era still rules sovereign in Gorki's late plays. The figures who are intended as heroes of the coming revolution have little effect. They are used merely for contrast. Gorki, too, is unable to create a synthesis of revolutionary heroics and an epic-dramatic painting of daily life. One cannot always be heroic, not even in times of revolt and social reorganization. The great revolutionary theater of the masses is an exception. This is also true in regard to the type of stage. Its layout is intended more for musical productions, for apotheosis, occasionally for oratorios. Here the deaths that occur have an emotional effect, but hardly a deep one because the figures who die in the course of the action secretly belong to the unreal sphere of the opera stage. All these works of this "genuine" heroic revolutionary drama (we are talking only about this form) are actually part of the ceremonial drama festival for the socialist society.

There is still a question about the presentation of daily life on the Soviet stage. For a time the genre of "heroic chamber plays" was possible. The dramatist Nikolai Pogodin portrayed daily life on the stage, but it was the daily life of Lenin. Classic European drama presented other possibilities which up to that time were relatively unknown on the Soviet stage. According to the substance of the play, the hero's change was the central theme. The harmony of an idealistic drama of change, as in Schiller. Moreover, the expressionists introduced new dramaturgical possibilities by stressing the transition from the bourgeois to the socialist society. The famous Professor Timirjasev acknowledges and joins the revolution; an important surgeon puts aside his reservations; the conflict between private life and public is reduced to satisfactory proportions; individual peasants give up their resistance to collectivization. With World War II and invasion the new exceptional situation becomes a literary theme. Ostensibly the daily life no longer exists. War and daily life are contradictions —when viewed superficially. It is only later that Norman Mailer and Heinrich Böll discover the daily life in the form of war.

The new Soviet daily life after 1945, however, hardly provided an opportunity for excitement. Stalin, Beria, Shdanov. Occasionally the shocks of the war had a delayed effect and could still be presented in a traditional manner. This was still genuine. Soon, however, everything fell apart—in the ceremonial drama in honor of the "miraculous man from the Georgian region" and in the dramatized council for production. The daily life of Stalin on the stage is idolatry and not a heroic chamber play. A bourgeois society that could have changed itself no longer existed. Change in the theater presupposes that the dramatic figure has the right to change his mind and life. Yet, when intellectual regression was supposed to be portrayed in Soviet literature, the right to change no longer came as the conclusion but rather as the call for the police. Stalin's police, however, was not a very fruitful literary theme.

"A few years ago I was told a story at the construction site of the Irkutsk power plant. It fascinated me because of its natural lyricism and purity. For a number of years this story continued to live in my imagination. It changed, transformed itself, and finally, without any apparent doing on my part, became the version that I have related. What actually happened at that time in Irkutsk and what my imagination unintentionally added to it —this is something that I myself cannot remember." Thus wrote the dramatist Alexi Nikolaievitch Arbuzov in 1959, reflecting on how his successful play *The Irkutsk Story* had originated. Aside from the fact that it was a success, the play can be viewed as a model work for a new experimental series by Soviet playwrights in their attempt to come to terms with literature and daily life under new conditions. Therefore, we can use Arbuzov to understand the situation of literature and the theater. He was born in 1908 in Moscow and received his training in the theater at an early age. He was an extra, drama student, actor, and director in the country, Leningrad, and Moscow. During the war he directed a theater on the front and emerged as a successful dramatist by the end of the Stalin era.

Since Arbuzov came from a theatrical family he was familiar with the dramatic principles that made the Soviet theater and film so important in the 1920's. He attempted to enlarge the dramatic realm in terms of time and space and to create mixed forms of dramatic literature while the majority of Soviet novelists (in all the republics) imitated Tolstoi and told stories that told themselves or were told by an omniscient narrator whom no one questioned as to how he knew every precise detail. Also the majority of Soviet dramatists returned to the traditional picture-frame stage as a setting for the actions of Soviet citizens, with their occasional little imperfections, or even Stalin, with no imperfections. Arbuzov had sought a link to the epic theater quite early without finding the direct path to Brecht—something that was not practically possible about 1950. Nonetheless, one of his plays after 1945 bore the title *European Chronicle*. Another, *The Long Way*, which takes place in the summer of 1945 and concerns some young people who become friends while constructing the Moscow subway, was classified a "lyric comedy." However, *The Irkutsk Story* signified a complete dramaturgical break with the picture-frame stage, with the unity of time, story, and place, and with the traditional present of the stage action.

Arbuzov borrowed certain techniques of the epic theater that were certainly not new, for there were commentators and narrators in the plays of Vishnevski thirty years before Arbuzov. But the epic forms of Vishnevski's *The First Cavalry* and *The Optimistic Tragedy* had the sole purpose of finding a new form for revolutionary heroics. Arbuzov, on the other hand, deals with daily life in the late 1950's in Siberia during the construction of a power station on the Angara River. Hence, a new attempt to present Russian daily life in the theater—with the stage techniques of the epic theater. Here we find Arbuzov suddenly moving in the same area as Thornton Wilder. The routine of daily events portrayed by means of an epic theater which rejects all the naturalism of scenic illusion and uses a stage manager to set the story and direct the actions of the characters. This was actually the same thing that was offered in *Our Town*. Without asking the secondary question as to the various literary influences, it is possible to infer that Arbuzov learned a great deal from Wilder. With him as with Wilder, the plot is not divided by the classic formula of a story rising to its climax and then declining anticlimactically, but rather it is arranged according to certain basic facts of man's survival in daily life: birth, love, marriage, work, death. Wilder's epic narrator is replaced in Arbuzov by a chorus: three men and three women speakers. This might look like a collective in place of the single "individualist" in Wilder. However, it is noteworthy that the chorus in *The Irkutsk Story* has several functions at one time—as the contrasting feelings of a figure, which are presented here not as a monologue but as conflict; as the voices of conscience in an attempt to bridge the tensions between natural drives and socially useful behavior; as the judgment of society about the occurrences. In short, the chorus represents "the others" in Sartre's sense.

A banal story as in Wilder. Whereas the American dramatist consciously withholds any conspicuous traits from his characters, Arbuzov, as a theater man, can hardly refrain from making some of his figures slightly exemplary, implying changes, or sketching ideological developments. A girl between two suitors. She does not marry the sympathetic rake whom she loves but the shy, serious worker who does not arouse her great passions but does enlist her trust. He then drowns in an attempt to save someone. Finally, she marries the rake, who has changed and become serious. This sounds terribly philistine, but it is not the case. One might have the same discomforting feeling if one wanted to characterize Wilder's family stories in the same way.

There is a problem in dramatizing daily life, and Arbuzov occasionally tries to remedy it with light heroization and the dramaturgy of change. All the supporting characters of the three main figures, Valya, Sergei, and Victor, are so consciously held in the roles of daily life that they forfeit the right to their own character in the sense of traditional realism. They are merely given a leitmotif basis by the author, and they have to show this constantly as a passport whenever they appear. One is a student from Leningrad, another was once a soldier and speaks only when he can tell stories about "his" captain. As in the tetralogy of Wagner, where the orchestra has a leitmotif for each figure and action. This use of the leitmotif for supporting characters goes back to the proven forms of character comedy, where the supporting characters can be presented with only one trait. Music on one string. Molière was often capable of creating beautiful music with this method. The bourgeois comedies of the nineteenth century usually did it more cheaply. It was sufficient if such a character just stuttered or was a little absentminded.

Arbuzov's technique is closer to the bourgeois nineteenth century than the character comedies of Molière. The three main characters are also closer to the conventional bourgeois dramaturgy than is usual in the epic theater. There is no character development in Wilder—the "planetary mind" forbids it, and accordingly, life is not to be fulfilled in life. In contrast, if it does not matter to Brecht whether Mother Courage develops, it is because he is interested in the development of the spectator. Of course, in two instances he did present a "change." In the case of Señora Carrar the action is presented in a decidedly Aristotelian, nonepic manner, whereas the dramatization of Gorki's novel *The Mother* presented the change of the heroine in an epic form. There, however, the matter concerned a revolutionary heroic drama and not a dramatization of daily life. Arbuzov is not a Christian, as is Wilder. For him, experience is fulfilled in living, not after death. His subject matter is taken from daily life, not from heroics, and here we see why the dramatist is stuck in a limbo: neither the dramaturgy of change nor the epic theater of Brecht, which allows the conclusion or moral to be drawn by the spectator. Arbuzov leaves very little for the spectator. The chorus comments and also directs the purpose of the play. This theater is not dialectical. Practically nothing is omitted. The first chorus speaker turns directly to the audience and emphatically declares: "We will place the ending of our story at the beginning in order to show that this is not an end but a new beginning." *The Irkutsk Story* is in its substance and in its dramaturgy a work from the transitional period of the country in which it was written. Neither reification nor idolatry. Neither idealistic change nor the logical presentation of the commonplace. Neither metaphysics as in Wilder nor dialectics as in Brecht. The portrayal of daily life, after many disappointments with false heroics.

In October 1961, Walter Jens spoke at the opening of the Frankfurt Book Fair about "The Writer and Totality," and made the following postulation: "The good is not a reservoir of mediocrity. Morality is not a nesting place for Bible-reading philistines. We cannot wish today that ethics and decency become taboo only because the ability of writers is not adequate to describe morality." It would be possible to use certain artistic devices in describing the monstrous and the off-beat, but "in focusing on the horror in daily monotony" one needs the talents of a genius. It is difficult to depict the joys of everyday life. On the other hand it is much easier to show the anxiety in modern society.

Admittedly, the falsity of the social statics which Wilder tried to utilize has long since become obvious. The socialist dynamics of Arbuzov will have a hard time in daily life if it wants to maintain itself against slogans and feature articles. Literature can no longer help where there is no impetus. A position that is merely negated negation is also worthless. It is possible to present daily life only if it is more than just the eternal recurrence of the same thing. If one looks closely, the theme "literature and daily life" is closely connected to the philosophical theme "Nietzsche and the consequences."

Steppenwolf and Everyman:
Literary Types of the Outsider

The Exception and the Rule

There is the exception and the rule, the opposition to the norm and the norm, the "troublemaker" and the "good guy." What happens, however, if the lines marking the differences between these opposites become vague, perhaps converge with one another without producing, let us say, a more sublime unity? Then the exception becomes the rule.

There is a well-known riddle that lawyers like to ask as a joke: What do you call that crime which carries a heavy punishment if one is caught in the act, but none at all if one carries it out successfully? The answer, of course, is high treason. In committing high treason, one attempts to replace a state order, that is, a legal order, by use of force. If the *coup d'état* is unsuccessful, the conspirators are sentenced to death. However, if it is successful, then a new legal order takes effect on the strength of the "normalization of present conditions." The rule is that of the traitors. The opposition to the norms becomes the norm.

Today even the lines distinguishing the good guy—the everyman—from the rejected outsider—the steppenwolf—show signs of becoming vague. Now that television has become a regular component of daily life, whole societies are familiar with every word and picture that is beamed from the screen. They know the unappealing image as well as the appealing one, the trouble-maker as well as the good guy. The troublemaker's image has, moreover, become a model for considerable segments of modern societies. Those things that appear to everyman as crude and disgusting—the provocative acts that dismiss all that is important to him—are now regarded by a sizable part of the community as socially correct behavior. At the restaurant of the Hotel Ritz the doorman will still refuse a guest entrance if he is not wearing a tie. But at mass meetings of outsiders, everyone will turn to look at a conventionally dressed person as an intruder. The outsiders have ostensibly set up their own communities in opposition to the predominantly bourgeois public. In fact, however, these outsiders, themselves products of a bourgeois society, have not repudiated their former modes of thought. They are not political radicals. They have merely adapted outlandish and antagonistic modes of behavior to uses that can easily be accepted in middle-class society, which thrives on pluralism. In short, the steppen-wolf has become the everyman.

A mutual accommodation is taking place. Long-held antagonisms are becoming softened. The so-called pluralistic society of the late bourgeois epoch is becoming incapable in its everyday life of making clear-cut distinctions. Borderlines between friend and foe can no longer be clearly drawn. When one can no longer decide for the exception or the rule, the steppenwolf or the everyman, all modes of social behavior become ambiguous. Everyman senses that the steppenwolves pose no real threat to his peaceful daily routine.

The ruling classes know well who the real enemy is. Steppen-wolves can be integrated and converted into everymen, but what of the everyman who suddenly turns against his own class? The everyman with his family car and his television set, an obvious representative of the rule and the norm, who changes himself into a proletarian. When the everyman breaks out of the structure of existing society (as when the servant Matti, in Brecht's play, declares war on Herr Puntila), a new community of everymen will be produced that is opposed to the everymen of the ruling class, and its members will address one another as "comrade." Then one will know who the friend is and who the enemy.

Decisions will be possible again; the lines of the class struggle will again be clear.

The everyman's conversion into proletarian is possible only if he is serious in his conflict with society and is not merely a steppenwolf who secretly yearns to discard his wolfishness and become a watchdog. There is no class struggle between a steppenwolf and an everyman. The artist and bohemian Tonio Kröger, in Thomas Mann's early story, pined away for the joys of an ordinary bourgeois existence. Literature has always preferred to depict the outsider and troublemaker. This was its prime domain. Thersites and Socrates; the melancholy hero, the fool, and the misanthrope; the eccentric, the madman, and the Bohemian. In all epochs of society up to the present, the issue has concerned the contradictions between the rational and the irrational in a given social system. The framework has almost always remained clearly delineated, revealing differences between the exception and the rule, the opposition to the norm and the norm. Only in the contemporary period, it seems, can things which were the exception become the rule, and steppenwolves transform themselves into everymen—and most likely also into philistines.

Thersites and Socrates

The ugly Thersites has become more immortal than the legendary Herostratos, who, out of revenge, set on fire the temple of Artemis at Ephesus. Homer refers to the troublemaker with disdain: Thersites is a coward; he abuses the heroes. Above all, he is distinguished by his ugliness. Recent scholarship suggests that Homer perhaps wanted to denigrate a type of the original inhabitants in his description of this inferior physical specimen so that the Greek conquerors and princes would shine the more gloriously. However that may be, the example of the sarcastic Thersites, the great classical "exception," has been shown very little understanding except by Shakespeare. Later classical versions carried on the tradition of the Homeric types. Achilles is said to have beaten or killed Thersites after the war with the Amazons because Thersites mocked Achilles' love for the corpse of the

Amazon queen Penthesileia. Yet Thersites apparently did not belong to the lower classes. He mixed with the heroes in his argumentative and zealous fashion. He was not submissive, and there is no doubt but that he secretly considered himself equal in rank to the others. Of course even here he would still be the great exception.

In *Troilus and Cressida,* Shakespeare lent Thersites the same Homeric attributes: cowardice, sarcasm, and ugliness. As a coward, and one who consciously plays this role, he refuses to participate in the heroic ritual of man-to-man combat with the bastard of Priam. He is often beaten, and continues to deride the warriors. In spite of this, he possesses greatness, and the dramatist seems to understand this in his creature. Shakespeare's cruel comedy takes the side of the Trojans, particularly of Hector. The general staff of the Greek conquerors proves to be much more foolish and less serious than the war council in Troy under the leadership of Priam. Thersites (obviously speaking for Shakespeare) never tires of denouncing the military campaign of the Greeks and their behavior: *wars and lechery.*

Nevertheless, posterity seems to have uniformly accepted Homer's condemnation of Thersites. It appears as though the absence of any positive features connected with the name and figure of Thersites in the Homeric world has continued to have an effect over the centuries. Friedrich Schiller summarized the unbearable swing of fortune in war like this:

> Without our choice and approbation
> Luck does give away its gifts.
> For Patroclus lies in his coffin
> And Thersites stands in our midst.

> Ohne Wahl verteilt die Gaben,
> Ohne Billigkeit das Glück,
> Denn Patroklus liegt begraben,
> Und Thersites kommt zurück!

This means that Achilles' handsome and heroic friend had to pass away while ugliness and cowardice survived. Shakespeare had depicted Patroclus sardonically in the arms of his lover, and

Thersites was not lax in describing this incident in as clear and vulgar a way as possible. There is no question but that Shakespeare in *Troilus and Cressida* made different value judgments from Homer and Schiller. In Shakespeare's work the handsome, beloved, and absurdly heroic Patroclus is an episode; Thersites represents a principle.

On the other hand, the astute Polish drama critic Jan Kott, who has clearly shown that *Troilus and Cressida* must end as a cruel type of comedy because of its denial of possible tragedy, fails to recognize the greatness of Shakespeare's Thersites. To be sure, he sees Thersites as a "bitter fool" who is free from illusions. Nor does he miss the remarkable rejection of the false-heroic world by Thersites, who is the only one not ready to participate: "I would croak like a raven; I would bode, I would bode. Patroclus will give me anything for the intelligence of this whore. The parrot will not do more for an almond than he for a commodious drab. Lechery, lechery still, wars and lechery! Nothing else holds fashion. A burning devil take them!" For Jan Kott, the figure of Thersites belongs to the realm of the grotesque: "The grotesque is crueler than the tragedy. Thersites is right. But what does it mean that he is right? Thersites is a scoundrel."

Is Thersites really a scoundrel? Is he one because of his cowardice, his sarcasm, or perhaps his ugliness? Ambiguity surrounds this character from the Greek epic up to our own day and age. We are dealing with someone who was not ready to participate. He was neither a slave nor a rebel, neither a martyr nor a prisoner. He belonged to a group—but he did not want to belong to it. The exception among a great many regular people. In a world which was disposed to equate physical beauty with moral values, destined as it were by nature and birth. The classical age could not conceive ugliness associated with heroism. Prometheus was tortured, Ajax went insane, Philoctetes had an incurable disease —but only Thersites was ugly and unheroic, and consequently he was robbed of any tragic stature from the very start. Nevertheless, he belonged to his world as the exception does to the rule and ugliness does to beauty.

Socrates' ugliness must also have been somewhat confusing for his contemporaries in Athens. Alcibiades' speech in Plato's

Symposium implies this: "For one could compare Brasidas and others generally to Achilles, Pericles to Nestor and Antenor. . . . Yet, one would have to hunt far and wide to find something similar to this strange man, both him and his conversation. There is nothing like him among our contemporaries or those in the past, unless someone were to compare him not with a human being, as I am doing, but with Silenus and the satyrs." The phenomenon of Socrates appears to have caused a certain hesitation in making the usual equation between physical beauty and moral worth, and hence a distrust of the *kalokagathia* (the standard values). Plato separates the phenomenological forms of *eros*. He connects Socrates' ugliness with the intellectual power of seduction; as a result of this ugliness, he is stronger and more potent.

Unlike Thersites, Socrates was unable to survive scandals. As compensation, he was saved the ignominious treatment of being categorized as a "poor exception" by posterity. For a conservative writer of comedies such as Aristophanes, who was still thoroughly committed to the old gods and the established aristocratic order, Socrates, the ugly son of a midwife who posed at the Agora, disturbing questions hostile to the gods, was as much a laughable figure as the avant-garde tragedian Euripides, who allowed gods to appear in his plays. It was apparent that Euripides did not believe in these gods and allowed them to show themselves up before a public whom he took into his confidence. Aristophanes' portrayal of Socrates in the *Clouds* may have helped lead to the philosopher's death sentence by poison. This is the reason why Socrates' disciple Plato has Aristophanes come under the influence of Socratic love in the *Symposium*.

However, because of Socrates, an exception became the rule. His ugliness played a role in causing the realms of sensuousness and intellect to split from one another. The history of philosophy has been affected in some strange ways by this phenomenon. The earlier Greek thinkers were suddenly downgraded to pre-Socratic thinkers. The exception set new rules. Perhaps Nietzsche was the first to estimate the historical importance of this event when he traced the slave morality of Christianity back to Socrates. The radical outsider had simultaneously exploded the old norms and set new ones. The disciples and followers of the man who developed an "intellectual art of obstetrics" knew later on how to prevent the Socratic irony from merely exposing and destroying. They learned to keep all questions open without providing for a new integration. The parallel developments of the Socratic school and Christianity have often been noted, not only by Nietzsche. In contrast to Thersites, Socrates did not remain categorized as a negative figure. The Socratic irony proved itself to be helpful, constructive, and open to integration even in social realms.

The Everyman and the Fool

The intrinsic theme of all literatures only seems to be that of the everyman—at any rate this is the case in the local sphere of Europe or the so-called Occident. In reality it is difficult to imagine a play like the Middle English text of Everyman (The Somonyhnge of Everyman) outside of its historical context, English society at the end of the fifteenth century. This is due not merely to the fact that Christianity as an institution and as the final spiritual and worldly authority is a precondition. What is more astounding about the text is that it shows hardly any sign of the feudal period. Everyman is a wealthy citizen who can afford to offer noteworthy sums to death to count as "good-dedes" in an accepted form of giving accounts. There is more to learn here than merely noting the medieval pattern of the dance of death. In the old plays about death, pope and king were not shown to be equals of rich commoners and poor peasants until the last moment before death fastened his grip. Everyman, on the other hand, is the work of a bourgeois mind which seems to be concerned only with bourgeois everymen, not with aristocrats and even less so with priests. It has often been noted that this medieval English play already reveals some opposition to the institution of priestly sacraments. There are thorough distinctions made between good and sinful priests in a worldly and rational manner:

> Synfull preestes gyveth the synners example bad,
> Theyr chyldren sytteth by other mennes fyres, I have harde,
> And some haunteth womens company,

With unclene lyfe as lustes of lechery;
These be with synne made blynde.

This play about the wealthy bourgeois Everyman produced the later basic categories of all bourgeois thinking in terms of a natural equation between humane and bourgeois life. This is true not only of the English *Everyman* but also of dramas from the Dutch play *Elckerlijc* up through Hans Sachs's *Comedi von dem reichen sterbenden Menschen, der Hecastus genannt* (*Comedy of the Rich Dying Man Named Hecastus*). The Catholic view that was the basic conception before the Reformation allows Everyman to fall back on good deeds that can be counted in terms of hard currency. After Luther and Calvin, the way to salvation through charitable deeds is blocked in the Everyman plays, including Hugo von Hofmannsthal's version. Everyman is told to take stock in faith. But, as is well known, the Calvinist faith was again able to place itself in the service of the bourgeois economy by the seventeenth century.

With this development, the opposition of the outsider and the everyman, understood as that between the exception and the rule, presented itself as a specific phenomenon of a growing bourgeois society.

Athenian and Roman comedies were also plays about the everyman, but with one basic requirement: that the slave society should not be treated as a theme. Comedies were possible only between men, and therefore could be essentially concerned only with patricians and plebeians. The slave was only *res*, an "object" according to Roman law. These everyman plays from Aristophanes up to Plautus evoked laughter over those neighbors in *polis* and *urbs* who, though they belonged to the society of everymen, failed to meet its standards because of some minor human deficiency—pretentiousness, cuckoldry, cowardice, unsociability. (Dyskolos belongs here too even though or because he strives to be different.)

The everyman of the Christian Middle Ages was guided by the separation of spiritual equality and a rigid, stratified social hierarchy. The self-consciousness of the everyman in that period was still quite far from the knowledge that Hegel formulated in his

Encyclopedia: "Christianity has become a reality through its followers. For example, they will be slave to no one. If they are made into slaves, if the decision about their persons is made arbitrarily and not according to the law and courts, then they would find the substance of their existence damaged."

The English play about Everyman's burden caused by death became possible only when the feudal War of the Roses had destroyed the basis of feudal domination and bourgeois self-consciousness could begin to defend itself, supported by wealth and numbers. The bourgeois plays about the rich Everyman postulated the demand for equality, in other words, equal citizenship with the feudal lords. The everyman's social rule presented itself as a new exception in opposition to the feudal world. On the other hand, these plays began to substitute a new form of economic inequality. They never dealt with the lives of poor peasants or propertyless city dwellers.

Aristocracy and feudalism were not prepared even in literature to accept the social postulates of the Everyman plays. The wealthy urban bourgeoisie in Shakespeare's plays do not in any instance stamp the course of a history, tragedy, or comedy. The protest of the rich London citizens against the usurper Richard Gloster was weak and ineffective. The feudal lords and the plebeians carry the action in the plays—and their strict separation is marked by their different forms and quality of speech.

Shakespeare acknowledges not the bourgeois everyman in his plays but rather eccentrics of all kinds—the melancholic, the misanthrope, the madman, the fool. He takes pleasure in confronting one form of eccentricity with another: the fool with the melancholy Jaques in *As You Like It*; melancholy with genuine and feigned madness in *Hamlet*; nonsense with genuine and feigned madness in *King Lear*.

But Shakespeare's fools and melancholy protagonists do not take a stand as exceptions to the social rule. They are completely integrated with society. They belong. In fact, obvious madness, as Michel Foucault has shown in his book *Madness and Civilization*, was recognized until the onset of the Enlightenment as a natural component of society, as part of a norm, not in a strict sense as opposition to that norm.

There are the fools—not merely the clowns in Shakespeare's works but the institutionalized fools created by absolutism, that is, the fools whom Velázquez painted at the court of the Spanish Hapsburgs, the court fools of Louis XIV, and even the Baron Gundling in Potsdam, whom Frederick William I kept as court fool and president of the academy.

Shakespeare's fools are the rule, not the exception. They are neither melancholy nor misanthropic. Only two characters of Shakespeare are complete social exceptions who cannot be classified or brought into harmony with the others. The fact that they appear in comedies makes the break even greater. The two are Shylock the Jew and Malvolio the Puritan. Malvolio's closing words are important: "I'll be reveng'd on the whole pack of you." The Puritan Cromwell demonstrated in the Revolution of 1648 how this was to be understood. Once again an exception transformed itself into a new set of rules.

The Misanthrope and Society

In his book *Der Sonderling in der deutschen Dichtung,* which deals with the eccentric figures in German literature, Herman Meyer does not overlook an interesting definition which Caspar Stieler had formulated at the end of the seventeenth century for a type of social eccentric. Stieler's reference work, *The Etymology and Development of the German Language (Der deutschen Sprache Stammbaum und Fortwachs, 1691),* classifies that person who withdraws from society as "homo singularis et peculiaris opinionis, alienus a consortio hominum, solitarius."

That curious word *alienus* appears here already. The word which is constantly used in contemporary English and French—*alien, alienation*—where "strangeness," "strange," and "estrangement" should be used instead.

The eccentric is connected with the idea of isolation (*Absonderung*) not alone in the linguistic realm. There are two forms of isolation. One is that of the eccentric who departs from a community; the other is that of the community which keeps the eccentric individual or special group at a distance and eventually isolates it.

Strangely enough, those eccentrics in society who voluntarily kept their distance from the ordinary routine were never seriously nor strictly isolated. On the contrary, such eccentrics were generally highly esteemed and secretly admired by those people whose society they disdained.

It must be remembered that the melancholy hero is a part of society and cannot base his spiteful attitude on any real and hostile condition of being an outsider. Shakespeare always showed his melancholy heroes, as well as his fools, in their exact function. He made a careful distinction between true, noble melancholy and melancholy that was tailored for an occasion and, hence, ignoble. The melancholy Jaques in the Forest of Arden with the exiled duke is noble and aristocratic. On the other hand, the melancholy of the illegitimate and comical Don Juan in *Much Ado about Nothing* is false. In either case, these characters belong to the world of comedy. They are not tragic. Even Hamlet's melancholy was not sufficient for tragedy; the tragedy rises from the conflict between the melancholy hero and the rotten state of Denmark.

Ever since antiquity, or, to be more exact, ever since Plato, the melancholy hero has been considered gifted, particularly in the fields of art and science. Aristotle was one of the first to see a connection between melancholy and artistic genius (as is demonstrated by Rudolf and Margot Wittkower in *Born under Saturn*, 1963), and the Italian Renaissance philosopher Marsilio Ficino compared the melancholy of the genius with that which Plato called the divine gift of "mania"; in other words, it was a type of obsession. Since the Renaissance, melancholy has come to mean "born under the sign of Saturn," as well as "isolated from the common people by birth and genius." Hamlet is both: prince and melancholy genius.

Even where the melancholy increases and becomes misanthropy, the complete isolation that is strived for by the misanthrope will be only seemingly effective. Once again, Shakespeare can help us see this with his repertory of social types. In *Timon of Athens*, his misanthrope is a superficial link between the real misanthrope and society. The weakness of the tragedy *Timon of Athens* consists in Timon's wanting to be too social. He keeps an open house, is considered immensely rich, seeks to buy friendship and affection by doing favors. The quick loss of his estates caused by misfortune, poor management, and waste does not drive him to make a horrible deal with a real outsider, as did the businessman Antonio of Venice with the Jew Shylock. Rather, Timon has fits of misanthropy. In fact, though Shakespeare does not fully define the contrast, he balances the superficial misanthropy of Timon engendered merely by misfortune and ingratitude by opposing him with the cynical misanthrope Apemantus, whose hatred of mankind stems organically from his philosophy. In Act IV, Scene 3, Apemantus states:

> This is in thee a nature but infected,
> A poor unmanly melancholy sprung
> From change of fortune. Why this spade? this place?
> This slave-like habit and these looks of care?
> Thy flatterers yet wear silk, drink wine, lie soft,
> Hug their diseas'd perfumes, and have forgot
> That ever Timon was. Shame not these woods
> By putting on the cunning of a carper.

Molière's play about the misanthrope Alceste is considered a highlight of French drama. French actors have set certain standards and qualifications for the roles of the misanthrope and Célimène which are used to judge and measure all new actors. The work is deemed a genuine French configuration of art and life, a counterpart to *Hamlet* and *Faust*. However, the worlds of the Danish prince and the German professor between heaven and hell are tragic realms; the misanthrope's realm remains, in spite of everything, a comic play, a *dramma giocoso*, like Mozart's *Don Giovanni*.

The world of French theater is a world of comedy. In fact, it is almost programmatic. When Bergson attempts to interpret the laughter and the intellectual motivating forces of the phenomenon in comedy, he takes examples from Molière's works and continually falls back on the case of the misanthrope Alceste. Bergson sees a certain rigidity and lifelessness in Alceste's passion for honesty. This brings him into conflict with the social norms that in turn always bring decency and propriety into opposition with each other.

Molière's Alceste wants to be a man of society, remain true to its norms in the age of the radiant monarch Louis XIV, and at the same time enjoy his passion for decency through voluntary isolation. His misanthropy is mere dissatisfaction with the fixed, almost ballet-like, forms of French aristocracy's social behavior. This is the reason why that society laughs over this unfortunate misanthrope—with good reason and in accordance with Molière's will. Shakespeare, on the other hand, did not jeopardize the tragic situation of Timon by emphasizing his counterpart Apemantus.

Molière's Alceste is a comic figure. Society demands conformity. Instead of just refusing, Alceste compromises. He goes through all sorts of contortions to remain polite while hearing Orontes' silly verses, he is a courtier without wanting to be courtly, he strives for genuineness and loves a fashionable woman, he detests his judges and places himself before them in their court. In this way, the power of society is directly acknowledged by him, its detester, and Molière makes himself its laughing commentator. There is also no solution, either tragic or comical. The play about the misanthrope ends *en queue de poisson*—it fizzles in the end. Alceste retreats to his estates (like the nobles of the Fronde or the Duke de La Rochefoucauld) or returns to society, nothing is decided. A century later Rousseau was more inexorable. He refused to compromise at all and lived a life of protest to the very end. Though he may have seemed bizarre, he was definitely not comical. And, it was just this Rousseau who argued Alceste's case against Molière. In the "Letter to D'Alembert" he defended the honor of the misanthrope against those who laughed at him.

As the melancholy of Renaissance artists and aristocrats of absolutism was replaced by bourgeois melancholy, the conduct of the new bourgeois everyman in the Age of Enlightenment proved to be more and more incomprehensible, as in the case of Molière's Alceste. The everyman had made a career for himself since the end of the Middle Ages. Cromwell's Puritans in the English revolution of the seventeenth century had toppled, if only for a short period, the aristocratic world and its fools, melancholy characters, and misanthropes. The citizen of Geneva, Jean-Jacques Rousseau, was in his turn misanthrope, fool, and melancholy hero all in one. He contributed two things at the same time to the bourgeois emancipation: the authoritative thinking of bourgeois everymen who strove for the honorary title of *citoyen* and the melancholy solitude of the eccentric on the Isle de Saint-Pierre in the Lake of Biel in Switzerland, the solitude of the *promeneur solitaire*.

A paradox seems to dictate the situation here. Rousseau may have wanted to be a fool, a melancholy genius, a literary teller of lies, and a hermit addicted to audiences. If so, these feelings were a part of the personal side of Rousseau's life. That life had a social side, also, that was much more important. Rousseau's special way of existence—the mania for solitude that was also a declaration of war in the name of equality and the bourgeoisie against the hierarchical structure of society—proved to be a pure incarnation of bourgeois enlightenment. This is why Rousseau's views could be politically influential with a diversity of types that ranged from Duke Philippe of Orléans, who dubbed himself "Philippe Egalité," to Robespierre. With the storming of the Bastille, the everyman stormed the bulwark of feudal society with the apparent goal of establishing equality. As members of the bourgeoisie, they strove at the same time for full self-development as individuals. Equality and individuality moved toward each other in contradiction. The bourgeois individuality triumphed because of the class situation. The *citoyen* became the bourgeois.

However, he soon wanted once again the irreconcilable: the stabilization of the newly ruling bourgeois class *and* the freedom of individual development that was necessarily antibourgeois. This contradiction could not be relieved, as in Molière's play, by laughter, and this is the reason why *The Misanthrope* immediately became suspect in the eyes of the new citizens.

Goethe pondered the case of this play time and time again. Along with *Troilus and Cressida*, *The Misanthrope* was one of his favorite plays. Even as late as 1828 he wrote in a letter to the musician Zelter that he was happy that his friend had discovered Molière and had not accepted Schlegel's rejection of Alceste.

Goethe went on to state in this letter of July 27, 1828: "The French themselves are not completely clear about the misanthrope. On the one hand, Molière is said to have taken a rude, aggressive courtier as his model. Others say he portrayed himself. Naturally he had to mold this character from himself. He had to depict his own relations vis-à-vis the world. And they were remarkable relations! There can be none that are more common. I'd like to bet that you found yourself in more than one place in the play. And don't you play the same role with your daily associates? I have become old enough and have yet to reach the point of placing myself on the side of the epicurean gods."

Here we have the grand privy councillor of Weimar designating himself a descendant of all the early misanthropes. He clearly separates the human position of the misanthrope from his coincidental integration within any society. Goethe would like to concede to Alceste that one can be both at the same time: a model courtier and a misanthrope. In other words, a grand ducal minister and a misanthrope. Here the clear isolation from society which Rousseau had practiced, however theatrically, becomes changed into mere subjectivity. The bourgeois misanthropy presents itself, like the bourgeois melancholy, as mere reservations of the intellect and the heart.

Bourgeois Steppenwolves in the Nineteenth Century

Goethe himself probably felt misanthropy quite early. He knew all kinds of isolation—the melancholy of the bourgeois heroes Werther and Tasso, the clownish antics of Mephistopheles. Whereas Shakespeare and Molière needed no emotional involvement to portray Timon and Alceste, Goethe had to be able to feel the misanthropy of Doctor Faust and the difficulty of bearing communal life with people in general, not merely with one class. No direct line leads from the suffering, protest, and suicide of the young Werther to the bourgeois eccentric characters of the nineteenth century, the forebears of Hermann Hesse's Harry

Haller. Werther's melancholy was not bourgeois subjectivism. Goethe's friend, the playwright Lenz, who knew all about this, showed in a satirical scene how the pastor and sexton would have preferred to dig up the bones of the suicide Werther, burn them, and spread the ashes on the sea. It was this Lenz who undertook the defense of Werther and Goethe against charges of sentimentalism and subjectivism. In his *Letters on the Morality of Young Werther,* the author of the comedy *Der Hofmeister* makes the following assertion: "Werther is a picture, gentlemen, of a crucified Prometheus, by whose example you could measure yourselves, and it is left to your own genius to make the best possible use of it." Here Werther begins to be understood by contemporaries as a sacrificial Prometheus, a forerunner of those protesters who burn themselves because they would like to bear witness to their convictions.

In his poem "The Harz Journey in Winter" (*Harzreise im Winter*), 1777, Goethe made use of an alternative for the protesting Wertherians—distancing oneself from society through passive resistance so that the protest has to turn quickly into isolation:

> Who is it, off the beaten track?
> His path loses itself in the bush.
> Behind him the shrubs
> Fall into place.
> The grass stands up again.
> The solitude swallows him.
>
> Oh, who heals the pain
> Of him whose balm became poison?
> Who drank a hate of man
> Out of fullness of love.
>
> First despised, now a despiser.
> Secretly he tears apart
> His own worth
> In insufficient egotism.
>
> Aber abseits, wer ist's?
> Ins Gebüsch verliert sich sein Pfad,
> Hinter ihm schlagen

Die Straüche zusammen,
Das Gras steht wieder auf,
Die Öde verschlingt ihn.

Ach, wer heilet die Schmerzen
Des, dem Balsam zu Gift ward?
Der sich Menschenhass
Aus der Fülle der Liebe trank.

Erst verachtet, nun ein Verächter,
Zehrt er heimlich auf
Seinen eignen Wert
In ungenügender Selbstsucht.

Werther and the consequences. Yet even here the misanthropy is exactly fixed in relation to society, as in the works of Shakespeare and Molière. The isolation is made sharper by the fact that the individual must isolate himself from now on from a society which on the surface no longer takes the common welfare and unity of its citizens as seriously as it does the personality of the individual. The outsider in Goethe's poem achieves his individuality by isolating himself from a society of alleged individuals. In a later interpretation of his poem (1821), Goethe understood his earlier poetic attitude toward the misanthrope of the Werther period in this way: "His [Goethe's] hearty sympathy for him [Werther] pours forth in prayer." But this prayer is secularized, remains poetry.

Later in the nineteenth century, Johannes Brahms used harmony in an attempt to make a musical exorcism out of this. In his "Alt-Rhapsodie" a deep woman's voice sings the role of the outsider. Then a chorus of men commences with "prayer and hearty sympathy" in order to bring the individual back into society. In Brahms's time, in the second half of the nineteenth century, the individual, the eccentric, and the crank were already tame, thrown back into themselves and socially integrated.

Hermann Hesse had good reasons in *Steppenwolf* to confront the loner Haller, who is apparently quite radical and wolfish, with two forms of music that deal with the overcoming of solitude. On the one hand there is Mozart; on the other, Johannes Brahms, who composed music for "The Harz Journey in Winter" and now drags the many superfluous notes behind him like heavy chains. The bourgeois individualism of the nineteenth century needs the eccentric as a bourgeois form of self-respect, especially where it finds itself at the mercy of undeveloped social forms, as in Germany. The eccentric in the literature of that epoch did not stand for protest but for the highest form of adjustment. A spiritual reservation of subjectivism confirms the social passivity.

Austrian literature in the imperial realm of the Hapsburgs was the first to turn to these new forms of bourgeois confirmation in the form of subjective reservation. Under the restoration of Prince Metternich, they assumed literary form—the delicate steppenwolves of Franz Grillparzer and Adalbert Stifter.

This is the reason why there is little to compare between the bourgeois and Austrian misanthrope and his predecessors in the works of Shakespeare and Molière. Ferdinand Raimund's play *Der Alpenkönig und der Menschenfeind* (The King of the Alps and the Misanthrope) originated in the same year that Goethe had once again emphatically defended Molière's *Misanthrope*. Just the name of the misanthrope Rappelkopf (Hothead) in Raimund's play implies sickness. In the works of Shakespeare and Molière misanthropy had represented awareness of the pathological condition of society. In the era of bourgeois individualism it is interpreted as a symptom of disease and is dismissed in this way simply as a special case. Heinz Politzer has demonstrated, in a study of Raimund's play, that Raimund, in contrast to Shakespeare and Molière, does not attempt to define the causes of his protagonist's misanthropy. Apparently the bourgeois life in itself is sufficient cause. Yet as a result, a dangerous component of the eccentric that was always present can develop itself and unfold freely—a feeling of superiority and elitism in being an eccentric. Politzer makes the following comment about Rappelkopf: "The ego of the man causes separation and isolation. Rappelkopf's flight into the wilderness is done only to create an obvious setting for this isolation. His misanthropy is to a large extent a mania for greatness. Only a small step is needed from misanthrope to overman (*Übermensch*). And just as the *Übermensch* portrays only the glorious reverse side of European nihilism, as it were, this misanthrope is also a nihilist in chrysalis condition."

However, it is exactly here for the first time that an element becomes visible which should have a stronger bearing on the character of the steppenwolves after Hesse. Opposition to society is converted not only into aggression against the bourgeois everymen but also into the will and desire to rule them.

Timon and Alceste belonged to their social systems as negation does to affirmation. Even in death, Werther was a bourgeois man of the Enlightenment who protested merely by sacrificing himself. He was not yet capable of using the terror of the later moralists and disciples of Rousseau, Robespierre, and Saint-Just. In the nineteenth-century German works of Jean Paul, the author secretly sympathizes with his demonic rebels and men who do the work of the devil, yet the humor is aimed at protecting the petty bourgeois idyll from their intrusion. On the other hand, many of the eccentrics in the later development of bourgeois literature understand the attitude of the loner as regression, as a yearning for conditions which preceded the bourgeois epoch, as horror of the large city, the monetary economy, modern traffic, and the transformation of intellectual production into goods.

Hermann Hesse constantly called upon Goethe as well as Jean Paul and the German romantics for support. Yet, this intellectual synthesis and "symbiosis" was not possible. One cannot take a strong stand for enlightenment and at the same time for the countermovement, for resistance and the escape into subjectivism. It was exactly this way of life that was practiced by Harry Haller, the man who wanted to be everything in one: an enemy of the bourgeois society and its techniques, an artist of the old times while living under the sign of a more modern cultural industry, a madman and eccentric of the elite.

Once again we have a paradox. On the one hand, the eccentrics and loners represented the petty bourgeois opponents of a development which led to imperialism. It was the protest of those who strove for the promise of complete self-development against a social system which began to prevent this more and more strongly and completely. Such resistance through passivity, subjectivity, and the careful cultivation of traits of eccentricity and loyalty to a private philosophy was more or less harmless, so these eccentrics were treated with general benevolence. What was more serious was the fact that the individualistic and objective petty bourgeois refused to join their protest with the common cause of the proletariat, but preferred to practice antibourgeois protest in a manner that was not revolutionary or collective but superior, that is, individualistic. It has repeatedly been proved that this manner of resistance can be superbly exploited as an apology for undesirable conditions.

In France, Flaubert did not think of working for a common cause with the Paris Commune. He longed for the annihilation of the revolutionaries by the bourgeoisie whom he otherwise hated. He believed that he himself could determine who was bourgeois and who not: "I call that person bourgeois who has low thoughts." Who decides, however, what low thoughts are in individual cases? Flaubert, the artist of the elite, quickly became a genuine bourgeois ideologist when the bourgeois world that he supposedly detested was threatened for a moment.

Thus the two dominant traits of the bourgeois steppenwolves in the late period of bourgeois society are determined by the course of action they take: the way of total individual subjectivity or the way that leads toward an aristocracy of artists wherein the elite can be used to vindicate bourgeois society.

However, there was still a third way. It was *not* the transition made by certain bourgeois intellectuals into the proletarian camp—the way of a Karl Marx or a Friedrich Engels. Nor was this third way chosen out of feelings of loneliness and isolation. It is a combination of artistic individualism in the traditional bourgeois sense and a decision not for subjectivism but for revolution.

Bohemianism and Revolution

Either the Count Czernin or the Count Berchtold, ministers of the imperial Austrian government at the outbreak of World War I, is credited with a famous remark. Someone predicted that the war could lead to a revolution if there was an unfortunate turn of events. The count replied, "Please, be serious. Who do you think will start a revolution here in Vienna? Someone like our Herr Trotsky in the Café Central?"

The point of this anecdote is not the understandable ignorance of a Viennese nobleman, but the apparent disparity that existed between speeches in a café by a foreign troublemaker with the alias Trotsky—a man who had long been shadowed by the police, who did not have a profession other than that of revolutionary, who read newspapers, carried on political discussions, and wrote articles and brochures for others of his own ilk—and the fact that there was to be a social and political revolution on the soil of a great European power. Czernin and Berchtold knew that there were many such café-revolutionaries in London and Paris, Geneva and Zurich, and even in Vienna. They saw no reason to do more than leave them to the police as usual.

The power that stood behind Trotsky was difficult to estimate. As a frequenter of cafés he had, in effect, made himself unrecognizable to the Viennese authorities in the summer of 1914. Then suddenly, in October 1917, Trotsky made his true self recognizable as a leader of a world revolution that would change history. As Jew, as political writer, and as revolutionary he had been triply an outsider, yet, until now, he had seemed to belong within society, indistinguishable from the steppenwolves who inveighed against society but remained a part of it. From this moment on he was seen to be a *true* outsider, from the viewpoint of bourgeois society. Unlike the steppenwolves, Trotsky had firmly aligned himself with the proletariat.

Such is not the way of the "bohemian," who has learned nothing from the lesson of Trotsky. Characteristically, the bohemian who engages in politics, however extreme his radicalism may be, is unwilling to admit that revolution and resistance are everyman's concern. He remains an outsider in every social class.

The most recent scholarly studies of the bohemian—meaning here the outsider who is a radical critic of the political structure—show that this dualism remains characteristic today. It is demonstrated in the roles of the outsiders and bohemians in Tankred Dorst's recent play *Toller*, about the short-lived Munich *Räterepublik* of 1919. If the disdain of the Viennese count had been directed against the leaders of this abortive revolution, Ernst Toller, Gustav Landauer, and Erich Mühsam, it would have been justified. This raises a question: Is the difference between the political effectiveness of these men and that of Trotsky due merely to Trotsky's charisma? Or does it arise from basic differences of ideology—the difference between, on the one hand, a mixture of feelings and thoughts brewed from sympathy and self-sympathy, ethical socialism, and anarchical hatred of the state, and, on the other hand, Bolshevism.

The political bohemian is isolated from the social processes of production, though he is generally guaranteed a minimal sale of his goods. This fact gives him the right to his radical theories that grow out of hatred of society. Yet his way of life and his ideology isolate him from the everyman producers—the only members of his society who hold within their hands the means to bring about effective political change.

For the bohemian who is unwilling or unable to ally himself with the everyman producers, all roads open to him will lead him back into the society which, ostensibly, he wishes to flee. For example, he may concentrate on an intellectual subject in a field outside the economic and political sphere. He should recall, however, that, according to tradition, Archimedes died because he was unwilling to see his geometrical figures disturbed by soldiers during the war at Syracuse. Then there is the activity of the aesthetic outcast exemplified by Stephane Mallarmé or Stefan George. Their protest against society was solely concerned with form and forms. Only very rarely can this strict renunciation of "common affairs" in favor of intellectual realms where absolute standards may prevail be converted into political activity, as it was in the case of the Austrian writer Karl Kraus. It has been clearly documented by sociologists that the outsider with a radical but nonpolitical stance is firmly integrated with society. Helmut Kreuzer, in his study of bohemianism, *Die Boheme* (1968), gives examples of such integration. Similarly, Colin Wilson, in analyzing the attitude of the aesthetic outcasts in the cafés of Soho around 1960, offers the following manifesto: "I am interested in making men change, not in changing their social conditions or curing their immediate ills. A man who sets out to 'influence society' is a scoundrel, for his real aim is power; his real driving force, the most puerile kind of ambition."

This form of outcast state, although it can be thoroughly radical in its scientific and aesthetic practice, cannot lead to a constructive relationship between bohemianism and revolution precisely because those who are attracted to this way of life are neither willing nor able to relinquish their alienation. The single steppenwolf does not seek a community with others of his kind. Ludwig Wittgenstein, it is true, was able to establish a community of scholars, much as Mallarmé and George formed communities and cliques of artists. Still, the dominant way of life in the political cafés of the outsiders is the free-for-all fight. The slogan "Steppenwolves of the world, unite!" would have no significance in their world.

It does not follow from this that it is unimportant to understand possible future connections between contemporary forms of an intellectual and social outcast state and contemporary forms of social change. Rudolf Hagelstange, a critic of German development since 1933, has asserted, "We howled with the wolves whom we should have torn apart. It would have been better for us if we had howled with the Steppenwolf." Still, the question remains whether it is possible to howl with the steppenwolves. Or desirable.

Steppenwolf Becomes Everyman

In *The Communist Manifesto* of 1848, Marx and Engels record how children of the bourgeoisie renounce their class and their previous class consciousness—that is, the bourgeois ideology— once they have recognized the sharp divisions of the class conflict. They do this in order to take the side of the proletarian class in a complete sense. Karl Marx seems to have understood this process as resulting from intellectual learning rather than emotions. Later, Bertolt Brecht also asserted that his Marxism was based on theory and was not motivated by sympathy or hate. This statement can be verified by studying the manner in which Brecht presents the common people in most of his works. In contrast, the outsider who never really distances himself from his bourgeois origins (notwithstanding his revolutionary rhetoric) maintains a hate for the establishment and sympathy for the oppressed and wronged. This was Ernst Toller's reason for assuming the role of a revolutionary, and this was the motivation behind Gustav Landauer's "ethical socialism." In recalling his beginnings as a revolutionary, the eminent theoretician Georg Lukács in 1967 still talked about the difficulties which he encountered in the conflict between scientific knowledge and ethical motivation: "Insofar as I am in a position to remember those years, I find that there were two simultaneous tendencies in my world of thought at that time: on the one hand, the leaning toward Marxism and political activism, and on the other, a constant intensification in the formulation of questions which were idealistic and ethical."

It happened to be Trotsky who warned rather early in his career about the political dangers that could spring from a connection between intellectuals who had lost their social roots and become outsiders and the revolutionary proletarian movement. Helmut Kreuzer quotes this remarkable passage written by Trotsky, who settled his account with the intelligentsia that had become rootless: "In that they joined the proletarian party, they brought all their social characteristics with them into the party: a sectarian spirit, an intellectual individualism, and an ideological fetishism."

Kreuzer writes, "The conflicts were unavoidable for members of the marginal intelligentsia. Due to special historical conditions they had pushed their way into the Marxist camp of the masses, and their ready opposition to the ruling class emanated from antibourgeois feelings colored by individualism and bohemianism, or it stemmed primarily from idealistic and ethical motives." In such cases, the bohemian became a revolutionary according to the model of the heretic of old times who remained ready to repent and sacrifice his outcast state. In his heart the revolutionary steppenwolf did not want to be anything more than Comrade Everyman.

What is more serious today for those who act this way is that we now are experiencing the opposite development: *everyman is becoming steppenwolf.*

Those of the younger generation who are designated in German as *Gammler* and in English as hippie or yippie arouse a pleasant feeling of abhorrence. The outward forms of their way of life are only superficially new and unusual. The Italian Renaissance artist Giorgio Vasari described a group of young artists about the middle of the sixteenth century in Florence in the groups which formed around painters like Pontormo and Andrea del Sarto "who under the pretense of living like philosophers existed like pigs and wild animals. They washed neither hands nor face. They did not comb and shave themselves. They did not clean their homes and only made their beds once every two months at the most. They covered their tables with designs for their paintings and drank only out of the bottle or pitcher. This miserable existence, this living from hand to mouth—as one says—was considered by them to be the most splendid life in the world."

It is well known that this way of life quickly turned into an ostentatious dandyism. All these forms of a provocative isolation have one thing in common: they always allow for the opposite attitude, depending on external circumstances. The flower cult of passive resisters can suddenly change into the bomb cult of the terrorists. The cult of extreme ugliness was immediately understood by the expressionists as a new form of aestheticism. The religious implications beneath the shrill atheism of Friedrich Nietzsche is apparent. The protest of the hippie against the conditions of social alienation create stabilization because it is really not a protest against these conditions. Because of Bérenger's passive decision in Ionesco's play not to become a rhinoceros, he at once reveals himself to be one. Where everyman, as it were, turns to these token forms of romantic alienation like the steppenwolf Harry Haller, the old opposition between Haller's madness and the reason which he detests in his bourgeois counterpart becomes meaningless. Then one declares the old irrational standard to be the new rational standard, the outcast state as the normal social situation. Even though this is not without justification, it changes nothing. The steppenwolfish everyman remains affirmative and harmless.

Norman Mailer, in his essay "The White Negro," in *Advertisements for Myself,* discusses the attitudes of that group of Americans who suddenly discovered *Steppenwolf* and eventually Hesse's entire work. He distinguishes between the beatnik type and the hipster. The first group is composed of young men from the middle class in America, often from the Jewish milieu in a large city which forms the background of the novels of Bellow and Malamud and of Arthur Miller's *Death of a Salesman.*

The other type, as Mailer presumes, is often a product of the underworld of the huge cities of contemporary America: "The beatnik, gentle, disembodied from the race, is often a radical pacifist, he has sworn the vow of no violence—in fact, his violence is sealed within, and he has no way of using it. His act of violence is suicide even as the hipster's is toward murder, but in his mind-lost way, the beatnik is the torchbearer of those all-but-lost values of freedom, self-expression, and equality which first turned him against the hypocrisies and barren cultureless flats of the middle class."

There is also ambivalence here. The transition from one type to another is possible at any time. Still, the outcast state of the beatnik develops itself in a situation where all outsiders strive for unity and participation in such a unity, which leads in the direction of disciplined politically active organizations whose activities are responsive to current conditions. The conflicts which then arise are no longer those of the outsider from the bourgeois class but those of the American proletarian movement.

On the other side there is the steppenwolf who would like to remain one in the community with those of his kind, a steppenwolfish everyman of a new sort. He remains open to all sides, for enlightenment and also against it. This is the reason why one should be careful in citing Hermann Hesse, who asked in the "Treatise on the Steppenwolf" section of his famous book "how it could be possible that a bourgeois world which had become culturally so unproductive and reified could continue to exist just as before."

The answer reads: "Because of the steppenwolves."